HIDDEN POWER

OTHER BOOKS BY CHARLES DERBER

*Regime Change Begins at Home: Freeing America
from Corporate Rule*

*The Wilding of America: Money, Mayhem and the
New American Dream*

*People Before Profit: The New Globalization in an
Age of Terror, Big Money and Economic Crisis*

*Corporation Nation: How Corporations Are Taking
Over Our Lives and What We Can Do About It*

The Pursuit of Attention: Power and Ego in Everyday Life

*The Nuclear Seduction: Why the Arms Race Doesn't Matter—
And What Does* (with William Schwartz)

What's Left?: Radical Politics in the Post-Communist Era

*Power in the Highest Degree: Professionals and the Rise of a New
Mandarin Order* (with William Schwartz and Yale Magrass)

Professionals as Workers: Mental Labor in Advanced Capitalism

CHARLES DERBER

HIDDEN POWER

WHAT YOU NEED TO KNOW TO SAVE OUR DEMOCRACY

BK

BERRETT-KOEHLER PUBLISHERS, INC.
San Francisco
a BK Currents book

BERRETT-KOEHLER PUBLISHERS, INC.
235 Montgomery Street, Suite 650 San Francisco, CA 94104-2916
TEL: 415-288-0260 FAX: 415-362-2512 www.bkconnection.com

ORDERING INFORMATION
QUANTITY SALES Special discounts are available on quantity purchases by corporations, associations, and others. For details, contact the "Special Sales Department" at the Berrett-Koehler address above.
INDIVIDUAL SALES Berrett-Koehler publications are available through most bookstores. They can also be ordered direct from Berrett-Koehler:
TEL: 800-929-2929; FAX: 802-864-7626; www.bkconnection.com
ORDERS FOR COLLEGE TEXTBOOK/COURSE ADOPTION USE
Please contact Berrett-Koehler: TEL: 800-929-2929; FAX: 802-864-7626.
ORDERS BY U.S. TRADE BOOKSTORES AND WHOLESALERS
Please contact Publishers Group West, 1700 Fourth Street,
Berkeley, CA 94710. TEL: 510-528-1444; FAX: 510-528-3444.

Berrett-Koehler and the BK logo are registered trademarks of Berrett-Koehler Publishers, Inc.

Printed in the United States of America

Berrett-Koehler books are printed on long-lasting acid-free paper. When it is available, we choose paper that has been manufactured by environmentally responsible processes. These may include using trees grown in sustainable forests, incorporating recycled paper, minimizing chlorine in bleaching, or recycling the energy produced at the paper mill.

Library of Congress Cataloging-in-Publication Data
Derber, Charles.
      Hidden power : what you need to know to save our democracy / by Charles Derber.
         p. cm.
      Includes index.
      ISBN-10: 1-57675-345-X; ISBN-13: 978-1-57675-345-3
         1. Business and politics—United States.   2. Corporate power—United States.
3. Democracy—United States.   4. United States—Politics and government.
5. Political participation—United States.   I. Title.

      JK467.D468 2005
      320.973'09'0511—dc22

                                                                        2005045263
FIRST EDITION
10 09 08 07 06 05   10 9 8 7 6 5 4 3 2 1

Produced by Wilsted & Taylor Publishing Services
   Production management by Christine Taylor
   Copyediting by Nancy Evans
   Design by Jeff Clark
   Composition by Yvonne Tsang

TO MY STUDENTS

who give me hope

CONTENTS

ACKNOWLEDGMENTS

I am grateful to Steve Piersanti, my editor and publisher of Berrett-Koehler, who has made this book possible. Steve gave me unflagging support for this work and many keen insights into how to make it better. The whole staff of Berrett-Koehler is an author's dream, working collaboratively with me to get this book out to the largest audience possible.

Berrett-Koehler's thematic series, called Currents, has provided a perfect context in which to publish my writing about politics and social change. This book is a sequel to my earlier Berrett-Koehler book, *Regime Change Begins at Home*. I have reintroduced some basic concepts and passages from Chapters 1, 3, and 10 of *Regime Change*, so that new readers can jump right in. But it will be a new and provocative read to those who have read *Regime Change* or my earlier books, since I turn my attention to a cluster of new concerns: the role of elections and democratic rhetoric in hiding the very existence of regimes, the cultural and religious strategies that the regime uses to legitimate itself, the nightmarish prospects for an extreme right-wing turn, and a new, in-depth look at the social movements that could take the country in a more progressive direction.

I want to thank Ted Nace, whose authoritative work on the history of corporate power helped educate me. Ted reviewed the whole manuscript with exceptional care and gave me many important insights about how to improve it. I also want to thank Yale Magrass, an old friend and learned scholar of U.S. history and political economy, for reading the chapters and offering a wealth of observations that helped give the book more depth. And I thank Joseph Webb, who also reviewed the entire book and offered valuable substantive and stylistic comments.

As always, my friends David Karp and John Williamson

helped get me through the intensity of this new project. They listened with their customary patience, read and commented on chapters, and gave me the encouragement that kept me at it.

Finally, I want to thank Elena Kolesnikova, who inspired and warmed me on every step of the journey. Elena's own talents as a thinker, writer, and editor grace these chapters. Elena has been endlessly patient, always willing to hear me rehearse the latest argument. I am always grateful for her loving patience, for food, films and fun, and for awakening my heart.

WHO REALLY RULES AMERICA

*I*n the 1980s comic film, *Moscow on the Hudson,* a visiting Russian defects to America while touring with his Soviet group in a Manhattan Bloomingdale's. The Russian, played by Robin Williams, rejoices in his newfound freedom. But as he learns about his new country, he gets confused. He's free to shop at Bloomingdale's but he can't afford it. He appreciates that Americans are free to vote in their leaders, but he can't tell the "bad guys" from the good guys. In the Soviet Union, at least you knew who the "bad guys" were and you had no doubt that they ran the country.

A friend of mine who immigrated from Eastern Europe tells me he feels a bit like Williams. In the Soviet era, everyone in the Eastern Bloc knew who was running the show. Nobody believed in their phony elections. Few in East Germany or Poland thought their gray, aging presidents in their big bulky suits were anything but puppets of Soviet rulers. And nobody believed the newspapers or television because everyone knew they were pure propaganda.

In the United States, my friend says, things are much more confusing. There are "real" elections, but he isn't sure who is really running the country. Is it the president? Is it the Republican Party? Is it "special interest" groups playing behind the scenes? Is it truly the American public?

Many of my students at Boston College are beginning to ask similar questions. They know the president—currently George W. Bush—has great power but they are not sure if he is really making the decisions. They cannot answer with confidence the questions about who really rules America. They are not sure about what stories to believe in the media. They are not sure why the country has gone to war in Iraq. They are not sure that democracy is still alive and well and they wonder whether their vote matters.

This is not the way democracy is supposed to work. Democracy should be transparent. It should lead voters to have faith that the leaders they elect are in charge, that these leaders are accountable to the people, and that the media are not publishing propaganda. They should be getting the truth about who rules their country—and it should be the people themselves.

I am writing this book because I think Americans are not getting the real story. I believe their questions and fears are based on reality, reflecting a dangerous deterioration of American democracy. I am not a conspiracy theorist and I am disturbed by the wild conspiracy ideas floating around on the Internet and in ordinary conversation. But there *is* a system of hidden power in America.

This book explains the hidden power structure, but it is not just the existence and power of the ruling regime that is hidden. The capacity of ordinary Americans to make the kind of democratic change that inspired Thomas Paine and Thomas Jefferson has itself become veiled. My goal in this book is to pull back the curtain to reveal *both* forms of hidden power: the power of those who govern and the power of ordinary Americans like you, the reader. The hidden rulers are not the small cabal of evil plotters imagined in most conspiracy theories but are deeply entrenched social forces and institutions with far more power and sophistication. The hidden power of the people is part of a democratic tradition of political participation and dissent that has been represessed and forgotten. When the curtain is torn down, the promise of American freedom that Robin Williams was looking for can become real.

THE REGIME

In discussing the hidden power of who really rules America, I am talking about a complex, historically entrenched system that is now almost seamlessly integrated with our elections and our official leaders. I call it a regime. When American leaders talk about regimes, it is usually about the evil governments of North Korea, Iran, Syria, or Cuba. As U.S. power brokers see it, a regime is a repressive government somewhere else in the world that the American public ought to distrust. Regime change, by the same logic, is about how the United States can rid the planet—as it did Saddam Hussein's regime in Iraq—of a government that it portrays as a threat to civilization.

The dictionary defines a regime as "a manner, method, or system of rule or government." If we take this more sober approach and view any "system of rule" as a regime, then the U.S. government is also a regime and the history of the United States—as of other nations—can be seen as a succession of regimes. American regimes are entrenched systems of power and ideology, and regime changes at home, while not revolutions, are great dramas, creating seismic shifts in power and social values.[1]

Our current regime is a corporate one, and I start this book by describing what a corporate regime is and how it is weakening our democracy. This is the third corporate regime in American history and, while more global and hazardous than its predecessors, it is not entirely new.

Theodore Roosevelt points to a key difference between our corporate democracy and a dictatorship. In a dictator-

THE INVISIBLE GOVERNMENT

"Behind the ostensible government sits enthroned an invisible government owing no allegiance and acknowledging no responsibility to the people. To destroy this invisible government, to befoul the unholy alliance between corrupt business and corrupt politics, is the first task of the statesmanship of the day."[2]

PRESIDENT THEODORE ROOSEVELT

ship, the real government is visible. In our democratic regime, hidden power reigns.

The roots of our current regime lie in the Gilded Age of John D. Rockefeller, J. P. Morgan, and other early captains of industry, who helped shape the first corporate regime, and in the Roaring Twenties of Warren Harding, Calvin Coolidge, and Herbert Hoover, the leaders who presided over the second corporate regime. Conceived in the 1970s and shaped by the election of President Ronald Reagan in 1980, the current corporate regime has been steadily consolidating power, whichever party is in office. The result so far: profits grow and democracy shrinks. Bush has pushed the envelope, taking the regime in more radical directions as Washington becomes a money swamp and people like you and me have too many days when we feel helpless to change it.

The American system wasn't supposed to work this way. The Founders crafted the Constitution to ensure that "We, the People" would have a voice in our own affairs—and in those of the nation. The Constitution embraced an elaborate set of checks and balances that were to separate government agencies and prevent concentration of private power. James Madison, the author of the Constitution, wrote that "There is an evil which ought to be guarded against. . . . The power of all corporations ought to be limited. . . . The growing wealth acquired by them never fails to be a source of abuses."[3] In today's regime, the world's biggest global firms have accomplished what the Founding Fathers most feared. They have hollowed out the institutions that enabled ordinary Americans to have a say in how their land is governed. To cover up this hijacking of our constitutional and democratic gains, the regime has targeted you and me with a classy Madison Avenue arsenal of manipulation techniques—including democratic rhetoric and practices that have helped hide the very existence of the regime.

FROM THE ELECTION TRAP TO REGIME CHANGE

Most Americans understand that individual corporations —such as Nike, Wal-Mart, General Motors, and Citigroup —have great power. But they see only the skimpiest outlines of the hidden connections that weave together these huge companies with one another, with the political leaders of both parties, with the media, with schools and hospitals, and with the military—the systemic connections that create a regime. Because they barely see the shadows of this ruling system, it is even harder for them to see their own hidden power to create regime change.

In all nations, regimes spin elaborate myths that disguise their own power. Sometimes this comes in the form of obvious propaganda systems. In such societies, it is actually easier, as Robin Williams discovers, to figure out who is ruling and the lies they are telling. In democracies like the United States, it is much harder to tell who really is in charge and to distinguish truth from propaganda. This is partly because a corporatized government and media work together to create and market some of the world's most sophisticated deceptions and illusions. It is also because the regime is so intertwined with democratic rhetoric and procedures, and because people see democracy and change itself as tied mainly to voting the bums out of office.

This linking of power and change with winning elections is part of a set of misperceptions about democracy that I call the Election Trap. It has taken root among Democrats and Republicans, reds and blues, liberals and conservatives, even many radicals and libertarians. In short, nearly all Americans are ensnared in the Election Trap, and I have discovered myself sometimes seduced into it, too.[4]

The Election Trap inflates and distorts the role of the horse race in democratic politics. It makes near-term elections the primary object of political struggle and electoral victory the criterion for measuring power. Strategically, winning becomes everything. The Election Trap was on full display during the 2004 presidential elections, most tragically by the Democratic Party. Party leaders and most voters in the Democratic primaries selected John Kerry as their nominee because they knew he was a war hero and thought he had the best chance of winning. They didn't know much else about him. The philosophy of the party was summed up in one phrase: "Anybody but Bush."

The Democrats were caught—like a hungry mouse who sees nothing but the cheese in the mousetrap—in the Election Trap. The Party was focused like a laser on winning the election. It would choose anyone who could win, even if ordinary voters knew virtually nothing about what he stood for. This has been the story not just of Kerry but of the Democratic Party leadership over most of the last three decades. Its whole identity was about winning. This led to two predictable consequences. First, it led the party to lose the elections. Second, it meant that even if the Democrats had won, the party would not have created regime change.

The problem was not that Kerry and other Democrat

leaders tried so hard to defeat Bush and win the election. It was that their obsession with winning helped undermine their ability to set forth a principled agenda that might have actually persuaded people to vote for them. For the Democrats to win, they have to convince ordinary citizens that they are going to help make their lives better. They need a philosophy of governing and of regime change, not just of winning. The Republicans are better at the horse race, with more efficient operatives and hacks, more money, and more sophisticated propaganda. The politics of the Election Trap almost always favor Republicans, especially in the current era where elections are driven by money. Given these realities, the Democrats could have won recent elections only if they had actually advanced a politics of conviction.

The sad Democratic experience in 2004 is just one example of the way the Election Trap works. The larger story is about how democracy itself has become a vehicle for undermining itself. The regime is the winner and the people the loser.

The main catalysts of regime change in America have not been parties glued to the next election, but social movements that operate on the scale of decades rather than two- and four-year electoral cycles. Political parties have historically become agents of democratic change only when movements infuse the parties with their own long-term vision, moral conviction, and resources. Abolitionists, suffragettes, minorities, or labor movements have sometimes succeeded in creating more democratic systems, as in the New Deal. The lessons of their past successes for today is one major theme of this book. Evangelical religious groups and social movements of corporations themselves have created their own forms of regime change, most recently in 1980 when they came together to create the current governing regime. They also have much to teach us about hidden power and how to change it.

HIDDEN POWER, DEMOCRACY, AND HEGEMONY

Hidden power exists in many societies, but, as Teddy Roosevelt pointed out, it can be particularly severe in capitalist democracies. Our political leaders and millions of Americans celebrate the increasing spread of elections around the world. They believe these new elected regimes make power transparent and give people far more democratic control over their own nations and lives. This has some truth in many countries, and our celebration reflects how we understand our own democracy. The cherished sovereignty of "we the people" is enshrined in our own elections, and we yearn to believe in it. But looking behind the parchment and ideals, we see that popular control in our own democracy and in much of the world is increasingly a fantasy.

Part of the disconnect between democratic ideals and reality arises out of the nature of capitalism. In every society, but especially in capitalism, it is impossible to separate economic and political power. As Karl Marx, the most famous critic of capitalist societies, observed more than a century ago, setting up formal political mechanisms for representative democracy—including constitutions, elections, and rule of law—does not ensure that the people's elected representatives will be accountable to them; in fact, Marx believed that the whole point of capitalist democracy was to create a visible government as a cover for the invisible one.[5] If economic power is skewed, and the gap between rich and poor is great, elected leaders will have other masters in the shadows and true democracy will wither. In a different context, Thomas Jefferson also saw how inequality shaped politics when he observed the corrupt and economically polarized aristocratic societies of Europe. Jefferson believed that the United States could become and remain democratic only if the new nation could create and sustain relative equality of land and wealth.[6]

The gap between rich and poor is always large in capitalist countries and has become vast today, greater than at any time since the Roaring Twenties and growing rapidly enough to make Jefferson roll over in his grave. In March 2005, Bill Gates, the world's richest person, was worth $60.6 billion.[7] *Forbes* magazine, in its 2004 account of the four hundred richest Americans, noted that as the number of poor Americans rose to 36 million, the net worth of America's four hundred richest people rose to an unprecedented $1 trillion. *Forbes* magazine noted that this astronomical sum was more than double the federal budget deficit in that year and equal to the gross domestic product (GDP) of Canada.[8] Gates's corporation, Microsoft, is just one of two hundred gigantic, interlocked, and politically active firms who produce and control approximately 25 percent of the world's wealth.[9] Such concentrated economic power subverts the power of elections to create rulers who serve ordinary people, both in America and around the world. It inevitably makes corporations major players in our new global regime.

The hidden power structure of the regime, though, is

more than just a wealth pyramid. Politics is simultaneously about economic and moral authority. The power structures of capitalist democracies reflect underlying economic hierarchies as well as politically orchestrated moral values and cultural identities that give meaning to people's lives. A good way to view U.S. regimes is as a blended hierarchic system of money and morality whose outlines are only vaguely seen or understood by the population. To see these regimes clearly, you need to put on 3-D glasses that allow you to see beneath the surface of the politics in the headlines.[10]

In his recent best-seller, *What's the Matter with Kansas?*, Thomas Frank asked how red staters could keep electing Republicans who dish out economic policies ruinous to their own jobs and standard of living.[11] The answer to his question involves culture and ideology, but goes far beyond the discussion of religion and moral values that dominated much of the country after the 2004 elections. It is a question central to almost all societies and regimes: how hidden and exploitative power is disguised and justified in any governing system, whether democratic or not.

Ruling regimes have always worked hard to produce what Antonio Gramsci, a great early twentieth-century Italian social thinker, called *hegemony*.[12] By this he meant the system of thought and persuasion that led people to assign moral virtue and pledge allegiance to the existing order, no matter how much they are suffering. Gramsci was writing from a prison in Mussolini's fascist Italy, where he struggled to understand why so many Italians flocked to the dictator's oppressive cause.[13]

All power structures seek to draw their consent from the

people. This is because ruling by the barrel of a gun is costly and inefficient. In the United States, creating hegemony has moved to the very heart of hidden power. Our formal democratic procedures have become one of several key hegemonic tools for disguising the eroding democratic substance of our current regime.

Despite Mussolini's hegemonic success, creating hegemony in dictatorships, slave societies, fascist orders, and other nakedly coercive regimes can be very difficult. The power structure itself is typically transparent and people submit to it because they have no alternative. But they may resist internally, just waiting for the moment when the rulers put down their guns or sleep.

In capitalist democracies, though, creating hegemony can be easier, even if the regime acts against the interests of its own people. This is because all the elements of Western democracies—elections, constitutions, and the rule of law—are astonishingly powerful hegemonic instruments. By vesting citizens with voting power and rights under the law, the regime disguises the hidden and unaccountable power that remains vested in itself. If voters are suffering, they appear to have only themselves to blame for voting the bums in—and presumably can vote them out. This disguises the reality that whoever citizens vote in—the current bums or the next ones—may owe their allegiance less to the voters than to the corporate regime. It also veils the fact that the substantial freedom the regime offers is no justification for the freedom that it denies.

In 1956, C. Wright Mills wrote the classic book *The Power Elite*.[14] It was a devastating critique, arguing that U.S. democracy was mainly a cover for a power elite made up of corporate leaders, top military officers, and political elites. Mills believed that this elite, despite its great power, could be changed by social movements, a view that I expand in some detail. But he thought this possible only if the power elite was exposed and its ruling ideology discredited. This is a daunting task, precisely because of the hegemonic power of elections and constitutionalism in America, as well as the growing corporate control of the media and new technological powers for controlling popular thought.[15]

The task of sociologists is to peek behind the curtain of hidden power. In this book, I look at the new systemic character of today's hidden power and hegemony. It is by far the most corporatized and globalized regime in all of history, and it operates with great hegemonic sophistication and innovation. But the regime has vulnerabilities, and I draw heavily on the history of earlier regimes and regime changes as a window into our current system. Only by understanding how social movements created regime change in earlier eras is it possible to see a hopeful future today.

WHERE WE GO FROM HERE

Many Americans are disenchanted with the current system of power but don't see any realistic alternatives. The idea that there is no alternative is a self-fulfilling prophecy. We can create regime change only when we believe that a better alternative exists. The great question of the twenty-first century is what a post-corporate regime will look like. What is an America freed from corporate rule? We are so accustomed to the reign of big corporations that we scarcely bother to ask the question.

Here, I try to ask and answer it. I offer a vision of the new regime that lies within our grasp. While many will find my agenda idealistic, it seems so only because it is not achievable within the current regime. Regimes are systems for limiting the imagination and locking us into the current terms of discourse. When a regime falls, as it did in 1932 and 1980, changes that looked impossible can become common sense.

New crises are already fanning the flames of new social movements seeking regime change. Regime change happens because of serious cracks that fracture the system and weaken its power. Such cracks are emerging today and can produce a frightening regime change to the right, leading to the Orwellian scenario I call "fascism lite." Many new developments, including terrorism and the war against it, have helped to make this a real possibility. But today's regime crises can also lead to a more hopeful transformation.

Regimes change when their crises get so acute that new social movements arise from among the ordinary people harmed by the ruling regime. True, the hidden power of the people to change the regime—which produces great popular cynicism—makes progressive regime change very difficult, as does the great power of the corporations themselves. But new movements are already on the scene that are helping to reconnect ordinary citizens with their long-lost traditions of challenge to the ruling system. Despite their lack of big money, the new movements are worthy challengers of the new global corporate goliaths. In the last few chapters of this book, I show how they and the Democratic Party can work together to change the country.

Einstein said that "the world is a dangerous place, not because of those who do evil, but because of those who look on and do nothing." Today, this is a call for Americans who are not happy with their government to recognize and exercise their own hidden power. I show here how hidden power works, how it could lurch to the right or left in unexpected ways, and how you can make a difference.

CHAPTER I

AMERICAN REGIMES

*E*very regime is like a political house built around five great pillars.[1]

When you go to buy a house, you usually have to get it inspected. You want to make sure that you understand the structure and that the house is safe. The inspectors will tell you something about the history of the house and what you might have to repair or rebuild.

Since we all live in our current regime's house, we need to inspect it, too. We urgently need to understand its pillars and its history. But there is no official inspector to call and we have to do our own analysis. Since the house is shaded and partly hidden, this is a challenge. We need to do some serious investigative work to see the house clearly and know what kinds of repairs and rebuilding it might need.

Pillar 1: A Dominant Institution (e.g., the corporation, the government, the church)
The dominant institution is the foundation of the house.

Pillar 2: A Mode of Politics (e.g., corporate sovereignty, theocracy, representative democracy)
The mode of politics determines how the house is run.

Pillar 3: A Social Contract (e.g., the welfare state, laissez-faire, libertarianism)
The social contract sets the terms for the tenants.

Pillar 4: A Foreign Policy (e.g., isolationism, empire, multilateralism)
The foreign policy dictates the relation to the neighbors.

Pillar 5: An Ideology (e.g., social Darwinism, socialism, individualism, democracy)
The ideology spells out the creed of the household.

I am writing this chapter to offer some general observations about the architecture and history of political regimes in America. They are a first step in a citizen's guide to regime houses. As a warning, most such houses have mainly been owned and managed by a select few with their own agenda, so we have reasons to be very cautious. But in democratic regimes, ordinary dwellers can empower themselves to run the house. The architecture of the house and the design of its pillars reflect the underlying and changing balance of power in society and the spirit of the era that might be called the zeitgeist.

While you won't read about regimes and political houses

in most history books, American history is a series of fascinating regimes and regime changes. The modern history of U.S. regimes began immediately after the Civil War, when the earliest American corporate regime was born. Simon and Garfunkel sang a catchy, popular American song, "What a Wonderful World," originally written and performed by Sam Cook, that began "Don't know much about history." Many readers may have little taste for history and feel an urge to fast forward to the next chapter that tells the story of today's regime. But if you want to understand the regime house you live in today, and how it endangers you, you have to know its history, one largely hidden from most Americans.

U.S. MODERN REGIMES

First Corporate Regime, 1865–1901—Gilded Age
John D. Rockefeller and J. P. Morgan build this house.

Progressive Regime, 1901–1921—Progressive Era
Teddy Roosevelt busts the trusts in this house.

Second Corporate Regime, 1921–1933—Roaring Twenties
Harding and Hoover turn the house back to big business.

New Deal Regime, 1933–1980—New Deal
Franklin D. Roosevelt designs a people's house.

Third Corporate Regime, 1980–?—Reagan Revolution
Global corporations build this house for themselves.

In this chapter, I briefly tell the story of the four regimes before today's third corporate regime. All these regimes are historical twists and turns of an American capitalist system. Since they are all houses with the same broad capitalist architecture, you may ask, Why is it important to introduce the idea of regimes at all, and distinguish between corporate and non-corporate models?

The idea of regime helps capture the changing balance of power and different zeitgeists of different U.S. capitalist eras. The change from one regime to another is a political tidal wave—for better or for worse—in the lives of ordinary Americans and in the fate of American democracy and American morality. In corporate regimes, the balance of power swings toward money and away from democracy. The zeitgeist is *overwhelmingly* corporate, promoting profit over everything else. In other regimes, such as the New Deal during and after the Great Depression, the balance of power shifted away from corporations and empowered ordinary people to renew the American democratic dream. The passion for social justice and the strong anti-corporate sentiments of the New Deal regime were a revolutionary change from the selfishness and greed of the Roaring Twenties regime—showing how Americans can dramatically rebuild their political house.

American regimes change because capitalism creates many internal crises that weaken the architecture and threaten the tenants, and we have strong social movements that respond to these crises and can repair or transform our political house. The U.S. government is an institution spiced with contradictions and marked by "relative autonomy."[2] That's a fancy sociological term for saying that we have a capitalist U.S. government but one that is far from being a puppet of the ruling class.[3] While it is always strongly influenced by corporations, it can also be swayed by popular movements opposing corporate regimes and seeking to build a very different house.

In some periods, notably the Progressive Era and New Deal, the state moves in often bewildering, opposite directions at the same time, tugged variously by corporations, liberal and socialist reformers, workers' and farmers' grassroots movements, and progressive intellectuals and bureaucrats. A relatively autonomous capitalist state—open to influences both from big business and from people's movements—makes possible major regime changes within capitalism itself. The New Dealers had business supporters and reconstructed America partly to save corporate capitalism, but they were mainly movements of liberal elites, workers, the poor, and ordinary citizens like you and me, who managed to topple a corporate regime and build a new political house, a historic achievement that could happen again.

Regime changes in America are not revolutions, with the exception of the American Revolution itself. But they represent important shifts in the direction of the nation, creating major changes in power and spirit, and opening up possibilities for more fundamental change still on the American agenda. When we understand the story of earlier American regimes, we get a clearer view of our current hidden power system and how we might move beyond it.

THE FIRST CORPORATE REGIME

The Regime of the Gilded Age

DOMINANT INSTITUTION The Unregulated
   National Corporation
MODE OF POLITICS Naked Corpocracy
SOCIAL CONTRACT Sink or Swim
FOREIGN POLICY Manifest Destiny
IDEOLOGY Social Darwinism

Spanning the quarter century after the Civil War, the
Gilded Age, known for its robber barons and great fortunes, gave birth to the first American corporate regime.
It was quite a house! Swashbuckling railroad barons like
Commodore Vanderbilt, William Henry Vanderbilt, Jay
Gould, and E. H. Harriman helped build the new regime.
In the 1860s, they exploited government credit and land
grants, banking deals, speculative investments, arms dealing, and political connections to construct the new conti-
nental railroad that tied together the nation's first national
market. In successive decades, John D. Rockefeller, J. P.
Morgan, and the rest of the robber barons built the great
national corporations that became the dominant institutions of America.[4] President Rutherford B. Hayes, himself
a railroad lawyer, marveled at the power of the railroad
companies, asking, "Do the railroads own the people or the
people own the railroads?"[5]

The hidden power within this regime lay mainly in the
web of relationships the corporations built among themselves and with the state. Railroad barons such as Vanderbilt and Gould constantly realigned themselves with each
other and with financiers like Morgan to gain competitive

advantage and corner the market. The trend was toward ever-larger alliances, culminating in the marriage of the Rockefeller and Morgan corporate empires. Rockefeller sat on thirty-seven corporate boards and Morgan on forty-eight. When they merged in the first few years of the twentieth century, the corporate system involved 341 interlocking directorships linking more than a hundred of America's top corporations. The first corporate regime was a very close *family* of very big corporations.[6]

The regime also housed from the beginning a tight marriage between the robber barons and the national government. Presidents Grant, Hayes, Garfield, Arthur, Harrison, and McKinley, all Republican, and Grover Cleveland, the only Democrat, all carried water for the new national captains of industry. Rockefeller's aides, with briefcases literally stuffed with greenbacks, worked in the offices of senators who wrote legislation on oil, banking, and other industries. Senator Joseph Foraker of Ohio got about $50,000 from Standard Oil during the six-month period he spent preparing the corporate policy planks of the Republican policy.[7]

The captains of industry used their influence over both the Democratic (take note, Democrats today) and Republican presidents to send in troops when workers tried to organize. At the famous 1894 Pullman strike, Democratic President Grover Cleveland sent in federal troops to attack the workers. When they pleaded for his support, he told them, "you might as well ask me to dissolve the federal government of the United States."[8] The regime pioneered the ruthless assault on unions that has become a staple of our own political house today.

I dub the regime's political system a *corpocracy* because

it maintained the formality of popular sovereignty while serving effectively as a system of corporate rule. Corpocracy joins corporations and a formally democratic government in house ownership and management, with corporations enjoying the leading role and gaining their legitimacy through control of elected politicians. In different corporate regimes, the marriage between corporation and government varies in terms of its turbulence and equality of partners. In the first corporate regime, the corporations ran roughshod over their government partners, with the robber barons barely concealing their iron grip on the political wheels of government. Of all American regimes, this one was least concerned with hiding power behind a curtain. Listen to President Rutherford B. Hayes, a Republican, again, who saw it all clearly: "This is no longer a government of the people, by the people, and for the people. It is a government of corporations, for corporations and by corporations."[9]

Nonetheless, not all the power of the new corpocracy was visible. Gilded Age presidents appointed Supreme Court justices who redefined the corporation in a dramatic way. For the first time ever, in the 1886 Santa Clara decision involving a railroad case, the judges ruled that the corporation was defined as a "legal person" entitled to constitutional protection under the Fourteenth Amendment. This had several major transformative effects, largely unseen by the public, that boosted corpocracy at the expense of democracy. By building corporate power under the umbrella of constitutional rights, the first corporate regime weakened democratic popular control in the name of the very democratic rights that most Americans believe the Constitution is supposed to protect.[10] This equating of corporate rights with the rights of ordinary citizens has become one of the great hegemonic strategies of corpocracy in today's regime, as I discuss in the next chapter.

The robber barons dominated American society from the end of the Civil War until 1900. As Matthew Josephson, the great chronicler of the Gilded Age, put it, "Like earlier invading hosts arriving from the hills, the steppes or the sea," the robber barons "overran all the existing institutions which buttress society, taking control of the political government, of the School, the Press, the Church, and . . . the world of opinions or of the people."[11]

The social contract of the era was "sink or swim." At a time when John D. Rockefeller became the country's first billionaire, 90 percent of Americans were poor and in constant danger of drowning. There was no social safety net and the robber barons opposed the unions or social programs that might have brought some security to ordinary workers and farmers. In slums like Pittsburgh's Painter Mill, people cooked in dark cellar kitchens in houses without ventilation or drinking water. Eighty percent of the regime's workers, many working sixteen hours a day, were poor.[12] As an "anxious class," never sure whether they would have a job tomorrow, they accepted whatever the robber barons paid, something many workers today can well understand.

The regime had an expansionist foreign policy of Manifest Destiny that viewed the regime's conquest of an endless American frontier as opening endless opportunity for ordinary Americans. America was not yet focused on global pursuits, but the conquest of the South and West was essential to the new national corporations. It created their new vast markets and opportunity for profits.[13] The idea of land and resources for every American helped legitimate the system.

Social Darwinism was the reigning ideology. John D. Rockefeller said it clearly: "The growth of a large business is merely a survival of the fittest. . . . It is merely a working out of a law of nature and law of God." He concluded "God gave me my money."[14] The gross disparities between rich and poor were seen as part of the natural order of things. Darwinist ideology and religion were powerful hegemonic forces stabilizing a regime in which so many workers were brutally exploited.

The parallels between this first corporate regime and the one today are haunting. President Clinton made the comparison himself, saying that both the Gilded Age and our own era are corporate periods of great opportunity, with millions being left behind. Then as now, Clinton said, "vast fortunes are being made. . . . But a lot of people are being dislocated."[15] It has become fashionable to call this the second Gilded Age.[16]

The late-nineteenth-century robber-baron regime created many of the great historic companies, such as Chase National Bank (now J. P. Morgan Chase), First National Bank and National City Banks of New York (now Citigroup), Standard Oil (now called Exxon Mobil), and U.S. Steel, which, after various mergers, still dominate America. It was the first regime to flood politics with corporate money and create all-powerful corporate lobbies in Washington, constructing a corpocracy whose legacy would threaten democracy long after the robber barons passed from the scene.

This first corporate regime, despite its awesome power, faced a radical challenge by the Populists, fiery farmers and plain-spoken people from the heartland who created the People's Party in 1892 and launched one of the country's most important politics of regime change. They proclaimed in 1892 that corporations were being used "to enslave and impoverish the people. Corporate feudality has taken the place of chattel slavery."[17] The Populists were the most important of a cast of colorful social movements emerging in the 1870s, including the Knights of Labor, urban anarchists, Christian socialists, the Grange (known as the Patrons of Husbandry, discontented farmers who pushed for expansive credit), railroad unionism led by Eugene Debs and other socialist labor groups, and other regime-changing visionaries linked to the Populists whose activities I describe in Chapter 6. Suffice it to say here that the United States has rarely witnessed an outcropping of such diverse and radical democratic movements that brought hidden power into the spotlight and fought for the abolition of the first corporate regime. They were motivated by many forces: an extended depression in the 1870s and one of the country's worst financial crises in 1893, growing farm debt and credit crises linked to high interest rates imposed by Wall Street, skyrocketing shipping, storage, and transportation costs for farmers imposed by railroads and other corporate middlemen, and the sense of loss of control to new giant corporate entities who had never before ruled the country. They sought to break up trusts and monopolies, create government control over the banking system, and build a new alternative economy of farmer and worker cooperatives.[18]

THE PROGRESSIVE REGIME

The House the Progressives Built

DOMINANT INSTITUTION The Regulated Corporation
MODE OF POLITICS Liberal Corpocracy
SOCIAL CONTRACT Social Reformism
FOREIGN POLICY Early Empire
IDEOLOGY Progressivism

Many of the anticorporate grassroots groups faded, including the Populists, who melted away with their 1896 presidential endorsement of the defeated Democratic nominee, William Jennings Bryan. But they helped give rise to the reform movement of the Progressive Era under the "trust-buster," President Theodore Roosevelt. Since many readers may think of themselves as progressives, it is particularly important to understand the deep contradictions and complex blend of liberalism and conservatism that defined the progressive regime.

In 1907, Roosevelt called for "the effective and thorough-going supervision by the National Government of all the operations of the big interstate business concerns," a direct challenge to the "free market" regime discourse of the robber barons. Roosevelt was no revolutionary but he did engineer his own regime-change politics.

Roosevelt sought to create a Bureau of Corporations that would put limits on the biggest Rockefeller, Morgan, and other robber-baron fiefdoms. Corporations had to restructure themselves and embrace a measure of public accountability, as the Progressive Era consolidated political power in a new regulatory regime. As historian Martin J.

TEDDY ROOSEVELT'S PROGRESSIVE CREED

"The true friend of property, the true conservative, is he who insists that property shall be the servant and not the master of the commonwealth; who insists that the creature of man's making shall be the servant and not the master of the man who made it. The citizens of the United States must effectively control the mighty commercial forces which they have themselves called into being."

Theodore Roosevelt, speech at
Ossowatomie, Kansas, August 31, 1910

Sklar put it, Roosevelt sought to subordinate corporate power to the state to a dramatic degree: "The state would not simply police or regulate the economy. . . corporations would become," in Roosevelt's vision, "agents, 'controlled and governed,' of the state and public policy."[19]

Roosevelt did not create the radical dismantling of corporate rule that the Populists envisioned, and indeed his new regime restructured government not just to protect workers but to provide more stability and regulatory support for the corporations themselves. Gabriel Kolko, a historian of the Progressive Era, calls his classic book on the era *The Triumph of Conservatism.*[20] He shows that the new regulatory state created by the Progressives actually delivered precisely what the growing national corporations needed to survive and prosper. The Progressive state would regulate and weed out cheap competition, stabilize the business cycle, and provide the social reform the corporations needed to defuse populist discontent. No less a financier than Henry Davison, J. P. Morgan's partner, told Congress in 1912: "I would rather have regulation and control [of the banking sector] than free competition."[21] Could there have been a more ringing corporate endorsement of the Progressive agenda?

The benefits corporations secured during the Progressive regime show how subtly and forcefully capitalist hidden power exerts itself in all historical eras. As Progressives, driven by liberal and reformist sentiments, sought to build a regulated capitalism, they both strengthened and constrained the corporate order. The state gained its own regulatory powers, a rewiring of the first corporate regime that reined in corporate excesses and offered meaningful protections for ordinary Americans. But regulation also helped legitimate corporations by appearing to subject them to democratic control. The regulatory system built by Progressives has become one of the corporate system's most powerful hegemonic tools for securing the hearts and minds of ordinary workers and citizens.[22]

The Progressives, nonetheless, created a radically different zeitgeist from the Gilded Age period. It challenged many reigning corporate values and was bitterly opposed by large sectors of business. The regime replaced the old "sink or swim" social contract with a new system of progressive reforms regulating abuse of workers, especially children and the poor. Progressive muckrakers like Upton Sinclair and Lincoln Steffens, in their vivid exposés of the meat factories and urban slums, helped build a deep anticorporate sensibility that spread widely in the population. If corporate values of greed and laissez-faire defined the Gilded Age regime, the spirit of public interest, liberal reform and outrage at corporate abuse defined the zeitgeist of the Progressive regime.[23]

The New Deal would later mount a far deeper assault on corporate power. Nonetheless, the Progressive regime arose partly out of the Populist legacy of deep discontent with corporate power. Its profound contradictions remind us that all U.S. regimes serve corporations, but some do so in a way that opens up new popular horizons for challenging the corporate order.

The Progressive regime faded in the waning years of World War I, drastically weakened by the unpopularity of the war and President Woodrow Wilson's repressive measures to stifle antiwar dissent. In different ways, Theodore Roosevelt and Woodrow Wilson both advanced the regime's foreign policy of early empire. The United States was already a significant expansionist power, and by World War I was a significant world power. Roosevelt was an unreconstructed imperialist, as displayed both in the Spanish-American War and the colonization of the Philippines. Wilson was more like today's neoconservatives, cloaking expansionism in highly idealistic rhetoric about making the world safe for democracy.

Early empire served corporations seeking new foreign markets, but its excesses catalyzed the regime's collapse. In 1917, Wilson signed the Espionage Act and used it to silence peace activists, antiwar labor groups like the Industrial Workers of the World, and prominent anti-war socialists like Eugene Debs, who spoke for millions of Americans unenthused or opposed to the war. The regime moved harshly against dissidents. Vigilante groups, including the American Protective League sponsored by Wilson's Department of Justice, identified more than three million "dis-

loyal" Americans, several thousands of whom were prose-
cuted under the Espionage Act. This was followed by the
great "Red Scare" of 1919 and 1920, triggered by a bomb
at the home of Wilson's Attorney General A. Mitchell
Palmer. The infamous Palmer raids, backed by a Congressional Act permitting deportation of aliens, led to roundups
of more than four thousand people in January 1930, who
were held in seclusion for long periods, denied represen-
tation, and then deported. The general climate of repression created a right-wing drift that severely weakened the
liberal, reformist zeitgeist of the Progressive regime.[24]

Ironically, regime change occurred partly through the
political skill of isolationist Republicans, who exploited the
mass disenchantment with a bloody war that had never
been popular. When Wilson first announced the need for a
million Americans to enlist, only 73,000 did so. By the end
of the conflict, war-weary Americans, disaffected by the
idealist adventurism of the Progressive regime leaders, became receptive to Republican calls for rebuilding the good
life at home. Behind the scenes, in the regime that followed, the Republicans helped rebuild European colonial
empires that would secure foreign markets for their big-
business sponsors. In this sense, the new regime would not
be isolationist, as it is typically regarded, but a surrogate
empire, helping reinforce the battered European empires
after the war. To ordinary Americans, the Republicans argued for a postwar regime change that would create a new
consumer and corporate paradise at home.[25]

THE SECOND CORPORATE REGIME

The Regime of the Roaring Twenties

DOMINANT INSTITUTION The Monopoly Corporation
MODE OF POLITICS Deregulated Corpocracy
SOCIAL CONTRACT Corporate Paternalism
FOREIGN POLICY Surrogate Empire
IDEOLOGY Consumerism

The second corporate regime of the Roaring Twenties was a twentieth-century replay of the Gilded Age and another harbinger of today's corporate regime. The Harding, Coolidge, and Hoover administrations abandoned the regulatory impulse of the Progressive regime and turned Washington back to big business. While less constitutionally extreme than the Gilded Age presidents, they created a new regime of corporate hyper-power, dominated by an ideology of consumerism, corporate self-regulation, and paternalism.

Corporate self-government was the central political theme of the second corporate regime. When President Hoover, in the depths of the Depression, argued that the government budget should be slashed, he was expressing the regime's fierce counter-reaction to Theodore Roosevelt, rejecting forever the Progressive zeitgeist of government activism and reform.[26] Government was seen as the enemy and corporations were viewed as the invisible hand that could solve social problems. President Hoover said that the government "owes nothing" to himself or any citizen, since the business world had created opportunity for everyone and could police itself.[27]

While the second corporate regime pronounced itself

a laissez-faire order, it was actually a deregulated corpocracy. As in the Gilded Age, corporations had their snouts deep in the government trough and depended on government for subsidies, contracts, and opening of public lands and leases for exploiting public resources. The huge corporate scandals like Teapot Dome exposed the massive corruption and political links between big business and big government.

The new regime proclaimed a union-free world known as "Plan America," a social contract of corporate paternalism in which big business would house and educate workers and provide them with medical care and retirement. Plan America envisioned a whole society wrapped in a benign corporate cocoon, without any need for government regulation or unions, previewing some of the fashionable views about corporate responsibility in the current regime. The antiunion sentiment was fierce, with the courts in the 1920s issuing 2,130 injunctions against strikes compared to 835 between 1910 and 1920.[28] The Roaring Twenties regime created a corporate zeitgeist of postwar individualism, hedonism, and mass consumerism.

Consumerism—and the associated ethos of individualism—was the critical ideological contribution of the corporate second regime. As the historian of consumerism Stewart Ewen has shown graphically, modern advertising got its birth in this era, as did the industry of public relations that would reshape both the mass media and all government and corporate propaganda.[29] The regime's construction of consumerism was tied to corporate profitability: when Henry Ford argued for the $5 a day wage, it was to make sure that his workers could afford to buy the cars his company would produce. More broadly, though, consumerism fueled the regime's zeitgeist of hedonistic individualism that helped to legitimate twentieth-century capitalism. You might have to work hard, but you could be assured of your reward in this life, not the next one.[30]

Consumerism also helped undermine democracy, persuading people that their real voice could be heard with their buying power rather than acts of citizenship. Tying the sense of efficacy to consuming rather than voting or protesting was another great legitimating power for modern corporate capitalism. But the excessive hyper-hedonism and individualism of the Roaring Twenties helped to undermine it. The regime's zeitgeist of unregulated greed contributed to the huge stock market bubble that popped in 1929. The regime ended with market collapse and the victory of President Franklin Delano Roosevelt in 1932.[31]

THE NEW DEAL REGIME

The House the Workers Built

DOMINANT INSTITUTION The Federal Government
MODE OF POLITICS American Social Democracy
SOCIAL CONTRACT The Welfare State
FOREIGN POLICY The American Century
IDEOLOGY Social Justice

Spurred by the Depression and the recognition that capitalism could only be saved under a different order, Roosevelt created the New Deal, a new regime that established basic rights for labor codified in the Wagner Act, and created an entirely new social welfare system built around Social Security. As I show in Chapter 3, the New Deal was a continuing work in progress, the fruit of a dynamic interaction between regime-change movements of workers, veterans, farmers, and the poor, on the one hand, and progressive policy elites in Washington. The New Deal did not end corporate power but it turned the government into a limited agent of countervailing power and it sought to preserve a public sphere, whether in the health system or the public schools, safe from corporate predators. Economist John Kenneth Galbraith wrote at the height of the New Deal, "the major peacetime function of the federal government" is to rein in corporate power, a statement that no established thinker or politician could have entertained in the Gilded Age or Roaring Twenties regimes.[32]

The New Deal regime was the longest and most important in modern American history. FDR, an aristocrat, did not enter his presidency as an anticorporate reformer, but he created the American regime that most deeply challenged corporate power and the corporate zeitgeist. Much of big business came to hate him as a "class traitor," but FDR relished the confrontation. He was exuberant when he introduced the controversial 1937 Wealth Tax Act, which spurred corporate elites to sputter and rage about his treachery.[33]

The New Deal, of course, did not undermine corporate capitalism. Instead, it preserved corporate capitalism just as the Progressives had helped create it. Corporations remained a powerful force in America and the New Deal did not live up to the hopes of the left or even many of FDR's more liberal progressive advisors, such as Rexford Tugwell and Henry Wallace. Nonetheless, FDR radically shifted the balance of power and was the president who most fully legitimated a countervailing "big government" in a society of big business.

FDR did not start as a regime changer. In 1932 and 1933, he pursued a version of Hooverism and the earlier regime's corporate self-policing, establishing the National Recovery Administration (NRA), which required industries themselves to create their own new codes of conduct. But the failure of corporate self-regulation and the militant upsurge of popular activism pushed FDR and the regime in a new direction. The New Deal regime upended the Roaring Twenties vision of corporate self-government, replacing it with an activist federal government as the dominant institution.[34]

Franklin Roosevelt created a regime based on a new tie between organized labor and activist government. The new regime proved that while the bond between corporations and the state would not dissolve, the "relative autonomy" of the state allowed it to ally with popular forces to challenge corporate power. Roosevelt had always been deeply ambivalent about unions, but the power of labor activism and the deep labor sympathies of some of his closest advisors, such as Frances Perkins, Senator Robert Wagner, and Rexford Tugwell, led him to endorse the 1935 Wagner Act. Along with the Social Security Act, it was the foundation of regime change, pulling the state from its primary alliance with big business to a new intimate relation with labor.[35]

The new state-labor alliance was rife with strains and contradictions; the militant labor leader John L. Lewis was a Republican, and FDR had many close big-business associates. But the new tie to labor fused with the progressive sympathies of FDR's policy advisors to help create an American social democracy. Social democracy is the label typically used to characterize Western European systems characterized by activist government, strong labor movements, and universal social welfare policies. The new regime's version of social democracy was far less ambitious, reflecting the relative weakness of the new labor movement and the continuing great power of big business. But its zeitgeist was social activism, social justice, and relief for the long-suffering poor.

The New Deal regime lasted several decades after Roosevelt's death in 1945. In the 1950s and 1960s, labor membership peaked and did not start reversing until the 1970s. The social justice focus of Lyndon Johnson's Great Society, including the Civil Rights legislation of the early 1960s, was an extension of the original New Deal's social democratic promise. Even Republicans such as Richard Nixon were still bound by the terms of discourse of the New Deal, as when he supported a minimum income for all Americans and new environmental and social legislation.

In its post-Roosevelt phases, though, the contradictory character of the regime—its fundamentally conservative as well as liberal impetus—began to emerge. The Taft-Hartley Labor Act, a harshly antiunion measure passed in 1947, signaled the resurgence of corporate forces within the regime. Certain corporate sectors, including retail and finance, had helped build the New Deal early on. Retailers like Edward Filene, a major FDR supporter, believed that the New Deal was necessary to revive consumer spending for their department stores. Financiers, including Joseph Kennedy, had a broad overview of what was necessary to keep capitalism alive, and supported New Deal planning and social programs as a way to stimulate the economy and placate social discontent that could lead to socialism.[36]

In 1944, the choice of the centrist Harry Truman over left-leaning Henry Wallace for vice president would strengthen the corporate turn of the regime after FDR's death. Truman replaced Harry Dexter White, Roosevelt's left-leaning advisor on international economic affairs, with conservative advisors who transformed the regime's original plans for international economic cooperation and the United Nations into an agenda for an American Century.[37]

Truman's foreign policy, rooted in the new Cold War, supported a vision of a new global American era. It promised the global markets and resources that U.S. corporations were finally in a position to exploit after the collapse of the European empires. It also generated the "military Keynesianism"—or high Pentagon spending—that became the New Deal's main strategy for stimulating technological innovation, pump-priming the economy, and creating prosperity.[38] Military spending succeeded where the earlier New Deal failed, finally pulling the country out of the Depression by spending vastly more public funds in World War II than had been spent through the entire New Deal period before the war.[39] The seeds of both corporate globalization and global American Empire were thus firmly planted in the latter phases of the New Deal regime, though they would not fully germinate until the rise of our current third corporate regime. This demonstrates the continuities, particularly in foreign policy areas, that knit different regimes together. It also puts on full display the contradictions within regimes themselves, and the evolutionary stages they move through as they age.

The corporate and military sides of the New Deal regime ultimately helped to sink it. By the late 1970s, the United States suffered "stagflation"—a combination of high unemployment and high interest rates—that felt like a mini-Depression to many American workers. Corporate globalization, which the New Deal encouraged, was a critical factor in the deteriorating economic conditions. Corporations were using globalization to escape from the obligations to workers and communities—including good wages, benefits, and environmental regulation—that the New Deal itself had built. As jobs were being lost to stagflation, corporate flight, and global competition, and as wages and benefits declined, the American household survived only by sending women to work, and making two incomes do the business of one. The sharp decline in American working and living standards undercut the core agenda of the New Deal regime.

Military Keynesianism played a significant role in the New Deal economic slide. Military spending had helped pull the United States out of the Depression. But continued high Pentagon spending in the Vietnam era and beyond drained capital from the civilian side of the budget. It exacerbated the crisis faced by U.S. companies as they tried to cope with new competitive pressure from European and Japanese economies not saddled by high military costs. The New Deal's institutionalization of what economist Seymour Melman called the "permanent war economy" proved contradictory and ultimately lethal, initially boosting the New Deal economy and finally helping bring the entire regime down.[40]

Nonetheless, the New Deal, despite its serious limitations, still gives hope to many ordinary Americans. By realigning government with ordinary workers and citizens, it created foundations for economic growth and the creation of a middle class who could make good on the American Dream. While the New Deal was not a revolutionary anti-capitalist regime and far from an ideal democratic order, it resurrected the democratic dreams of the Declaration of Independence, reversed the corrupting legacy of two earlier corporate regimes, and demonstrated to skeptics that U.S. regime change can take back the government from the corporate moguls.

CHAPTER 2

THE POWERS THAT BE

ENTER THE THIRD CORPORATE REGIME

The *third* corporate regime is the house we live in today.
George W. Bush is just the current master of the mansion.
The architecture of the house is changing under Bush but
it follows the basic design established by Reagan a quarter
century ago.

Hidden power is still the story of our ruling regime. It is
a tale of anti-democratic power concentration that might
surprise even C. Wright Mills, who wrote about a veiled
power elite fifty years ago. Ironically, the regime's hegemonic ideology is that it is bringing American-inspired
democracy all over the world even as it erodes democracy
both abroad and at home.

I am not suggesting a past democratic paradise in the

Certificate of Birth

Name:	Third Corporate Regime
Date of Birth:	Election Day, 1980
Father:	Ronald Reagan
Mother:	Corporate America
Headquarters:	Washington, D.C.
Current Presider:	George W. Bush

Brief Biography

The regime is twenty-five years old.
It took form under the Reagan Administration. The regime consolidated itself
under Bush I, secured legitimacy from
Democrats under President Clinton, and
radicalized itself under Bush II. The aim
of the regime is to shift sovereignty
from citizens to transnational corporations, and to transform government into
a business partner committed to maximiz-
ing global profits for a small number
of global executives and shareholders.
It is showing signs of age and is viewed
by much of the world as dangerous.
Caution is advised.

Registry of Regimes, Washington, D.C.

United States. All corporate regimes have created a debilitated democracy in their own way. Nor am I implying that the current regime has stripped away all meaningful democracy. Quite the contrary. It is the very persistence of substantial democratic freedoms, including elections and constitutionalism, that allows the regime to persuade so many Americans that they are a shining hill of democracy when so many of our freedoms are now threatened.

THE TRANSNATIONAL CORPORATION

The foundation pillar of the regime is the transnational corporation, the biggest concentration of cold cash in human history. The companies dominating the regime—giants such as Wal-Mart, General Motors, General Electric, Exxon, Citigroup, Bank of America, Verizon Communications, Philip Morris, and Microsoft—are bigger than most countries. Citigroup has total assets over a *trillion* dollars![1] The top ten corporations have assets worth about $4 trillion. That is $4,000,000,000,000! Wal-Mart employed 1.34 *million* workers in 2003.[2] General Motors' annual sales are larger than the GDPs of Hong Kong, Denmark, Thailand, Norway, Poland, South Africa, and 158 other countries.[3] Big business has existed under every U.S. regime since the Civil War, but the third corporate regime is creating a world where companies are replacing countries as the super-powers. They make the companies of earlier regimes look like pygmies.

But while the size of the current regime's corporation is impressive, it is just one part of the story about what makes it new and uniquely dangerous to democracy. Today's corporation has a new transnational and constitutional identity that leads it to function more easily beyond the popular control of any government or people. The larger picture is about the structure of the corporate system itself that now links hundreds of transnational corporations with each other and the U.S. government into a global corpocracy, allowing the regime to constrain democracy over much of the planet in the name of promoting it.[4]

We have long had global corporations, but never the transnational form of today. Corporations of earlier regimes acquired raw materials abroad and sold to foreign markets. But their ownership was not global and they did not produce a significant fraction of their products with cheap foreign labor all over the world. When I walked into Toyota headquarters in Toyota City, Japan, I saw a world map lighting up the scores of different countries in which the tires, seats, engine parts, body, and other components were each produced. The entire globe was lit up like the Christmas tree in Rockefeller Center.

The transnational firm is a different and far more empowered entity than the corporation of the two earlier corporate regimes. A leading business group, the New York–based Conference Board, defined the earlier "multinational" firms as "national companies with units abroad."[5] In contrast, this regime's transnational is a firm whose identity lies in its global horizons. National borders are its enemy and national governments its handmaidens.[6] The new ethos of a transnational dream is well demonstrated by this quote from Dow Chemical's CEO in the 1970s:

> I have long dreamed of buying an island owned by no nation and of establishing the World Headquarters of the Dow Chemical Company on the truly neutral ground of such an island, beholden to no nation or society. If we were located on such truly neutral ground we could then really operate in the U.S. as U.S. citizens, in Japan as Japanese citizens and in Brazil as Brazilians rather than being governed in prime by the law of the United States. . . . We could even pay any natives handsomely to move somewhere else.[7]

This is truly a dream, for the current regime is based on a tight marriage between the transnational corporation and the U.S. government. But it accurately reflects changes in the identity and aspirations of the current corporation from those of earlier regimes. It also creates new tensions in the current corpocracy that did not exist in either the first or second regimes.

The transnational firm of the third corporate regime

feeds overwhelmingly on "exit power," one of the great sources of power in any social system. In a marriage, the partner who has the emotional or financial ability to leave wields power in the relationship. In prior corporate regimes, the American corporation used exit power by threatening to move from one state to another, a form of extortion that companies still use today to pit state governments or workers against one another. A big inequality in exit power is a recipe for abuse.[8]

This regime is constructing a new system of global exit power for the transnational firm. It threatens democracy far more powerfully than the exit power of earlier corporate regimes. If exit power is exercised across states, citizens can organize to ensure that the federal government, as in the New Deal, can step in to establish national minimum standards, such as a federal minimum wage. But since there is no true global government, that democratic option is currently off the table. Organizations most similar to global government, like the World Trade Organization (WTO), enforce international property rights, such as rights of equal treatment for foreign firms and global copyrights. But they view labor standards as beyond their constitutional purview, and there is no global agency with the teeth to enforce even the most minimal democratic worker protections.[9]

The United States and its allied global authorities, such as the WTO, formally strip away impediments to corporate mobility by enforcing unfettered trade requirements and open markets that are conditions for entry into the world economy and the WTO itself. In doing so, they erode democratic capacity in the nation-state, since the nation lacks exit power and is becoming more subordinate to the hypermobile transnational firm. The rights of the corporation to leave and protect its property rights globally are defined as part of a global constitutional order promoting freedom and democracy. If you challenge free trade, international property rights, or the corporation's freedom to exit, you are challenging freedom itself. Globalization is justified by the regime's ideology of global democracy that the regime itself is subverting.

A small number of transnational corporations sit at the heart of the regime, led by the Top Ten. Each of these Top Ten are bigger than one hundred countries. In 2004, eight of the top ten global companies in the *Wall Street Journal*'s ranking by market value were U.S. based, with GE, Exxon Mobil, Microsoft, Pfizer, Citigroup, and Wal-Mart being the six largest (BP and Royal Dutch/Shell were the only two non-American firms represented).[10] But you'd have to add on GM, Ford, J. P. Morgan Chase, and scores of other behemoths to get the picture. $4 trillion is just a fraction of the wealth controlled by the two hundred largest intertwined giant companies who rule the regime and produce slightly more than one-quarter of the world's total wealth.[11]

In the first corporate regime, Rockefeller and Morgan helped build the interlocking corporate web that knit together all major robber corporations into an integrated *system.*[12] It is this intercorporate spider web, with the capacity for collective corporate identity and action, that underpinned the regime. While the robber barons and their individual companies were highly visible, the interlocked system itself was less transparent, part of the earlier regime's partially hidden power grid.

In the current regime, we have a new corporate spider web that is also more hidden than the individual brand-name companies. It is a byzantine maze of interlocking directorships, contracting networks, and strategic alliances. Economist Bennett Harrison notes that the biggest corporations themselves have decentralized into a "network" system linking workers, designers, contractors, suppliers, and corporate headquarters.[13] But these networks have networked themselves into intercorporate alliances across global economic sectors. Nearly every top 200 firm is networked with every other, including its biggest competitors. Think of the collaboration between GM and Toyota, or the airline partners, or the cross-marketing collaborations between companies such as McDonald's and Toys R Us.

While this interlocked system, as in earlier corporate regimes, is most dense in the United States, it is rapidly becoming a global affair. British sociologist Leslie Sklair, the authoritative chronicler of this emergent global hidden power grid, believes that it is already dense enough to have created a "transnational capitalist class (TCC)."[14] Its inner circle, he says, has included some of the best-known global executives, such as Citibank's David Rockefeller, News Corporation's media mogul Rupert Murdoch, Sony's founder Akio Morita, and Nestlé's former CEO, Helmut Maucher. The inner circle is highly interlocked globally, just as the robber barons were interlocked nationally in the first corporate regime. They function, as Rockefeller and Morgan did a century ago, as Sklair puts it, as "a unity to the diverse economic interests, political organizations, and cultural and ideological formations" that sustain the current global regime.[15]

Popular movements have launched anticorporate campaigns against almost every individual Fortune 500 transnational corporation—from Wal-Mart to Nike to Philip Morris to Nestlé. But these attacks glance off the regime and barely scratch it. The underlying interwoven corporate spider web is largely off the public radar screen, a sign of its hidden power. The movements themselves can sometimes unwittingly reinforce the perverse hegemonic democratic ideology of the regime. By permitting attacks on individual firms, the regime shows its democratic colors, all the while realizing that the core of its hidden power remains secure. The stronger the anticorporate attacks on individual companies, the more the regime can proclaim its democratic credentials in giving them free rein.

GLOBAL CORPOCRACY

The global corporate grid, by itself, cannot create or sustain the regime without its relation to the U.S. government. As in earlier corporate regimes, it is the marriage between corporation and state, the corpocracy, that makes the regime tick. In the current regime, it is a fusion of the transnational firm and the American government. To see the current corpocracy, look at George W. Bush's cabinet:

PRESIDENT GEORGE W. BUSH
CEO, Texas Rangers; Board of Directors, Harken Energy

VICE PRESIDENT RICHARD CHENEY
CEO, Halliburton, Inc., the huge energy and defense conglomerate

SECRETARY OF DEFENSE DONALD RUMSFELD
CEO of General Instrument Company and the drug giant, G. D. Searle and Co.

PAUL O'NEILL, FIRST BUSH SECRETARY OF THE TREASURY
CEO of Alcoa and of International Paper Co.

SECRETARY OF THE TREASURY JOHN SNOW
CEO of CSX, the railroad giant, and Chairman
of the Business Roundtable, the leading big
business group in America

FIRST TRANSPORTATION SECRETARY NORMAN MINETA
Corporate Vice President, Lockheed Martin

LABOR SECRETARY ELAINE CHAO
Vice President, Bank of America

FIRST AGRICULTURE SECRETARY ANN VENEMAN
Board of Directors of Calgene, Inc., a subsidiary
of Monsanto Corporation[16]

Bush's cabinet illustrates the marriage between transnational corporations and the U.S. government that is
the second pillar of today's corporate regime. The corporations are giant transnationals, but all headquartered in
the United States. This reflects both the dominance of U.S.
firms among the world's largest corporations and the fact
that this is a regime rooted in the power of the U.S. government. The marriage of corporation and government, as
in earlier corporate regimes, is fundamentally antidemocratic, since it creates a governance system unaccountable
to the voters, who are not partners in the marriage and have
different interests than either spouse.

While this antidemocratic core is consistent with earlier
regimes, there is a new schizophrenic dimension at work
here. The transnationals in the marriage ultimately seek to
break down nation-states and create global corporate sovereignty. But they depend on the economic, political, and
military backing of an American state which has little in-

terest, at this stage, in eliminating the nation-state or national sovereignty.

In earlier corporate regimes, such schizophrenia was impossible, because the regime was rooted in national corporations and the corpocracy was a purely American affair with exclusively U.S. interests. Today, the corpocracy must wrestle to reconcile global corporate interests with the nationalist interests of the state. The government largely seeks to satisfy its transnational patrons but not so flagrantly that it openly breaks faith with the U.S. workers and voters to whom it is supposed to be democratically accountable.

In responding to this hegemonic challenge, the United States tilts globally but in a way that favors U.S. transnationals and the U.S. government itself. Rigging global rules threatens global hegemony, since around the world, the United States is seen as creating an unfair playing field. Nonetheless, hegemonic control of ordinary Americans is far more important to the regime than winning the hearts and minds of citizens around the world, who can be controlled militarily. The regime is prepared to tolerate strong anti-Americanism abroad to tamp down dissent from anxious American voters who fear for their jobs and need to believe that their government is still representing them.

Inside the United States, the antidemocratic structure of the corpocracy is similar to both the first and second corporate regimes. Big business representatives sit in the cabinet with the president, their lobbyists work with Congress, and together they all write the rules, under the hegemonic cover of American democracy and free elections. Consider the corpocracy's response to the outbreak of the mad cow epidemic. When the epidemic was discovered in the United States in December 2003, Alisa Harrison, the spokesperson for Agriculture Secretary Ann Veneman, was telling the American public not to worry—American beef is safe. She didn't say that she used to be the PR director of the National Cattlemen's Beef Association. In fact, the Department of Agriculture, which is supposed to protect the public from mad cow disease and other health risks, is packed with former lobbyists for the cattle and agriculture businesses. Dale Moore, who is Veneman's chief of staff, was previously chief of staff for the same Beef Assocation. And another high-ranking Agriculture Department official used to be president of the National Pork Producers Council.[17]

Give due credit to Reagan for the construction of today's corpocracy, the regime's second pillar. Despite Reagan's rhetoric that "big government is the enemy," the regime is a vast, unaccountable federal apparatus, hugely expanded by Reagan himself and so entangled with global big business as to be indistinguishable from it. Reagan's cabinet of former CEOs, like Bush's, functioned as a board of directors for corporate America.[18]

Today's corpocracy functions with the same brazen antidemocratic style as the robber-baron regime. Imagine a Las Vegas slot machine with a surefire chance of winning—and let's take the pharmaceutical industry as an example of a sure corporate winner in the regime. In 2000, the industry put millions in the Washington slot machine to help reelect Bush. The industry then used its lobbyists in the House of Representatives alone to draft the huge Medicare overhaul bill passed in 2003. See the schematic sum-

PLAY THE
CORPOCRACY GAME

DRUG COMPANIES

1. Give Bush $21 million in 2000 to elect him.
2. Spend $100 million in contributions, entertainment, and lobbying of Congress between elections (2000–2004).
3. Use your 467 lobbyists on the Hill to pressure representatives and draft the Medicare Overhaul Bill, which returns billions in new profits to you, enhancing your status as the most profitable industry in America, making more than five times the profit rate of the average U.S. industry. Just by restricting government bulk purchasing of drugs, your lobbyists deliver an extra $139 billion in profits to the industry.[19]
4. Spend $100 million in 2004 to reelect the president and make sure that the new Medicare program continues to deliver the goods.[20]

This is not just a game played by pharmaceuticals. With all corporations pulling together, it's even more profitable.

ALL CORPORATIONS

1. Give Bush $2 billion in 2000 to elect him.
2. Give Bush $2 billion in 2004 to reelect him.
3. Get Back: corporate-friendly legislation on energy, trade, media, pharmaceuticals, health care. Receive back, in 2004, a Congressional tax bill delivering an additional $210 billion in corporate tax breaks.[21]

mary of the corpocracy in action for the pharmaceutical companies.

The share of federal taxes paid by corporations dropped dramatically from the New Deal to the current regime, and it just keeps falling as ordinary citizens pick up the slack. The data are a measure of who the government really serves—and it isn't the ordinary taxpayers with the biggest and growing burden. In the New Deal regime, the corporate tax burden averaged about 30 percent. In the 1980s through the mid-1990s, as the new regime took hold, it fell to 15 percent. By 1998, it fell to 11.8 percent[22] and in that year Texaco, Chevron, PepsiCo, Enron, WorldCom, McKesson, and the world's biggest corporation, General Motors, paid no federal taxes at all.[23] Since then, the corporate tax burden has lightened even further. Robert McIntyre, director of the respected Washington-based center Citizens for Tax Justice, reported in 2005 that "large Fortune 500 companies now report less than half their actual profits to the IRS, and that almost a third of such big companies paid no income tax in at least one of President Bush's first three years in office. One company, General Electric, which enjoyed $9.5 billion in tax subsidies over the three years analyzed in the study, is widely conceded to be the biggest beneficiary of the just-passed corporate-tax-subsidy bill."[24]

How does the regime sustain hegemony and maintain the fiction of democracy in the light of such brazen corporate political influence over both the White House and Congress? The answer can be found partly by looking at the regime's courts, another part of the corpocracy that both creates and is driven by corporate power, all in the name of democratic constitutionalism.

In the first corporate regime of the robber barons, as discussed in Chapter 1, the courts helped redefine corporations as private persons with constitutional rights. During most of the New Deal, the Supreme Court did not extend any new constitutional rights to further empower companies. But as the New Deal faded in the 1970s and the current regime took over in the 1980s, the Supreme Court began finding new corporate constitutional rights that would cement new hidden power and dramatically erode democratic rights.

Corporate historian Ted Nace has chronicled the corporate constitutional rights emerging with the new regime:

- The Seventh Amendment right to a jury trial in a civil case (*Ross v Bernhard*, 1970)
- The First Amendment right of "commercial free speech" (*Virginia Board of Pharmacy v Virginia Citizens Consumer Council*, 1976, and *Central Hudson Gas*, 1980)
- The Fourth Amendment right against unwarranted regulatory searches (*Marshall v Barlow's*, 1978)
- The First Amendment right to spend money to influence a state referendum (*Bellotti*, 1978)
- The First Amendment right of "negative free speech" (*Pacific Gas and Electric Co. v Public Utilities Commission*, 1986)[25]

In these decisions, corporations gained new rights to corporate "free speech" that, as Nace suggests, give them a "megaphone" that can drown out speech by the rest of us. In the Pacific Gas and Electric case, the Court struck down a regulatory agency's ruling that the utility had to include a consumer rate-paying newsletter in its billing envelope.

THE POWERS THAT BE

The Court said that forcing the company to include the newsletter would violate its speech rights not to be associated with views that it doesn't support ("negative free speech"). But since Pacific Gas is a monopoly controlling information about the industry for millions of consumers, defending the free speech rights of the company muted the popular voices seeking to challenge the utility firm.[26]

This illustrates how this regime's constitutional corporate rights empower the companies in the name of the very democracy that they are weakening. The First Amendment rights give the corporations new power to control information and promote their own political agenda in the name of protecting the cherished speech rights of all of us. The Fourth Amendment rights allow the corporations to claim privacy rights restricting spot checks on its pollution in the name of protecting the privacy rights of you and me. As in the first corporate regime, the rights awarded by the courts dramatically increase hidden power in the sense that these landmark constitutional cases and their political implications are invisible to most Americans. The new power is dressed up in the third corporate regime's unique hegemonic strategy: constitutionally equate new corporate rights with the democratic rights of you and me. If you challenge the new constitutional corporate rights to speech, of a Nike or Philip Morris, you appear to be attacking your own constitutional rights to speak freely. The Supreme Court of the regime is, in fact, melding the two together. The Court thereby undermines democracy in the name of expanding it to protect both corporate citizens and real ones.

The regime is systematically dismantling the social contract of the New Deal that promised security to a generation traumatized by the Depression. That contract was expensive and protected people by regulating corporate excesses. The current regime seeks a new social contract—its third pillar—that trades the social security of workers and citizens for profit maximization, essentially a blow to social democracy.

Social insecurity begins with the job. The regime now aims to abolish the traditional concept of a job that developed under the New Deal regime, the secure full-time form of work prevailing at mid–twentieth century but now seen as an unacceptable limit on profits. "What is disappearing," writes organizational analyst William Bridges, "is not just a certain number of jobs—or jobs in certain industries . . . but the very thing itself: the job. That much sought after, much maligned social entity, a job, is vanishing like a species that has outlived its evolutionary time."[27]

Jobs survived in the new regime, but they wouldn't be government or union-protected. This required all-out assault on the 1935 New Deal Wagner Act, which enshrined unions as democratic counterweights to corporations. The regime has made a frontal attack on organized labor, and it has been the most consistent element in all three corporate regimes.

The third corporate regime wasted no time in busting unions, with Reagan's first act being the dismantling of PATCO, the air traffic–controller union. Reagan then started the long-standing regime policy of breaking unions: by making antiunion appointments to government labor boards, encouraging companies that broke union contracts and demanded concessions, and facilitating the ultimate corporate weapons against labor: exit power. As companies under the new regime fled overseas for cheap labor, aided by Reagan's new tax breaks for companies operating overseas, massive downsizing became the regime's signature,

I talked to Allen, who is forty and a software engineer freelancing with computer companies in the United States and living in Boston. Allen told me that his father "was a salesman for an electrical company and he worked for the same company his whole life." But Allen, although well educated with graduate degrees in business and accounting, has worked "for about forty companies," and he says "fifty percent of the employees on the payroll are temps or contractors like me. The companies don't want to pay benefits and they're greedy." Allen claims his father's era is finished, and Allen does not expect to ever get a permanent job.

By stripping away the protections and security of the New Deal job, the new regime is endangering the middle class. Allen declares flatly: "The middle class is disappearing." Allen says his own American dream is shrinking. "Lots of things I thought I was going to have I may never have. I may never own a home. I may never marry and I definitely will not have children." Allen is thinking not just of his own difficult economic circumstances but of his brother and wife, who have four children and are not making it. His brother has been downsized twice out of well-paying corporate jobs.

along with the creation of the new breed of contingent and outsourced jobs that have turned America's "middle class" into a new "anxious class."[28]

In a transnational corporate regime, corporate globalization becomes the ultimate hammer for beating down U.S. job protections and security in the name of "free trade." The U.S. social contract is dragged down toward the horrendous social contract long prevailing in Third World countries, thereby globalizing the third corporate regime's social contract on terms that favor the transnational corporation at the expense of workers in both rich and poor countries.[29]

The new social contract also requires dismantling the New Deal social welfare system—the American version of what Europeans call social democracy. Reagan attacked social democracy by taking a sledge hammer to domestic social spending and arguing that the New Deal's welfare system undermined the entrepreneurial spirit at the heart of the new regime. Reagan bled nearly every domestic program—education, health care, food stamps—to finance his tax cuts for the rich and his military spending.[30]

Reagan's social policies continued under Bush Sr. and into the Clinton years, when Newt Gingrich spearheaded the Contract for America that proposed cutting nearly all social spending and leaving a government devoted entirely to corporate welfare and the military. Clinton did his part by calling for "the end of welfare as we know it." Clinton targeted 130 federal programs for extinction, many for education, scientific research, or the environment, and proposed to abolish or radically downsize the Department of Housing, the Department of Transportation, and other agencies devoted to social ends. One Washington observer noted that "You expect to see Republicans when they are in power doing this—it's what they've been pushing for years. But to see the Democrats doing it, and to see the competition between the White House and the congress as they race to privatize—it's amazing."[31]

Bush is pursuing the regime's social contract in yet more brazen ways, openly pursuing tax cuts worth more than a trillion dollars for the rich while underfunding virtually all vital social needs, including his own touted education act, called "No Child Left Behind." The regime is moving under Bush toward its ultimate conclusion: privatizing Social Security itself and ultimately eliminating the concept of social insurance developed during the New Deal. While the collapse and scandals of the financial markets postponed Bush's plans to privatize Social Security for a second term, Bush announced after his reelection that "reforming" Social Security and turning it from a social insurance plan into a system of private accounts was his top domestic priority.

This plan was the pivotal assault on the New Deal legacy, since the 1935 Social Security Act was the central accomplishment of the New Deal regime. It created a retirement system based on the assumption of a pact between generations, on a commitment to redistribute wealth to ensure a decent retirement for all, and on the core New Deal idea that American individualism had to be balanced with strong commitments to community and solidarity.

Bush's proposal to create private accounts is a direct assault on all these New Deal precepts. It argues that each generation must now look out mainly for its own interests. A system of private accounts would lead to significantly less redistribution, across gender and class, as John B. Williamson and others have documented in rigorous studies.[32] And it would weaken the moral commitment to solidarity by individualizing the responsibility for retirement. Under a privatized system, how you fare in your retirement depends on your wealth and on your talent or luck as an investor. In the New Deal system, your individual retirement was determined by the contributions of the entire community. What could better sum up the difference in the social contract between the New Deal and the current regime? From a corporate regime's perspective, let us also not forget about the multibillion-dollar bonanza for the Wall Street managers who are salivating about the new money to be made on your retirement money and mine.

EMPIRE

The foreign policy aim of the current regime—its fourth pillar—is to shape a U.S.-led corporate *global* order: to be blunt, an American empire. Empire is by its nature anti-democratic but it is essential to transnational corporate interests. As in the progressive age of President Woodrow Wilson, empire is thus defined as a way to secure global democracy, even as it subverts democratic prospects both at home and abroad.

Empire has a long American history, beginning with the 1823 Monroe Doctrine. It picked up steam in the imperial adventures of the Progressive era, including the U.S. acquisition of the Philippines in 1904. But the creation of a fully global empire began in the New Deal regime after World War II. The collapse of European colonialism opened up a power vacuum that both U.S. corporations and the U.S.

government were eager to fill. By the early 1950s, the United States was busy building both the international economic institutions, such as the International Monetary Fund and the World Bank, and the global network of military bases and client states that was the first step toward full-scale global hegemony.[33]

The third corporate regime thus changed domestic policy far more than foreign policy. Rather than transforming the nation's foreign policy, it has accelerated and deepened the nation's antidemocratic, empire-building, expanding U.S. military presence and intervention, particularly in the Middle East, and justifying it with new neoconservative doctrines. It remains, however, as in the late 1940s, 1950s, and 1960s, a corporate-driven process for expanding markets and profits, making clear that corporations played a major role before the current regime in shaping New Deal foreign policy.[34] The best-selling book *Confessions of an Economic Hit-Man,* by John Perkins, offers a compelling personal account by a corporate insider of how this process played out from the New Deal through the current regime. Perkins describes himself as a "hit man" because he was personally collaborating from the 1960s to the 1990s in the dirty work of deceiving poor countries to accept loans that would force them to open and subordinate their economies to U.S. firms, backed by the U.S. military. The personal stories and Perkins's own deep spiritual remorse make clear how this practice has undermined democracy and moral principles in both the New Deal and current regimes.[35]

As the third corporate regime has aged, changes in corporate interests and political power, as well as in the ideology of the U.S. foreign policy establishment, have nonetheless produced some important new directions. Global capital has become more concentrated and powerful, while new technology has facilitated the move offshore, where cheap labor increases profit margins. The acceleration of corporate globalization during the current regime has increased the foreign policy and military U.S. government stakes in securing the entire planet as a friendly base for U.S. corporations, leading to the establishment of the now more than 700 U.S. military bases around the world. This ensures that the regime's global dominance will be enforced at the barrel of a gun if necessary.

During the New Deal, the U.S. acted in the service of nearly the entire range of U.S., Japanese, and European global companies to establish the beginnings of a corporate global order. Over the course of the current regime, and particularly since the Bush II years, U.S. oil and military companies, such as Halliburton, Exxon, and Lockheed-Martin, have gained power relative to other corporate sectors. While these firms have obviously benefited from the wars and enormous military expenditures in Iraq, the Gulf, and the broader Middle East, the broader costs of empire, including massive U.S. government deficits, fall not only on ordinary Americans but to some degree on corporations in other sectors. This could open up cracks within the current regime, not only between U.S. corporations and U.S. workers, but among different sectors of the American corporate world itself. Bush Sr. spoke more for the eastern Wall Street financial sector from which the Bush dynasty hails. Bush Jr.'s shift of the corporate center of gravity to Southwest military and oil companies has produced consternation among the New York–based traditional Republican elites, who fear that the son's "cowboy capitalism," symbolized by the unilateralism of the Iraq invasion, could help drive deficits disastrous to the financial system.[36]

The current regime is now in a phase of dismantling much of the multilateral framework and the system of international law created under the New Deal. Remember that Franklin Roosevelt helped to create the United Nations, and his regime successors, such as Truman and Eisenhower, pursued global power with some deference to multilateralism and U.N. conventions, seen as essential to a democratic world order. Like Bush II, Reagan was impatient with international treaties and other multilateral restraints on American power. He began the process of rejecting much of the New Deal international framework, and was openly contemptuous of the United Nations, of arms control, and of restraints on military spending. President George W. Bush has accelerated these regime tendencies begun under Reagan and pursued more quietly under his father and Clinton. Following Reagan's disdain for international law and his fondness for interventions and regime changes abroad, Bush has used the new climate after 9/11 mainly to institutionalize these long-standing regime policies. In its more extreme form, as former White House advisor William A. Galston described the regime's current approach, it "means the end of the system of international institutions, laws and norms that the U.S. has worked for more than half a century to build."[37] Princeton political scientist Richard Falk, one of the nation's leading scholars on international law, writes that the preemptive invasion of Iraq "repudiates the core idea of the United Nations charter. . . . It is a doctrine without limits, without accountability to the U.N. or international law."[38]

The neoconservatives' revival of Wilsonian idealism puts

on display the hegemonic function of democratic rhetoric and elections. Empire is once again justified as a way to make the world safe for democracy. As in the domestic sphere, the regime's spread of elections to the Middle East, symbolized by the 2005 election in Iraq, exploits democratic procedures abroad to disguise the continuing U.S. dominance of Iraqi politics and the enforced opening of the Iraqi economy to U.S. corporations and the International Monetary Fund.[39] Elections abroad have become the hegemonic wedge legitimating the U.S. empire, just as they are used to hide and legitimate corporate rule at home.

THE CORPORATE MYSTIQUE

Free markets! Free trade! Free people! Free Iraq! Free world! Free after-Thanksgiving sales! Freedom is the seductive mantra of the third corporate regime. Most Americans buy it.

Liberty, of course, has always been at the heart of American ideology. What is new is a rhetoric of freedom for all—at home and abroad as Bush proclaimed in his second bold Inaugural address—that translates into unimagined freedom for big business and big problems for the rest of us. Bush's rhetoric opens up new political opportunities for those who seek not just the rhetoric but the promise of new democracy, but I return to that much later in this book.

The expansion of freedom for the First Citizens of this regime, that is the corporations, is the real aim of the current regime and is now equated with personal freedom and the expansion of democracy. It is all part of the corporate mystique, the regime's ideology telling us that a "free market" based on unfettered corporate liberty is the best of all possible worlds. The mystique says there really is no other way. The freedom of the market is the cornerstone of the freedom of every citizen and a free corporation is the precondition of a free society. The corporation is the Golden Goose, but it needs free range. When freed to do what it wants, it delivers the goods. If we shackle it, we shackle ourselves and our prospects for the good life. Kill corporate freedom and we kill off democracy.[40]

The mystique, while rhetorically embracing personal liberty, in truth nourishes mainly one form of personal freedom: the right to splurge at the mall. Consumerism! It is the highest form of freedom in the corporate mystique, and the regime encourages us to use our plastic cards to keep consuming long after we can afford to. Consumerism replaces citizenship as the operative value in the regime. *I buy, therefore I am. I am what I buy!*

The freedom dreamed of by the Founders is at high risk. Citizen choice in this regime is the right to decide between Coke and Pepsi. The regime argues that choice at the marketplace is the most powerful act of citizenship. One dollar, one vote. That is the democracy of the corporate mystique, which legitimates the regime. The current regime's hegemonic strategy knits together the rhetoric of democracy and elections with the ideology of consumerism—all under the rubric of freedom. If we are free to vote and to consume, how can we not regard ourselves as a genuinely free society? The corporate mystique manufactures the consent of the people, in the name of freedom and democracy, to a system that is less and less free and democratic. And it continues to hide *systemic* corporate power, an astonishing accomplishment in a regime of such brazen and open corporate influence.

Citizenship is effectively redefined as freedom in the mall, not the town hall. A corporate regime makes this seductive since we grow up as kids addicted to magical corporate goodies, whether Disney films or PCs. Creature comforts are the great blessings of the regime, and they are not easily dismissed by anyone, especially a population brought up on Toys R Us and Big Macs. How can you challenge the producers of the Magic Kingdom, who have brought you happiness your whole life? How can you challenge the makers of Mickey Mouse, our best friend for life?

The corporate mystique, and its consumerist brand of democracy, was born in the first corporate regime and turned into a national religion in the second corporate regime of the Roaring Twenties. But in the earlier corporate regimes, leading ideologues were busy enough persuading just Americans to embrace the new corporation and get serious about consuming. Now, they have turned their attention to persuading the rest of the world. Globalization is the spread of the corporate mystique as the universal religion of the planet, and it is the cutting edge of the third corporate regime's ideology.

Global democracy is the corporate mystique as God's way. The third corporate regime aims to make everyone on the planet a believer.

CHAPTER 3

THE RULES
OF CHANGE

*T*homas Kuhn, the philosopher of science who wrote *The Structure of Scientific Revolutions,* showed that science develops through surprising transformations.[1] Kuhn says that science, rather than being a slow evolutionary process, moves in dramatic leaps from one basic paradigm to another. These quantum leaps in science are something like regime changes in politics: they are disruptive and radical.

Kuhn says there are two ways to do science. In most periods, scientists play by the rules of normal science. They accept the reigning theoretical paradigm and try to solve the small puzzles yet to be resolved. But over time, inexplicable contradictions—Kuhn calls them "anomalies" —begin to accumulate. A few brave scientists question whether the reigning paradigm can explain the contradictions and embark on a heretical quest to topple it and construct a new paradigm. In the process, they move beyond normal science, a shift from defending and patching up the old order to creating a new one. A Newton or an Einstein eventually emerges and proposes a revolutionary theory. A growing number of radical scientists embrace it and work to establish it as a new regime.[2]

Politics is no science. But like normal science, there is the game of *normal politics*: Republicans played it through most of the New Deal and Democrats have been playing it ever since FDR died. When you play the game of normal politics, you treat the big questions as settled, making most political contests about small matters that do not shake the regime and do not change the lives of ordinary Americans.

But politicians sometimes become paradigm-breakers. During the 1930s, the Democrats were regime changers and in the 1970s and 1980s insurgent Republicans were the quantum leapers. New Dealers during the Depression and New Rightists at the opening of the Reagan Revolution made politics a more "out of the box" game than in normal eras. Even couch potatoes got inspired—they may have listened to FDR's fireside chats on their couch, but they were really paying attention and promising to work with the president to change the country!

In this chapter, I describe the rules of regime-change politics. I draw on examples from the New Dealers and the New Rightists. They are the two masters of the regime change game in the twentieth century.

NAME THEIR GAME: NORMAL POLITICS OR REGIME CHANGE?

- Franklin Roosevelt
- Ronald Reagan
- George Bush, Sr.
- Bill Clinton
- Al Gore
- George W. Bush
- Howard Dean
- John Kerry
- Dennis Kucinich
- Ralph Nader

See the answers at the end of this chapter. Expect some surprises!

RULE 1: EMBRACE DEFEAT

It's hard enough to accept defeat, let alone enthusiastically embrace it! But this is precisely what the New Righters did in 1964, when President Johnson crushed Arizona Republican Senator Barry Goldwater in a landslide. Goldwater had rejected the normal politics of Eisenhower Republicans in the 1950s and campaigned on a radical platform to overthrow the New Deal regime (well, he didn't quite put it that way but that's what he wanted to do). It was a premature strategy and Johnson flattened Goldwater like a pancake in one of the biggest Democratic victories of all time. The genius of the New Right—and particularly of the grassroots antitax organizers and activist evangelical preachers in the South and West—was to reject conventional wisdom about Goldwater's humiliating defeat, refusing to skulk back to normal politics. Instead, they embraced this big loser as a hero and saw in his candidacy the route to regime change in the decade to come. Democrats, take note!

The Goldwater loyalists, sensing the vulnerabilities of the New Deal regime, saw that Goldwater had aroused a new constituency in the Bible Belt that could revolutionize the country. While Goldwater suffered a catastrophic national defeat, he had won all the deep South states, largely because the Democrats passed major civil rights legislation. Goldwater thereby both inherited and created a situation for a major political realignment, a sea change central to regime change today. The New Deal regime had been based on the coalition between the historically rock-solid Democratic South and the new industrial labor base in the Midwest. By winning the South, Goldwater shattered the political foundation of the New Deal and opened the path to the emergent coalition between Wall Street, Southwest military and energy corporations, and Southern religious fundamentalists that would become the base of the Reagan-Bush new regime.[3]

While the Republican establishment still hewed to a more mainstream conservative path in the candidacy of Richard Nixon, the New Right activists, ignited by the Goldwater campaign, shifted to regime-change politics and gradually infiltrated the Republican Party at the base.

Their eventual success led to the Reagan Revolution and today's regime. In the process, they created a historic political realignment that we desperately need again today.

RULE 2: PLAY OFFENSE, THINK BIG

BIG-THINKING REPUBLICANS: SMALL-THINKING DEMOCRATS

In normal politics, the rule is to think small and play defense. It's an understandable strategy on the Boston highways and in many marriages, and it's the standard approach in most political eras. Since the regime is well established and parties seek to contest the White House without changing regimes, politics is about small ideas. With big ideas out of play, parties play defense by moving to the center and politics loses its intellectual interest; it becomes entertainment, about personalities and partisan horse races.

Paradoxically, thinking small and playing defense have been embraced by the Democratic leadership for most of the last few decades, while the Bush Republicans are doing the opposite, playing offense as they seek to push the envelope of the current corporate regime. This is a dramatic historical reversal of roles, with the party that should be challenging the regime playing normal politics and those running the regime exploiting a cardinal rule of regime change. The Bush Republicans are still following Goldwater, most famously remembered for his phrase: "Extremism in the pursuit of liberty is no vice." The 1970s brash New Rightists, still in power today and still pushing big ideas, happily embraced extremism from the begin-

ning, forming new corporate-funded foundations and jour-
nals and filling them with radical ideas. Some of their big
(and mostly very bad) ideas, many of which they have now
accomplished, are:

Privatize Medicare
Privatize Social Security
Deregulate the mass media
Vouchers for private schools
Home schooling
Abolish the estate tax
Institute the flat tax
Abolish taxes on corporate dividends
Eliminate most environmental regulations
Eliminate unions
Ban abortion
Eliminate state-church separation
Roll back gay rights
Abolish the United Nations
Abolish the federal government (except the Pentagon
    and corporate welfare)

There was nothing modest or centrist in the thinking of
these activist conservatives, nor of the Reagan Administration itself, whose intent was to dismantle the New Deal
once and for all while destroying the Soviet "Evil Empire."
Today the neoconservatives, now the leading lights of the
Bush Administration, are still not playing normal politics,
and still winning by refusing to move to the center and
think small.

The New Dealers were also thinking big in the 1930s. Franklin D. Roosevelt knew it was no time for normal politics. In the Roaring Twenties, big ideas about laissez-faire, corporate self-regulation, and corporate paternalism had become deeply entrenched in the mainstream. By 1936, Roosevelt had attacked all these ideas, willing to risk the label of class warfare that intimidates Democrats in eras of normal politics. Roosevelt became the first president ever to launch a European-style social democracy in America, and his raft of new ideas saved capitalism but only by radically changing the political conversation. His regime-changing ideas—normal politics in Europe but almost revolutionary in the United States—inspired the most important legislation of the twentieth century:

> Create Social Security (Social Security Act)
> Legalize unions and collective bargaining (Wagner Act)
> Create government programs to employ millions of jobless workers (Public Works Administration, Emergency Relief Appropriations Act)
> Strictly regulate banking and Wall Street (Glass-Steagall Act)
> Break up big utilities and other big holding companies (Holding Company Act)
> Create public utilities (Rural Electrification Act)[4]

Some of these ideas may seem quite pedestrian today, but after the Hooverist "hands off" philosophy of the Roaring Twenties regime, they were mind-bending. The rich attacked it as socialism, but workers all over America found that politics finally meant something: a job, a voice, a little respect. These laws *created* the American middle class. No wonder so many people cried openly when they heard of FDR's death. Roosevelt turned the government from a handmaiden of the corporation into a countervailing power of and by the people, prepared to challenge business on key issues, including constitutional ones. Roosevelt's willingness to "pack the court" to shift the constitutionalism of the Gilded Age and the Roaring Twenties makes clear that FDR had rejected the politics of defense and small ideas.

Throughout the four terms of FDR, the Democratic Party played offense, seeking to reverse the legacy of two prior corporate regimes. *This was the only time that the Democratic Party has ever embraced militant regime-change politics and it produced the only sustained period of Democratic ascendancy in American history.* Shouldn't the Democratic Party leaders today be forced to repeat this lesson ten times at breakfast, ten times at lunch, ten times at dinner, and a hundred times before going to bed?

WHEN THE DEMOCRATS STOPPED THINKING BIG

The New Deal declined partly because Roosevelt's successors did not continue the spirit of thinking big that Roosevelt himself pioneered. Despite Democratic Congressional majorities in the 1950s, 1960s, and 1970s, they did not pursue the ambitious social goals that FDR himself might have embraced. The Democrats didn't try to build or democratize the labor movement. They didn't pass universal health care and they didn't attack corporate power.

They bought into the Cold War and—with the very important exception of major civil rights legislation, a genuine
advance of New Deal "big thinking"—mainstream Democrats turned against the Left in the 1960s, as it was pushing for participatory democracy and social justice at home
and peace and human rights in foreign policy—precisely
what the Democratic Party should have been doing. As
corporate historian Ted Nace put it, "Franklin Roosevelt
introduced notions of social democracy into American politics, but his successors dropped the ball."[5]

Thinking big and going on the offense is necessary both
to create regime change and sustain the regime over the
long term. Admittedly, it is easier for Republicans to get
major funding for their visionary ideas and politics, and
Democratic visionaries have had to run their institutes,
magazines, and organizations on a shoestring. Democrats
get corporate funding when they play the regime's game
and play the role of incremental reformers or the "loyal opposition." This explains the seductions of thinking small for
the Democratic establishment, but it doesn't make it a
good idea—in fact, it's criminal that the Democrats have
prostituted themselves to their own corporate patrons. If
it wants to win elections, the Democratic Party has to find
other ways to spread the big ideas it needs. Fortunately, the
rise of the Internet as an inexpensive way to reach millions
of people with bold new ideas, and raising small contributions, as Howard Dean did from large numbers of "little
people," suggest there are new ways for Democrats to think
big and play offense.

Ironically, in the last quarter century, the Democratic
Party has remained in the defense mode and small ideas of
normal politics, at the very historic moment when condi-

tions are emerging for new big ideas and regime change. Of course, unlike big-thinking activist leftists, the New Rightists are well funded for creating and promoting their radical ideas, and their political efficacy lies not just in the "bigness" of their ideas but in the twenty-four-hour cable media exposure and enormous financial backing they get. The New Right is a triumph of both big ideas and big money.

RULE 3: MAKE YOUR PARTY A SOCIAL MOVEMENT

Most of us like parties, but we tend to stay home when it comes to the big political parties these days. How many party caucuses or conventions have you been to? In normal politics, parties are establishments of professional politicians, not a home for ordinary citizens. Politics becomes a spectator sport for all but the political class. Citizens keep their distance from the parties because they are stifling bureaucracies with little to offer ordinary people.

REVOLT OF THE BIBLE BELT

In regime-change politics, new grassroots groups force themselves onto the political scene and penetrate the bureaucracy of the parties. The second phrase of Goldwater's famous declaration about extremism was that "Moderation in the pursuit of justice is no virtue." This sounds more like a social movement credo than a political party platform. The New Right of the 1970s was very much a social movement of fire-and-brimstone Bible Belt preachers tied to an insurgent class of grassroots Southern conservative workers, gun owners, religious fundamentalists, brilliant New Right policy wonks, and political organizers (such as the direct-mail expert Richard Viguerie, and Paul Weyrich, a founder of the Moral Majority). In addition, a major new movement of Fortune 500 and Wall Street corporate elites, who organized themselves to help dig the final grave of the New Deal and create a new corporate regime, led and financed this new regime-change politics.

The New Right learned the tools of regime-change activism in Goldwater's campaign. Here's how one New Rightist described it:

> It was learning how to act: how letters got written, how doors got knocked on, how co-workers could be won over on the coffee break, how to print a bumper sticker and how to pry one off with a razor blade. . . . How to talk to a reporter, how to picket, and how, if need be, to infiltrate—how to make the anger boiling inside you ennobling, productive, powerful, instead of embittering."[6]

Doesn't this sound like social activism to you? It was exactly what I was learning as a civil rights activist in Mississippi at about the same time.

The religious-based New Right movement deserves special attention because it is the origin of the "red state" activism that still fuels some of the most potent grassroots organizing in the nation—and represents the melding of economic and moral politics essential to regime change. For decades, the New Deal Democrats could count on ordinary Southerners, despite their social and religious conservatism, as the regime's most reliable voting base. But in the late 1960s and 1970s, as corporate globalization began to threaten U.S. jobs throughout the nation, the New Deal Democrats wounded themselves mortally, failing to take the extraordinary steps necessary to protect the economic and social security of ordinary Americans. The creation of a new "anxious class" of conservative Southern and heartland workers was the beginning of the end of the New Deal regime.

As globalization threatened job security and wages, so too did the rising movement of civil rights and feminists who wanted their own place at the table. White workers, already deeply economically threatened, saw the New Deal liberals who backed these movements as betraying them. The cultural radicalism and antiwar activism of students and hippies enraged many of the new anxious class, especially white male workers, whose place in society was increasingly threatened not only by globalization, but by high technology and job competition from women and minorities. New Right organizers brilliantly seized the moment, realizing that a politics of standing up for God and country against liberal anti–Vietnam War activists could became part of the anxious class's way of redeeming its own wounded pride, and standing against affirmative action could become its way of protecting traditional white male privileges. The enemy was the 1960s liberals who had taken over the New Deal, aligned themselves with blacks and women, and were desecrating the traditional values and patriotism of America. The political solution: regime change that would restore America's great moral values and provide the place in America for hard-working patriotic Americans who played by the old rules.

The Christian New Right grassroots groups soon began to cross paths and cross-fertilize the thinking of more established regime-change conservatives inside the Nixon and Ford Administrations, including Donald Rumsfeld, Paul Wolfowitz, and Dick Cheney, as well as with the corporate elites on Wall Street. The Christian preachers fired up a new Republican populist base in the churches of the South; the political organizers linked them in a new nationally coordinated and corporate-funded movement for change in Washington; and the policy wonks and intellectuals created the big neoconservative vision[7] to guide the movement and link it securely to the interests of the corporate and military establishment—as well as to the moral values and resentments of the new anxious class in the heartland.

THE SOCIAL MOVEMENT OF THE BOSSES

The New Right social activists would have been a footnote in history without the regime-change campaign from the boardrooms. By the early 1970s, business had concluded that its relative weakness since the Roosevelt era meant that it was finally time to counter-attack to end the New Deal. The influential corporate attorney Lewis Powell, later appointed to be a Supreme Court justice by Richard Nixon, wrote a memo to the national U.S. Chamber of Commerce in 1971 saying that "As every business executive knows, few elements of American society today have as little influence in government as American business. . . . The business executive is truly 'the forgotten man.' " At 1974 and 1975 meetings of corporate leaders sponsored by the New York Conference Board, one participant continued this theme, saying "At this rate business can soon expect support from the environmentalists. We can get them to put the corporation on the endangered species list."[8]

A full-scale corporate campaign began in the early 1970s, brilliantly chronicled by corporate historian Ted Nace, who dubbed it "The Revolt of the Bosses." It proves the critical point that social movements for regime change can arise among elites as well as the grassroots. "Corporations of the World, Unite!" shows some of the critical launching phases of the corporate social movement, which could be called "Justice for Billionaires"!

If you didn't think corporations could become a social movement, think again! Corporations, working individually and through trade associations, began networking into numerous coalitions for specific legislation and ideological campaigns, whether for deregulation or against "global warming" initiatives. Corporations such as Enron joined scores of such coalitions, including Americans for Fair Taxation, Business Council for Sustainable Energy, Direct Access Alliance, and many others promoting procorporate aims.[9]

The New Right regime change reflected the orchestrated efforts of America's biggest corporations, who understood, as Powell put in his Chamber of Commerce memo, that "The day is long past when the chief executive officer of a major corporation discharges his responsibility by maintaining a satisfactory growth of profits. . . . If our system is to survive, top management must be equally concerned with protecting and preserving the system itself."[10] The transformation of big corporations into a social movement was the key to regime change, and turned the Republican Party itself into a movement fueled by the money contributed by the big companies as well as the Bible Belt

CORPORATIONS OF THE WORLD, UNITE!

1972   CEO Frederick Borch of General Electric and CEO John Harper of Alcoa formed the Business Roundtable, an organization made up exclusively of CEOs from the biggest corporations of America.[11] The Business Roundtable became a forum for corporate coordination at the highest levels, lobbying for anti-union policies and procorporate tax, regulatory, and macroeconomic policies.

1972   Joseph Coors, the wealthy activist brewer, helped to found right-wing watering holes like the Heritage Foundation (originally the Analysis and Research Association). Along with the American Enterprise Institute, the Heritage Foundation is one of the most important of a new group of Washington-based conservative think tanks, policy institutes, political magazines, lobbies, and other bodies devoted to corporate regime change.

1973   Paul Weyrich, the New Right firebrand and tireless organizer, founded the American Legislative Exchange Council (ALEC) to lead conservative initiatives at the state level. ALEC originally was concerned with issues of abortion and school prayer but quickly evolved into a focus on corporate concerns as large companies began pouring money into the council. ALEC drafted bills such as the "Private Property Protection Act," and it helped business introduce more than 3,100 bills during 1999 and 2000 alone in state legislatures.

tele-preachers. The hidden power here was the synergy of corporate funding and grassroots moral anxiety and resentment, blended into a magically powerful economic and moral movement.

The movement flourished because of the vast money available, the commitment of the corporate elites, the extremely serious economic crisis created by stagflation, global competition, and military Keynesianism, and the insurgent New Right organizers' skill at exploiting new technologies and moral resentments. Viguerie was the mastermind of political direct mail that became a spectacular new tool of educating the grassroots and raising money. The Bible Belt preachers, such as Pat Robertson and Jerry Falwell, whom Viguerie and Weyrich helped persuade to get politically involved, used Christian television and electronic ministry as a remarkable new political apparatus, mixing fundamentalism and conservative populism to raise spectacular amounts of money for the cause. At the heart of it all was the construction of a new vision that—in one of the great triumphs of modern political propaganda discussed in Chapter 5—linked the interests of the world's largest corporations with the moral anxieties and resentments of U.S. workers that the corporations themselves were busy abandoning for cheaper labor abroad.[12]

As in most regime-change movements, the coalition between the religious grassroots base and the corporate Republican Party elites was not entirely comfortable on either side. The evangelicals suspected the Republicans and corporate elites were not fully in their corner on abortion, secularism, and other core social issues. The corporate elites and leaders of the Republican Party were eager to capitalize on the huge new political base of evangelicals, but were uneasy with some of the evangelicals' social and spiritual demands, which could be easily turned against the materialism of capitalism itself. Thus in many respects this was a marriage of convenience that required compromise by the grassroot zealots and zealous, sophisticated propaganda and political persuasion by the party elites.

The economic crises helped to cement a potentially shaky regime-changing coalition against the New Deal. The religious activists sought regime change for social and moral reasons; the corporations did so for economic aims. If the New Deal regime had still been economically stable, it might have been able to fight off the challenge of this potentially shaky coalition. But as severe stagflation and corporate flight undermined the ability of the New Deal to deliver and survive, the new coalition felt it had the wind at its back, sensing in its unity the prospect of victory, which it achieved in 1980 with Reagan's election. Despite the inherent tension in the alliance, which could ultimately lead to a split between corporations and the religious Right, it has survived thus far over the entire course of the third corporate regime, and has helped transform the country in a way that neither partner could have achieved on its own.

THE NEW DEAL AS A SOCIAL MOVEMENT

The same intoxicating brew of fiery new grassroots social movements and insurgent policy elites (but lacking the big money and organization of the corporate elites themselves) transformed the Democratic Party in the early 1930s. What were some of these movements?

Labor organizers, especially the CIO
Southern and Dust Bowl farmers and farmer unions
Miners, mill workers, and auto workers
Socialists
Communists
Veterans of World War I
Muckraking journalists
Wildcat strikers all over the country
Tenant organizers for the evicted and homeless
Welfare activists and relief workers
The unemployed

The New Deal regime change was the product of a dynamic interplay between militant grassroots activists and the Democratic Party. FDR was central, but regime change began with grassroots anger and activism against President Herbert Hoover after the 1929 market crash, who assumed the corporate regime could save itself and the country. Hoover's corporate friends, like John Edgerton, president of the National Association of Manufacturers, blamed the workers and unemployed for their own plight in the Depression, and agreed with him when he said in his presidential address in October 1930, that "if they do not . . . practice the habits of thrift and conservation, or if they gamble away their savings in the stock market or elsewhere, is our economic system, or government or industry to blame?"[13] The rise of angry popular revolts and movements against Hoover and his big-business allies helped elect FDR, who put into place as early as 1932 the beginnings of a regime-change agenda.

Hoover's unwillingness to change course and provide government relief after three years of Depression culmi-

THE RULES OF CHANGE

nated in a series of popular uprisings in 1932 that laid the groundwork for regime change. One of the most important was the Veterans' Bonus movement, an organization of World War I veterans who had been promised but never paid a bonus for their service. In June 1932, they descended on Washington and set up a tent city, a ragtag group with placards that proclaimed "Cheered in '17, Jeered in '32." Some stayed on and squatted in unused government buildings. Hoover responded by using federal troops against the veterans, killing at least one and physically removing hundreds of them and their families. He authorized tear gas against their camps and torched their squatter homes. This created a huge public response, with the Washington *News* reporting "What a pitiful spectacle is that of the great American government, mightiest in the world, chasing unarmed men, women and children with army tanks."[14]

Heartland farmers faced with foreclosures in 1931 and 1932 responded with violence against banks, railroads, local governments, and corporate lawyers. Farmers in Iowa "blocked highways with logs and spiked telegraph poles, smashed windshields and headlights and punctured tires with their pitchforks."[15] In Nebraska, farmers carried signs saying "Be pickets or peasants."[16] Back in Iowa, things got even more intense when farmers almost lynched a lawyer seeking a foreclosure and several hundred other farmers attacked a sheriff and an agent of a mortgage company. "If we don't get beneficial service from the Legislature," said a leader of the Nebraska farmers, "200,000 of us are coming to Lincoln and we'll tear that new State Capitol Building to pieces."[17] A second version of "red-state" populism thus contributed to the end of the second corporate regime, just as the original red-state populists led the charge against the first one during the Gilded Age.

Revolts of striking and unemployed workers in mid-1932 contributed to a sense of a country near revolution. In southern Illinois, Communists led a militant demonstration of ten thousand striking miners in a "coal caravan." In Detroit, unemployed workers broke into grocery stores together and carted off food without paying. In Des Moines, a group of workers got on streetcars and told the conductors to "charge the fares to the mayor." And in a sign of the regime-threatening character of the revolt, jobless miners in Wyoming sank their own shafts on company property and "bootlegged" $100,000 of coal for themselves daily. As historian William Leuchtenberg notes, "When the owners went to court, juries in mining towns would not convict."[18]

The majority of Americans remained relatively passive, though their faith in government big business had clearly declined as more than 25 million Americans, one-third of the labor force, lost their jobs. But the social movement scared regime elites, who understood it could pave the way to a Democratic victory and erosion of corporate power. One financier, Rudolph Spreckels, wrote in 1932, "I am alarmed at the increasing undercurrent of hate directed against our bankers and big industrial leaders." He added, with a bit of hyperbole, "the word revolution is heard at every hand."[19]

The popular movements, combined with the banking crisis and the depth of the Depression, propelled FDR into the first phases of a regime-change Democratic politics. In spring 1933, in the first hundred days of his presidency, he passed the largest legislative reform package in American history. As New Deal historian William E. Leuchtenburg summarized it, FDR had "promised to distribute stupendous sums to millions of staple farmers; accepted responsibility for the welfare of millions of unemployed; ... pledged billions of dollars to save homes and farms from foreclosure, undertaken huge public works spending; guaranteed the small bank deposits of the country; and had, for the first time, established federal regulation of Wall Street."[20]

At the same time, FDR and the Democrats were far from seeking or achieving full regime change. As is typically the case, the new leaders initially carried over much of the philosophy of the earlier regime. In 1933, FDR joined Hoover's crusade against government spending and slashed funds to veterans. Moreover, his 1933 National Recovery Administration regulatory scheme, known for the Blue Eagle insignia that symbolized a corporation's embrace of its own trade association's code of conduct, was rooted in the second corporate regime's idea of business self-regulation rather than public control. FDR was far from persuaded during these early years that he should offer state support for unions, something that was critical to regime change. In his first years, FDR remained committed to a government-business partnership heavily shaped by the earlier regime's vision of corporate self-government.[21]

The most important regime-changing element of FDR's first two years was his mobilization of popular hope rather than the legislation itself. Over half a million people wrote the president after his famous first inaugural speech, in which he declared that "the only thing we have to fear is fear itself." This mobilization of popular hope helped catalyze a second round of more militant populist grassroots activity, beginning in 1933, that moved the Democrats toward full-blown regime change in 1935 and 1936.

The charismatic miner John L. Lewis, supported by many socialists and Communists seeking a regime-changing labor movement, was the spark plug for the new social movement of industrial unions. In the summer of 1933, Lewis led an astonishing revival of the dying coal miners' union, adding more than 500,000 members to the 150,000 base membership of the United Mine Workers within a year. Lewis's success—partly generated by invoking FDR's magic name as a support of unions, a sign of the dialectic between the movements and the Democratic leadership—increased labor militancy around the country, leading in 1934 to some of the most radical labor activity in American history. This included demands for jobs, wages, welfare relief, unemployment benefits, union recognition, and even general strikes, backed up by dramatic acts:

> Milwaukee streetcar workers assaulted transport
> stations and pulled out trolley poles, assisted
> by socialist groups of unemployed workers.
> Striking Philadelphia cabbies burned one hundred
> taxis, leading fellow New York cabbies to drive
> 15,000 taxis out of service.
> Iowa union electrical workers pulled a switch that
> plunged Des Moines into total darkness.
> Copper miners in Butte, Montana, closed down the
> pits for months.
> In Toledo, Ohio, members of the fledgling American
> Workers' party battled police and national guards-
> men and threatened a general strike.
> On Labor Day 1934, textile workers from Rhode Island

and Massachusetts to the Carolinas launched the biggest single strike in American history, with pitched battles between strikers and soldiers in several states.[22]

All of this reflected the failure of the first hundred days to solve the urgent problems of millions of American workers and farmers who remained unemployed, bankrupt, or foreclosed. In 1934, nearly one-third of the workers attending the craft-based conservative American Federation of Labor (AFL) joined Lewis's crusade for a new, militant form of industry-wide organizing, leading eventually to a regime change in the labor movement itself: the creation of the Congress of Industrial Organizations (CIO). As the Depression deepened and labor militancy grew, new popular unrest grew in even more threatening forms, including the unruly Southern populism of Louisiana's Huey Long and the reactionary pseudopopulism of Father Charles Coughlin. These popular movements threatened the New Deal coalition and its ability to maintain electoral control and popular stability. The Democratic Party had to push the envelope.[23]

This led to the "second hundred days" of FDR's new term in 1936, after his landslide reelection, when the Democrats moved toward genuine regime change. The more progressive Democratic advisors now had the opportunity they needed to champion true regime change. These included the Kitchen Cabinet of intellectuals, many of whom were socialists or left-leaning progressives—including Raymond Moley, Rexford Tugwell, Louis Brandeis, Henry Wallace, Frances Perkins, Robert Wagner, and Eleanor Roosevelt herself—who had been pushing FDR to move beyond the corporate self-government model of the earlier regime toward a a new regulatory order and social welfare system based on institutionalized union power.

The full thrust of regime change began a bit earlier, in 1935, when the Democratic Congress passed the Social Security Act, which was the cornerstone of the new regime's social contract based on solidarity rather than individualism. By the summer of 1936, the Wagner Act, which institutionalized the right of unions to form and bargain collectively, put into place the second great legislative pillar of the New Deal regime. This was a dramatic regime-change move, signaling a change in FDR's own long-standing ambivalence about unions, ultimately brought about by the combination of grassroots labor movement militancy and the dedication of Senator Wagner and other progressive political and policy elites. Spurred by labor militancy, the Wagner Act created a magical new momentum for the labor movement; by 1939, there were 6.5 million union members, compared to 3.4 million in 1929 and 5.0 million in 1920.[24] FDR also introduced a pioneering tax measure, the Wealth Tax Act, that signaled a clear intent to redistribute wealth, increasing estate, gift, and capital stock taxes, as well as creating an excess profit tax and a surtax on the highest income brackets. The most controversial of all New Deal legislation, despite its relatively modest dimensions, the tax measure put the rich on notice that this was a new regime committed to a capitalism based on far greater equality. In 1937, the Fair Standards Labor Act put in place the third great pillar of the new regime, linking the rights of labor to state standards, and further cementing the marriage of state and labor movement that defined the new regime.[25]

The New Deal regime change illustrated the complex and often frustrating relationship between social movements and the Democratic Party that have historically marked shifts away from corporate regimes. The movements force the party away from politics as usual, and become successful in creating regime change only when they align with progressive policy elites in the party who can translate the grassroots demands into legislative packages and presidential agendas that carry the popular will. The tension between the movements and the party is never resolved, with popular movements almost always disappointed by the timidity of the party, and the political leadership constantly seeking to tame the more radical instincts of the movements. Nonetheless, the movements, while they don't capture the party, play a central role in regime change. In the New Deal case, they moved FDR from his initial corporate mind-set formed during the earlier regime to a regime-changing agenda that defined his legacy. They transformed the entire party in the process, not into a radical social movement but into America's first labor-based mainstream party. It would bring a form of social democracy to the United States and offer the most compelling and successful alternative to corporate rule yet seen in America.

RULE 4: IT'S ALL ABOUT CREDIBILITY

Just like you and me, regimes age over time—and the afflictions that will eventually destroy them become increasingly severe. Politicians playing by the normal rules paper over the crises, pretending they will go away or don't really exist (think of the current regime's approach to global warming or Iraq). As the contradictions intensify, the explanations and remedies offered by leaders become less honest and plausible and create a regime crisis of credibility.

In U.S. corporate regimes, as noted earlier, such credibility crises are endemic, stemming from the fact that the regimes proclaim themselves to be democratic but serve the interests of financial elites. Corporate regimes have credibility problems even in their early phases because of this inherent gap between democratic rhetoric and practice. As is evident today, the credibility problem worsens over time as recessions, job loss, debt, and other economic problems mount.[26]

Credibility crises in failing regimes are both systemic and personal. Systemic credibility crises involve erosion of faith in the basic institutions of society. Antonio Gramsci called the systemic crisis in capitalism a *crisis of hegemony,* when people no longer have faith in the corporate order. Enron is a mini-example of a hegemonic crisis, bringing into question faith in the markets even among the investor class that gets the payoffs.[27]

Regime-change politics is fueled by systemic credibility crises, with insurgent movements seeking to expose the regime's fundamental deceptions and awaken the public to the need for a more credible order. The nineteenth-century populists, who challenged the robber-baron regime, mounted the most radical challenge to the credibility of a corporate regime in U.S. history. They made a powerful case that the Rockefellers and Morgans were fleecing the country, impoverishing the majority of farmers and immigrant workers, and lying about the corruption and greed that lay at the heart of the regime. The populists ultimately failed but laid the groundwork for the progressive reforms under Teddy Roosevelt that eventually toppled the robber-baron regime.[28]

The New Dealers didn't have to work as hard to challenge the 1920s corporate regime's credibility. After the 1929 market crash, systemic credibility melted away with the Great Depression. Nonetheless, corporate leaders continued to proclaim that the corporate order could heal itself, and Roosevelt had to wage a major campaign to discredit these claims. The establishment of the New Deal became a bloody battle of credibility between Roosevelt and the conservative corporate establishment. Roosevelt won only because he was tenacious, aligned himself with mass popular movements, and made alliances with powerful sectors of the business elite itself. Ultimately, he successfully undermined the credibility of the old order because it had collapsed so spectacularly in the Depression and could no longer paper over its own failures.[29]

The New Righters had to wage a similar credibility battle against the declining New Dealers in the 1970s. The New Right learned from populists of the 1890s, embracing their own rhetoric of populism and calling for a people's crusade against big government rather than big business. The New Right won the credibility battle that the nineteenth-century populists lost because the New Deal was collapsing in the 1970s under the weight of an energy crisis, a major recession combining high unemployment and skyrocketing interest rates, and a shifting balance of power from government to corporations fueled by globalization and the "revolt of the bosses." The right-wing populists also had access to the huge coffers of the corporate elites while the 1890s populists were small landholders or dirt poor.

Credibility crises are personal as well as systemic. As systemic crises intensify, political leaders have to personally make claims about regime viability as the regime begins to unravel. Toward the middle and late phases of regimes, presidents and other regime leaders typically get ensnared in a web of lies, deceptions, and misrepresentations essential to papering over the crises and maintaining the credibility of a failing regime. When a credibility crisis gets personal, and the president's own credibility is compromised, the endgame of the regime may be approaching.

ANSWERS TO NAME THEIR GAME (P. 70)

Bush Sr., Clinton, Gore, and Kerry all play normal politics. Roosevelt, Reagan, Kucinich, and Nader played regime-change politics. Interestingly, George W. Bush and Howard Dean are ambiguous cases, who might be called regime-tippers: those who play normal politics but who could tip the regime right, in Bush's case, or left, in Dean's (but only if pushed by the grassroots).

CHAPTER 4

CRACKS IN
THE REGIME

I have conversations with my students that run something like this:

ME: Is our current corporate regime going to crack up?

STUDENT A: No. Americans are just too comfortable right now.

STUDENT B: And they voted to re-elect George W. Bush, the ultimate corporate president.

ME: Do you see any cracks or crises that might eventually lead to regime change?

STUDENT C: I bet that economic and social problems— like jobs and health care—could eventually cause real problems.

STUDENT D: And the war in Iraq or other wars could help bankrupt the country.

ME: How bad do you think things will have to get before we see regime change?

STUDENT E: I think it will take another Great Depression.

MANY STUDENTS AT ONCE: She's right!

All U.S. regimes before the current one have eventually cracked up. Almost from the beginning, small cracks opened up in each regime and widened over time. Eventually, certain cracks became big chasms that created large-scale popular discontent and major social movements seeking to create regime change. This could happen again.

My students are no dummies. They know it took a Depression to crack open the last corporate regime in the 1920s. They are also right that most Americans are not mobilizing to topple the current corporate regime. Some are too comfortable; others are too propagandized; others want change but feel helpless. And while polls tell us that most Americans worry about the huge influence of corporations and big money in politics, they do not want to kill the corporate golden goose and they see no alternative to the corporate regime.

But despite what my students think, it does not take a Depression to topple a regime. The first corporate regime of the robber barons succumbed in 1900 to the Progressive regime without the help of a depression. And Ronald Reagan put an end to the New Deal regime also without any depression, although in both 1900 and 1980 economic cracks—in the form of recessions and stagflation that played havoc with workers' lives—played a major role.

My students may also be wrong about the implications of Bush's 2004 reelection. The Election Trap leads Americans to read the results of elections as indicators of the stability of the existing order. This is another illusion. Elections like Bush's 2004 victory can mask serious regime cracks. Herbert Hoover cruised to victory in 1928, an apparent resounding triumph for the corporate regime of his day. A year later, the markets crashed, and three years later the second corporate regime was history.

You are becoming a victim of the Election Trap if you believe that Bush's two wins show that the regime is in good shape. Do not view the results of elections as reliable signs of how stable the regime is. When presidents lose, as Bush Sr. did in 1992, it does not mean the regime is cracking. And when presidents are reelected, as his son was, the regime cracks might be growing bigger.

In this chapter, I will show that significant cracks have opened up in the third corporate regime. But they will have to get worse before we see regime change and nobody can predict how long the process will take or whether these cracks will bring the regime down. The cracks will lead to regime change only if they become so severe that the elites cannot fix them and if social movements arise out of the suffering and dislocations and successfully organize to change the regime.

Nor can we be sure that any future regime change will be progressive rather than reactionary. If the current corporate regime cracks up, the country could lurch dramatically to the right rather than to the left—toward an Orwellian regime that I call "Fascism Lite." But while the outcome is in doubt, the cracks are already visible and they spell trouble for the regime.

WHY REGIMES CRACK UP

Karl Marx predicted internal contradictions that would destroy capitalism, but he was only half-right. Contradictions emerge in U.S. regimes but they typically create different versions of capitalism itself—sometimes more humane, sometimes more ruthless. While multiple U.S. regime crack-ups have not ended capitalism, they have delivered big changes in the direction of the country. When a regime cracks up, watch out: it will change your life dramatically.[1]

In fact, regime cracks are a principal basis for system change in America. They provide the opening that social movements need to bring down a regime and create one they prefer. Regime-busting cracks include:

Economic cracks (the 1890s recessions or the 1970s
    stagflation)
Political cracks (the 1920s huge Teapot Dome corruption
    scandal)
Social cracks (the 1890s huge gap between the rich
    and poor)
Military cracks (unwinnable wars like Vietnam)
Cracks in the elite (the 1901 GOP schism between
    Theodore Roosevelt progressives and Taft
    conservatives)

There is no historical formula about how quickly the cracks open up and blow the regime apart. It can happen precipitously, as in 1929 with the market crash, or over several decades, as in the case of the economic, political, cultural, and military crises that brought down the New Deal. But no American regime thus far has survived more than four or five decades.

At the core of every regime change is what I call the central contradiction of the regime, a deep source of the cracks that can lead to regime change. It cannot be resolved within the framework of the regime itself and becomes more transparent and lethal as new historical conditions make the regime increasingly obsolete. While each corporate regime has its own unique contradictions, they all are related to the pursuit of profit and power at the cost of the well-being of ordinary workers and democracy itself. Corpocracy and democracy are incompatible. Corporate regimes crack up when the harm to citizens becomes so great that they become "mad as hell and won't take it anymore."[2]

But why have all corporate regimes failed in this way? After all, if productivity grows, it can produce major improvements in workers' standard of living, as happened even in the ruthless corporate regime of the nineteenth-century robber barons. The problem has been that all corporate regimes eventually lose their capacity to create growth and productivity at a level that sustains both the regime and ordinary workers. This often arises partly because of the excessive power and greed of the elites, who take more than their fair share and torpedo their own systems, an obvious problem displayed nakedly by the Enrons and WorldComs of today.

All corporate regimes, though, have failed to meet the needs of *both* their workers *and* elites because they have not been able to adapt to changing conditions. History suggests that regimes ultimately fall on their own swords, unable to manage the changing and contradictory conditions of the very systems they create. Again, this creates quite different but closely related central contradictions in different corporate regimes. The robber barons of the first corporate regime knit together a national market, but could not create—indeed often opposed—the complex national government apparatus necessary to manage competition, create uniform national standards, and stabilize severe national business cycles. Similarly, the huge global corporations of today toppled the New Deal by creating globalization, but have failed to produce the global governing structures to manage a profoundly unstable global economy. This has put unsustainable burdens on the U.S. government, the American military, and American workers.[3]

As cracks widen, the regime ultimately reaches a tipping point. The regime contradictions reach a level of intensity that makes the regime lurch toward the precipice. Before the tipping point, regime elites are typically capable of patching up the cracks. The population falls into the Election Trap, focused on near-term elections rather than the long-term crises of the regime. But at the tipping point, the patchwork fails and the regime politics boil over into a struggle for regime change.

HISTORY OF A CRACK UP

Before looking at the deepening cracks in the current regime, consider how an earlier regime—the first corporate regime in the age of the robber barons—cracked up. It is a useful introduction to the cracks arising in the current regime—and how they might bring it down and transform America.

HOW REGIMES CRACK UP

Central Contradiction

↓

Economic Cracks   Political Cracks
Military Cracks   Cultural Cracks

↓

Tipping Point

↓

Regime Death and Regime Change

The central contradiction of the first corporate regime involved the mismatch between the new national corporation and the national government. That mismatch allowed the corporation to run roughshod over the country. There was no regulatory system that could restrain the robber barons' greed for profit and power. This weakened democracy and harmed millions of poor and immigrant workers. Ninety percent of working Americans lived in poverty, turning them against the regime. The regime's legitimacy and credibility—its hegemony among the population—eroded.

While this is well understood, there is a second, equally important side of this contradiction. The absence of a regulatory state system—or what I call the regulatory vacuum—also hurt the corporations themselves, even as it allowed

THE FIRST CORPORATE REGIME

Central Contradiction: Regulatory vacuum

Economic Cracks: Multiple recessions; Deepening business cycles

Political Cracks: Massive corruption; Clamor for antitrust and corporate regulation

Social Cracks: Mass poverty; Huge gap between rich and poor

Splits in the Elite: Schism in Republican Party between progressives and conservatives

Tipping Point: Assassination of President William McKinley, leading to presidency of Vice President and Progressive leader Teddy Roosevelt

them to plunder the country. Despite their antigovernment rhetoric, corporations have always needed a large national government to help them weed out or regulate low-cost competitors at home and abroad, to subsidize the training of workers and the building of roads and communications systems, and to manage the business cycles and keep the economy from tanking into recessions or a depression.[4]

The absence of a regulatory state was thus a crisis not only for the workers but for the corporate system itself. The robber barons who ran the first corporate regime were caught in a central contradiction of their own making. On the one hand, they promoted laissez-faire rhetoric and opposed the growth of government so that they could create monopolies and gouge as much profit from workers as possible without fear of regulation. But on the other hand, they needed a highly developed government for the purposes just mentioned. It would take a regime change to create a government that would simultaneously protect both the workers and the larger corporate order.[5]

Because the robber barons prevented the regulatory state that their system required, a whole set of cracks began to emerge early in the first corporate regime, becoming very pronounced just before Teddy Roosevelt became president. The economic cracks led to severe recessions in the 1870s, 1880s, and especially the 1890s, with 1893 bringing the worst financial crisis the country had seen. These business cycles took a severe toll on millions of workers, who suffered mass layoffs and became the nation's first "disposable" workforce. But they also cast a deepening economic shadow on the whole corporate regime, as investors began to question the stability of the system.

The absence of a developed regulatory apparatus meant that the robber barons had no political recourse but massive corruption—from the beginning of the regime—to try to save their skins. Rampant bribery became the order of the day and leading tycoons such as John D. Rockefeller openly bought the votes of senators to prevent antitrust laws. They also spent millions to elect corporate presidents who sent in troops when necessary to put down strikes. These puppet presidents also appointed blatantly pro-corporate Supreme Court justices who interpreted the

Constitution to give corporations legal personhood and constitutional protection of "equal protection" under the Fourteenth Amendment, a measure presumably passed to protect freed slaves, not corporations. All this created growing radical political dissent.

The social crises of the regime grew very serious in the 1880s and 1890s. In this period, Rockefeller, Morgan, and Carnegie became the country's first billionaires, while 90 percent of the workers lived in poverty. The gap between rich and poor made Gilded Age America seem a parody of the old European aristocratic order. The robber barons' estates were replicas of palaces like Versailles; at their parties one might see "monkeys seated between the guests, human gold fish swimming about in pools, or chorus girls hopping out of pies."[6] But as historian Richard Hofstadter writes, this wealth was achieved at "a terrible cost of values. . . . The land and the people had both been plundered."[7] A new class warfare bubbled up, led by rural populists and urban immigrant workers.

All these conditions set the stage for an unanticipated tipping point: the killing of President McKinley right after his reelection in 1900. Teddy Roosevelt, his vice president, was neither populist nor socialist, but he could not ignore the now nakedly exposed cracks in the corporate regime. Calling himself a progressive and a trust-buster, Roosevelt sided with the growing public sentiment against the naked power of the corporate robber barons.

This reflected a split among the elites, a very significant regime crack that often signals a coming regime change. The dominant Republican Party fractured into an old guard led by President Taft and the progressive wing represented by Roosevelt. Roosevelt recognized that the Gilded Age regime of the old Republican guard was doomed, and he set out to create regime change.[8]

CRACKS IN THE THIRD CORPORATE REGIME

Cracks in today's regime are widening rapidly, much like those of the robber baron regime in the 1880s and 1890s. Regime elites, now as then, are ensnared in contradictions of their own making that are leading them to grab what they can before the whole system comes apart. We have not yet reached a tipping point, but consider the current realities that could eventually create regime change.[9]

Today's cracks—involving unprecedented American debt, global economic crises, a new class of "anxious workers," and unwinnable wars—are more explosive than those that blew apart the robber-baron corporate regime a century ago. While we have not yet reached a tipping point, the cracks will get worse, because they are expressions of an underlying central contradiction that even the most brilliant corporate thinkers and their allies in Washington will never be able to untangle. The new contradiction is the mismatch between the new global economy and the old system of national sovereignty. Like the robber barons who opposed a stronger federal government, today's regime elites do not want a global government that can restrain their greed or regulate their global factories. They thus espouse the same religion of free markets and global laissez-faire that the robber barons enshrined in the United States. Yet they need a global government to manage global competition, harmonize conditions across countries, help stim-

THE THIRD
CORPORATE REGIME

Central Contradiction: American Overstretch

Economic Cracks: Debt; Recessions; Job security; Enron-type scandals

Political Cracks: Crises of credibility and legitimacy at home and abroad

Social Cracks: Growing poverty and inequality; Environmental crises

Military Cracks: Quagmire in Iraq; Endless war on terrorism

Splits in the Elite: Schisms in the Republican Party between moderates and radicals, and between religious and corporate conservatives

Tipping Point: Unknown

ulate global demand, and stabilize the new global markets they have created. Without such global governance, the entire global economy becomes increasingly vulnerable to financial crises, uncontrollable recessions, and deepening global poverty.[10]

True, regime elites have created global institutions like the World Trade Organization (WTO), the International Monetary Fund (IMF), and the World Bank. They are in a position to control these embryonic world governments, and thus have allowed them to grow. Yet they have kept them largely subordinate to U.S. dominance, precisely because they fear that they could lose control and face a global governing system that would limit their profits. Meanwhile, these organizations are losing global legitimacy, precisely because they are viewed by poor nations and the world's workers as corporate handmaidens.[11]

Corporate elites have looked to the U.S. government to step in and perform the regulatory functions of world government. American political leaders have been happy to oblige, eager to take on the role of "leader of the free world" or global hegemon. Since global corporations provide the money to get them elected, American political leaders of both parties have willingly embraced the need to support a global corporate regime. This not only buys greater funds for the next election, but offers the rationale for Empire.

American Empire may appear a happy solution for both corporate elites and Washington's political classes. But it is the flip side of the regime's global regulatory crisis: American overstretch. American overstretch is an inevitable consequence of asking a single nation—even one as powerful as the United States—to assume the role of global government. While the United States was capable of assuming such functions immediately after World War II, when Europe and Japan had been destroyed and the U.S. economy was an unchallenged powerhouse, things have changed. As Europe and Asia rebuilt after the war, the United States lost the economic dominance that would allow it to finance and manage the global order.

Acting as a global government is an extremely costly proposition. Uncle Sam has to:

Sustain the dollar as the world's reserve currency

Maintain global demand to ward off global recession

Bail out countries whose financial collapse might threaten the world's economy

Create a trade system assuring the global protection of corporate profits

Proffer a veneer of social regulation to gain legitimacy among the world's workers

Use military force to prevent serious disruptions of the corporate regime's global markets—from the Middle East to Latin America to Asia

All of this means spending a lot of money and, increasingly, a lot of blood. American overstretch is not identical to the classical imperial overstretch described by historian Paul Kennedy, in which the financial burdens of empire eventually sink it.[12] But the current American overstretch and the classical imperial forms are converging. American empire is creating heated anti-Americanism around the world, particularly since the unilateralism of the war in Iraq. The costs of maintaining U.S. hegemony after 9/11 are mounting in a period when U.S. deficits are spiraling and neoconservative ideology is promoting global U.S. overextension.

American overstretch is unsustainable for economic, political, military, and social reasons. But as long as there is no global government, America must do the job or the third corporate regime will unravel. Like their robber baron ancestors, the corporate leaders of the regime are impaling themselves on the horns of this dilemma. If they accept genuine global government, the third corporate regime will succumb to the will of the global majority and be replaced by a new order no longer based on national sovereignty and American hegemony. But if the regime's elites continue to rely on America as a surrogate for world government, American overstretch will eventually bankrupt the U.S. government and crack open the regime in a host of other ways. Either way, the regime faces extinction.[13]

We already see today glaring regime cracks that reflect American overstretch. Let's take a look.

ECONOMIC CRACKS

The regime is running up the largest national debt in U.S. history. Right after the 2004 election, in its first act on November 3, 2004, Congress had to raise the national debt ceiling to $8.18 trillion, the highest ever and destined to rise dramatically when the costs of the Iraqi war and the president's tax cuts were fully factored in. The president's proposed changes in Social Security, his highest domestic priority, would add another almost $2 trillion to the current debt. The nation's unfunded liabilities are projected in one of President Bush's own Treasury Department reports to run as high as $44 trillion over the next several decades.[14]

The United States spends billions to finance U.S. corporate expansion at home and abroad—through export subsidies, tax breaks, loopholes, and other forms of "corporate welfare." It is required to finance much of the efforts of the WTO, the IMF, and the World Bank, as well as to prop up the trade system and global financial order. As the United States sinks deeper into debt, it not only has to cut back on social services, research and development, and other infrastructure spending, but also has to worry about the collapse of faith in the dollar, as nervous foreign investors wonder whether the Euro might be a safer haven. Since foreigners now finance American debt—an untenable proposition for "the leader of the free world"—U.S. central bankers will inevitably have to ratchet up interest rates. This might eventually prove to be the tipping point for regime change as rising rates reduce U.S. consumer demand, cut into U.S. corporate profits, and cause recessions or even the new depression that my students view as the main catalyst for the regime crack-up. Princeton economist and *New York Times* columnist Paul Krugman agrees: "The crisis won't come immediately. . . . But at a certain moment we'll have a Wile E. Coyote moment. For those not familiar with the Road Runner cartoons, Mr. Coyote had a habit of running off cliffs and taking several steps on thin air before noticing that there was nothing underneath his feet. Only then would he plunge. . . . What will that plunge look like? It will certainly involve a sharp fall in the dollar and a sharp rise in interest rates. In the worst-case scenario, the government's access to borrowing will be cut off, creating a cash crisis that throws the nation in chaos."[15]

There are other related economic cracks in the regime, from unpredictable global financial crises to huge trade deficits and job insecurity at home. The new regulatory crisis has left the global economy and the U.S. economy increasingly vulnerable to financial swings and meltdowns, from the Asian flu that devastated much of East Asia in the late 1990s to the Argentine collapse in 2002. Overstretch has left the United States incapable of preserving global financial stability or bailing out nations in catastrophic fiscal crisis. At home, America's own trade deficit constitutes what MIT's Nobel prize–winning economists Franco Modigliani and Robert Solow call "the greatest potential danger facing the economy in the years to come." As economic analyst Jeff Faux observes, this form of debt "is now 22% of GDP. Assuming a recovery, the U.S. economy is on a trajectory to a [trade deficit] debt burden of roughly 40% of GDP within five years."[16]

Job insecurity is the Achilles heel of the regime at home. A global regime may be indispensable for American corporate profits, but it doesn't feel good to the millions of Americans who worry every day that their jobs will be outsourced or downsized. The hallmark of the New Deal regime was linking corporate profits with secure jobs and benefits for workers. But the current regime has cracked that link, creating a corporate economy at the expense of stable, well-paying jobs with secure benefits. This is the central economic crack of the third corporate regime, at least in the psyche of U.S. workers whom the regime has turned into a permanently anxious class. The U.S. worker's anxieties and resentments can undermine loyalty and productivity that the regime requires for its own profitability. The resentment of the anxious class—as jobs become ever more uncertain at home and U.S. workers see themselves as a "displaced class"—is the crack that could ultimately create *either* a far right-wing or progressive regime change, as I show in chapters to come.

POLITICAL, SOCIAL, AND ENVIRONMENTAL CRACKS

By serving as a surrogate global government for the corporations, U.S. political leaders switch their loyalty from American citizens and America itself toward a global order capable of securing global profits. But this switch opens up massive social and political cracks at home, as American citizens see their government undermine their own well-being. Social Security, Medicare, and Medicaid, the key social welfare programs that helped create the U.S. middle class, are now all under assault, no longer affordable because of the new priorities of the regime. As the American safety net at home is sacrificed to regime priorities, poverty and inequality grow dramatically in the United States, with the top 1 percent of the population being the main beneficiaries of government spending. The richest 1 percent now enjoy a higher percentage of U.S. wealth—about 40 percent—than at any time since the second corporate regime of the 1920s. Meanwhile, the U.S. poverty, homeless, and hunger rates increase, largely off the radar screen in a corporate media system. The majority of working Americans run harder to stay in place, working multiple jobs at lower wages while going deeper into consumer debt than ever in history. Remarkably, over the thirty years of the regime, the household income of ordinary Americans has remained largely stagnant, even though there are more working members of each household and the American worker toils on average a month longer than when the regime began.[17]

Naturally, all of this creates a problem of huge political legitimacy for the regime. American political leaders cannot survive if they are viewed as abandoning ordinary working Americans for their global corporate patrons. In a later chapter, I will show the political strategy that U.S. leaders, particularly the dominant Republican Party, have used to try to patch up this extreme political vulnerability. Suffice it to say here that American political leaders have exploited themes of patriotism in Iraq and the broader "war on terrorism" to reassure Americans that their primary commitment is to American security and Americans themselves. Ironically, the wars fought in the service of global companies become the symbols by which American political leaders display their commitment to American workers.

The environmental crisis is a historically unprecedented new fissure. Global warming is leading us toward ultimate environmental collapse. As globalization promotes unsustainable growth not only in the United States but in India, China, and other huge countries, the regime is already ushering in the conditions not only of its own demise but of life on the planet. The power of the fossil fuel industries, particularly the petrochemical industries, has risen as the regime ages. This makes it more difficult to produce the chances necessary to change environmental course and creates rising regime dissent among ordinary citizens and activist groups like the Sierra Club, who have recognized that there is no environmental solution without a broader political regime change. Moreover, corporations outside the petrochemical complex face not only rising fuel costs but also deteriorating environmental conditions for their own survival and profitability, and could become unexpected allies for environmentally driven regime change.

MILITARY CRACKS

While permanent war—another name for the "war on terror"—has become for the moment a useful political remedy for these problems, it creates its own dangerous regime cracks. Wars can sustain regimes but they also can bleed them to death. Vietnam became a lethal crack in the

New Deal regime, creating financial and political problems at home that contributed powerfully to the end of the New Deal era. Should it become a similar quagmire, Iraq could help crack up the third corporate regime.[18]

Permanent warfare has become a condition of life in the regime. This is because the third corporate regime depends on the U.S. government to keep markets open and friendly to U.S. business everywhere in the world. American Empire would breed anti-Americanism under the best of circumstances, and is a regime contradiction that has no obvious solution. But the problem has accelerated because the United States no longer has the resources or the will to sustain the global economy at a level that can reduce worldwide poverty and prevent the financial collapse or super-exploitation of poor and developing countries. As global poverty intensifies under the regime, and the United States maintains a major military presence in the Middle East and elsewhere to safeguard oil and other vital regime resources, opposition to U.S. foreign policy is spreading like a prairie fire. We are seeing the most fevered anti-Americanism in history, now spreading from the Middle East to Latin America, Africa, Asia and even, quite intensely, to our European allies.

This problem becomes even more serious when U.S. militarism and American Empire become perceived by Americans themselves as harmful to their pocketbooks or their security. The disaster of the Iraqi occupation has divided the country and created deep cracks in the regime's legitimacy at home. As 9/11 recedes, the real meaning of the war on terror has become itself a source of deep political debate. A growing number of Americans see the war on terror as increasing rather than decreasing the risks of another terrorist attack on the homeland. Moreover, more Americans, both Republican and Democrat, worry about the cost of permanent warfare and the intrusions on basic American rights and civil liberties that the war brings in its wake. A 2004 year-end ABC poll shortly after Bush's re-election showed 56 percent of the U.S. public saying the war in Iraq was "not worth fighting" and 57 percent disapproved of Bush's handling of the war. Moreover, almost half the country—47 percent—disapproved of Bush's conduct of the war on terrorism. Most polls over several years have confirmed the view of a growing crisis of political confidence in America's direction, not just abroad but at home.[19]

Loss of faith in war and U.S. militarism—at home and abroad—is a political crack in the regime akin to the economic crisis of debt. Essentially, the regime is being forced by its own contradictions to spend down its political capital as well as its financial assets. Yet Empire and militarism are integral to a global corporate regime which thus is ensnared in yet another unsolvable crisis. If the United States abandons its Empire, the global playing fields on which the corporations depend will be lost and the regime will be undermined. But if it perpetuates its Empire, it will eventually bankrupt itself both economically and politically. Once again, either choice will lead to regime death over the long haul.

SPLITS IN THE ELITE

All of these problems are beginning to create major schisms within regime elites, a sign of a regime in deep trouble. The intensely bitter partisanship between Republicans and Democrats is one expression of this schism.

Democratic Party leaders such as John Kerry are corporate Democrats who have embraced the third corporate regime and its global priorities. But the intensity of the difference between Democratic and Republican leaders is deep and consequential. Kerry believes that the unilateralism of the Bush team could torpedo the consensual global order that the regime itself requires. His domestic priorities also differ significantly, since he believes that Bush's naked favoritism of the rich and his effort to dismantle social welfare in America will itself undermine the domestic conditions for the survival of the regime.

Bush's right-wing radicalism is alienating not only Democrats but many of his fellow Republicans. Since the Republicans won decisive control over all three branches of government, the division among Republicans has created a more surprising and perhaps more consequential split among the elites. John McCain bears some resemblance to Teddy Roosevelt, who split off from the robber-baron Republicans to create a new Progressive regime. In his support of campaign finance reform, opposition to corporate welfare, and concern about corporate scandals and monopolies, McCain is part of a growing number of Republicans—including former New Jersey governor and EPA administrator Christie Whitman, Senator Lincoln Chafee of Rhode Island, Maine Senators Olympia Snowe and Susan Collins, and other New England moderate Republicans—who are deeply at odds with the conservative wing of the party represented by Bush. This split within the GOP represents the growing concentration of corporate regime power in narrower sectors of the corporate world, particularly in the petrochemical complex of oil companies and military firms centered in the Southwest. Divisions splitting this Southwest military and energy sector away from East Coast financial elites could become one of the most serious political regime breaches. Such a splitting of the Republican elites, along with the intense schism between the Republican and Democratic Parties, breaks down the sense of unity and purpose in the regime and exposes it to fratricidal wars that historically have proved dangerous to a regime.

The Republican Party faces a related, explosive crack between its religious and corporate supporters that could shake the regime at its foundations. As discussed in the last chapter, the third corporate regime was created by a coalition of Bible Belt religious conservatives and the world's largest global corporations. From the beginning, this was a coalition of convenience, fraught with potential stresses. Many of the religious evangelical conservatives were working class, poor and rural, whose jobs and wages were threatened by the huge companies that they were politically joining. Other tensions loom between religious and corporate Republicans, surfacing dramatically in early 2005 in three highly visible events. One was the Terry Schiavo case at the beginning of the year, where Republican religious conservatives asked President Bush and the Republican Congress to pass a law to save Schiavo's life, by reinserting a feeding tube, a move that many business and libertarian Republicans strongly opposed as government intervention in private life. In February 2005, Missouri's bio-tech Republican corporate elites clashed sharply with the state's religious GOP rank and file, who opposed stem cell research that the companies vigorously wanted to pursue. Shortly thereafter, Senate GOP Majority leader Bill Frist went to a widely publicized "Justice Sunday" event organized by evangelical leaders to build support for ending judicial filibusters. Many GOP business leaders opposed Frist's move, arguing he was crossing a line between politics and religion.

The coalition between religious and corporate conservatives is as shaky as the coalition between Southern racists and Northern liberals that underpinned the New Deal. While it can survive for some time, the scientific, materialistic, secular, and hedonistic values of the corporate world are at odds with the antimaterialistic, spiritual, and morally restrictive values of evangelical Christianity. The schism will grow, eventually creating a political realignment likely to weaken and perhaps undermine the current regime.

All of this might seem to suggest that regime change is just over the horizon. But while there are very serious cracks in the regime, regime leaders have developed political strategies to quell dissent and continue to win the allegiance of the majority of Americans. The Election Trap is just one tool in the arsenal of the regime that not only allows it to keep many Americans diverted from regime crises but also allows its very existence to remain largely invisible. Such hidden power can survive for a surprisingly long time, and I review in coming chapters the sophisticated strategies the regime uses to maintain its invisibility as well as to patch up its growing cracks and maintain the support of a majority of Americans.

The cracks discussed here will likely ultimately unglue the regime, even if it takes decades. But, as noted earlier, there is no assurance that this will lead to progressive regime change and a better world. We are already seeing a right-wing radicalization of the regime under George W.

Bush. When the cracks in the regime can no longer be patched, established leaders such as Bush—or new leaders from the evangelical or "anxious class" grassroots base —may be prepared to launch their own regime change toward a more authoritarian system. Recall that corpocracy in the current regime maintains the constitutional procedures of democracy, even if the substance of sovereignty has been turned over to corporations. But should the cracks in the regime become more acute, radical regime elites may seek to preserve their power and destroy growing dissent by dispensing with critical elements of constitutionalism itself. With the Patriot Act, the many voting irregularities of recent elections, and the general assault on civil liberties and constitutional rights advanced in the name of the war on terrorism, we are already witnessing early signs of a possible Orwellian regime change to the Right. Should that occur, we might look back fondly on the third corporate regime as the "good old days" and pine for its return.

CHAPTER 5

BLACK MAGIC

Do you believe in black magic? You should, because the regime survives through its own amazing form of it.

All regimes weave hegemonic myths and stories that help to win the allegiance of the people and keep the regime in power. These can be called regime ideologies or, more bluntly, propaganda. In democratic societies, the role of propaganda is partly to cloak what Teddy Roosevelt called the "invisible government" of the regime itself. In the third corporate regime, the mass media are not official organs of the state, but their relative freedom increases their power as propagandists. Along with the state itself and the broader education system, they are uniquely successful in helping the regime create its own myths both to hide and sustain its own ruling power. Rather than Goliath, the regime has made itself David. It is the underdog trying to protect the American people and civilization itself from enemies far more formidable than itself.

The black magic of the regime is not new. It is a variant of a very old propaganda system used by authoritarian or exploitative ruling elites to legitimate themselves. I call it pseudopopulism. It turns ruling elites who exploit the population into champions of ordinary people, allied with them to fight off powerful enemies who threaten America and all of the civilized world. Pseudopopulism transforms ruling regime elites into populist insurgents against foreign enemies and culturally alien establishments of their own society.

This propaganda strategy—based on a doctrine of "civilization under threat"—took on particularly toxic forms in the twentieth century. In Europe, it was used by radical nationalist regimes and in its most extreme form by the fascists in Germany and Italy, to create some of the most horrible regimes in history. Antonio Gramsci developed his concept of hegemony partly to understand how the Italian fascist regime that put him in prison created hegemony, but mainly to show how Western democracies disguised capitalist power through their own hegemonic ideologies.[1]

In the United States, pseudopopulism as a hegemonic ideology has had its own history, culminating most dramatically in the rise of the New Right and the Reagan Revolution that created the current regime.[2] Despite his alliance with the world's richest and most powerful corporate elite who financed his election, Reagan cast himself as a champion of the common people, vowing to join their populist struggle against the secular American liberal Establishment and the Communist enemy. George W. Bush, whose master black magician is Karl Rove, has also triumphed by identifying as the common man of simple faith in his struggle to defend American values against powerful enemies at home and abroad.[3]

The history of pseudopopulism tells us that it is powerful and compelling. As a propaganda system, especially when disseminated through a twenty-four-hour mass media apparatus with unprecedented electronic reach and propagandistic skills, it has the capacity to elicit enormous passion in the people and mobilize them to sustain regimes that are doing great damage to themselves and others. It takes the crisis of the regimes and the insecurities and resentments of those being hurt or displaced and turns them into red meat for the regime's continuing success and survival.

WHEN BLACK MAGIC GETS DANGEROUS

History—both in the United States and Europe—also tells us that pseudopopulism is exceedingly dangerous. Precisely because it appeals to the deepest moral and spiritual passions and fears of the people, and because it is a highly organized system of propaganda by regime rulers seeking to deceive and preserve power, pseudopopulism tends to breed scapegoating, hatred, and horrific violence. Although regimes turn to pseudopopulism and civilizational warfare (war between civilizations with different religions and cultures) to preserve their power, it can also be used to create a right-wing regime change and turn democratic societies toward fascism.[4]

Today there is fertile soil for a new kind of fascist turn. While pseudopopulism serves up black magic, it resonates among millions of Americans, much as a different version of it resonated among millions of Germans in the 1920s and 1930s.[5] The current resonance reflects long-standing cultural values in heartland America associated with "just plain folk" who are good because they live by simple rules of right and wrong that go back to the Bible. While the regime's master narrative that I describe in this chapter is propaganda, it would be a grave mistake not to recognize the culturally conservative mind-set and worldview, which is deeply embedded in American history and ideology, that gives it such power among the believers.

Today's pseudopopulism is a propaganda system woven around four interrelated core elements. Together, they tell a story of powerful domestic and foreign enemies of the common people. The black magic is making credible an incredulous story of how corporations and top political leaders are spearheading an insurgent rebellion of ordinary citizens to save them from evil ruling elites at home and abroad.

Despite the power of pseudopopulism, its deep resonance in sectors of the populace, and the enormous role of the media in spreading it over the airwaves every day, it has not converted all of America and remains a subject of intense ideological contestation. It has become a matter of faith among a highly mobilized religious conservative minority, and it energizes them toward fervent political engagement in support of the Republican Party. But most Democrats remain resistant to much of the regime's black magic, and there is also a significant sector of cynics who are skeptical about all political stories. Pseudopopulism is thus far from a dominant majority view, and can be challenged by social movements, but it has become the mobilizing tool for the Republican base and the regime's most ardent supporters.

The pseudopopulist story comes in four chapters.

THE PSEUDOPOPULIST STORY

1. Civilization Under Threat
2. The Alien Establishment
3. Permanent War
4. The Election Trap

CIVILIZATION UNDER THREAT

The idea of civilization under threat is the linchpin of this regime's story. 9/11 gives it special credibility today but it sustained the regime long before that—and it draws on a mythology that goes back deep into American history. It is a story of a siege of near-Biblical proportions that threatens the basic values of the nation and the values of civilized people around the world. It identifies enemies abroad and powerful elites at home and abroad who have little respect, even contempt, for ordinary Americans and seek to destroy their religion and way of life. The foreign threat has shifted from Indians, to racial groups (the Asian "yellow peril," or savage Africans, or Mexican aliens or immigrants), to Communists, and to terrorists over the course of American history. Pseudopopulists have tacitly allied these various foreign enemies with racial minorities and an alien secular liberal Establishment at home.

The regime has denied that it is engaged in the kind of civilizational war with Islam that has been proposed by Harvard's political scientist Samuel Huntington in his classic book, *Clash of Civilizations*.[6] President Bush himself claims the United States is fighting not Islam but a twisted version of it advanced by extremist groups in the Muslim world. The regime has found this denial necessary because it has to make alliance with Islamic governments to secure the oil necessary to fuel its global economy. The regime's official ideology of civilizational warfare is not an explicit war on Islam, of the kind Huntington seems to suggest, but a story that *all* civilizations are at risk, including both the Western and Muslim civilizations. The new enemies are barbaric and aim to subvert the values of all civilizations and religions.

Nonetheless, despite the official denial, a version of Huntington's civilizational conflict is a subtext of the regime's master narrative. It is American and Western values —freedom and liberty—that are most fully at risk. Alien civilizational forces, both abroad in the Middle East and at home in domestic cultural wars, are explicitly targeting American and Western civilization. Thus, the regime's story of civilizational warfare has two parts: 1) a generic threat to all civilizations and 2) a targeted threat to American and Western civilization.[7]

This new story is a dangerous twist of nationalism that puts both the nation and the values of all civilized people in the world at risk. It is nationalism raised to the global level—a mythological evolution not surprising for a global regime. The regime stipulates enemies who detest the values of family, God, and country that are shared, presumably, by all civilizations. Some of these enemies also hate the specifically Western ideals of freedom and liberty that are the bedrock of America and the West.

At stake is not just pocketbook issues or social policy questions but the survival of Western liberty and of all civilized order. For ordinary citizens, the danger is to their core identity: their religion, their freedom, their marriages, the values of their kids, their American Dream and freedom to work hard and get ahead, and their self-respect. Most political scientists define politics as a struggle over the allocation of resources and the power to decide who gets what. The regime's story elevates politics into something quite different: an epochal struggle over the future of civilization and the survival of Christianity and basic American values.

THE REGIME'S IDENTITY POLITICS

As a propaganda system, civilizational warfare has the potential to trump all other political issues because it speaks to the religious convictions and core values of the people. It makes the traditional material concerns of politics—about money, jobs, or wealth—seem secondary, almost trivial. It is spiritually driven politics, speaking to the heart. It is the right-wing politics of identity.

The new civilizational theme has become intensely compelling because of the skill of regime propagandists in conflating external and domestic religious and cultural "threats." Fighting Al Qaeda and Islamic terrorism would itself be a powerful way to persuade ordinary Americans that the ruling regime was fighting for their values and safety, as well as that of the world as a whole. Terrorism is the foreign threat most easily painted as a credible threat to all civilized values—terrorists are said to "hate freedom" and every other civilized value. But the regime has now managed to color America's own culture wars, now coded in terms of blue and red states, as a subtle domestic extension of the civilizational warfare being fought out in the struggle against civilizational enemies abroad. This melding of internal and external civilizational conflict has deeply stirred the anxieties of ordinary Americans in the heartland, who now worry that the threats to their basic Christian values and way of life are not just coming from fanatic Arabs but from secular liberal humanists in California or Massachusetts.

The regime's black magic changes politics from class warfare to civilizational warfare. This is an astonishing accomplishment for a corporate regime whose fundamental aims are, after all, economic. It takes a regime driven entirely by profit and redefines itself as a guardian of the people's religious values and the highest morality of Western civilization. By establishing civilizational warfare as the story of modern politics, regime leaders take their own ruthless economic agenda and staggering economic power off the political table.[8]

This is not to say that class and other economic issues disappear, but they get fantastically turned around—180 de-

grees—within the broader narrative of civilizational conflict. Divisions of economic power between workers and
increasingly ruthless corporations do not create the broad
class divisions imagined by Karl Marx but wed workers and
bosses together in a common struggle against the scape-
goats created by the regime's own propaganda machine.
Call this erasure of class conflict in an age of downsizing
and outsourcing the triumph of Groucho Marx over Karl
Marx, an absurdist comic plot worthy of a Marx Brothers
film rather than a depiction of reality.

The story of civilizational warfare aligns corporations
and their workers in a sacred bond against both the internal and external cultural enemy. Moreover, the anxieties
and insecurities now permeating the entire working and
middle classes become viewed as a function of cultural decay and the subversion of religion and society by an alien
cultural Establishment rather than the consequence of
predatory global corporations and their handmaidens in
Washington. The insecurity created by the regime ironically becomes the fertile seedbed for keeping the regime
alive.

THE ALIEN ESTABLISHMENT

The regime's hegemonic story of who actually rules America is true black magic. By positing a secular liberal Establishment that runs the country, the regime essentially
makes itself invisible and hides its own ruling power. The
alleged relation between the "Establishment" and the regime is one of the great triumphs of modern propaganda,
since it succeeds in turning America's most powerful corporate and political leaders, including the president of the

United States, into populist crusaders against the Establishment.

The Establishment, as painted by the regime, is an elite housed in Hollywood, mass media, top universities, the judiciary, many of the professions, and the Democratic Party, with branches in the large foundations, the foreign policy community and the State Department, the U.N., and even liberal sectors of Wall Street and international finance. According to the regime's propaganda system, and described repeatedly in the writing of conservative ideologues such as Ann Coulter, in the books and cable commentary of Fox's Sean Hannity, and in the speeches of the president of the United States, the Establishment rules even when it does not occupy the White House or control Congress by virtue of its dominance of the federal government's sprawling bureaucracy, the courts, the mass media, the educational system, and all the other central institutions that create our culture and ideas. The Establishment is a permanent power structure, enshrined since the New Deal and operating as a kind of entrenched bureaucratic elite, something like the mandarins of ancient China or the elite intelligentsia and civil service in France or Japan whose influence persists long after particular governments rise and fall.[9]

The Establishment is defined by a few central qualities of its members:

1. They possess cultural credentials, typically professional degrees or PhDs.
2. They live mainly in urban centers and on the West or East Coasts.

3. They are politically liberal and many are left-wing and far outside the mainstream.
4. They are anti-religious and culturally radical, embracing views on morality, faith, family, sexuality, abortion, and other social values that are subverting and destroying not only Christianity, America, and its cultural traditions but subtly threatening worldwide spiritual and civilizational ideals.
5. They speak and live in identifiable ways that clearly distinguish them from ordinary Americans; they are less likely to be married, have children, or go to church.
6. They view themselves as an elite and have little respect for those less educated than themselves.
7. They exercise perpetual power by virtue of their cultural authority and their positions in the federal government's bureaucracy, the "activist courts," and the cultural institutions they inhabit.

The leading institutional symbols of the Establishment include:

Hollywood
Harvard University
The *New York Times*
PBS
CBS
CNN
The NAACP
The ACLU
Saturday Night Live

Will and Grace
Tort lawyers
The judiciary and "activist judges"
Secular humanists, atheists, and antireligious activists
The AFL-CIO
The teachers' unions
Sierra Club and other environmentalists
University professors
The Democratic Party
Federal government civil service
The U.N.

Some of the famous people symbolizing the Establishment are:

Ted Kennedy
John Kerry
Bill Clinton
Hillary Clinton
Dan Rather
Ted Turner
Jane Fonda
Paul Krugman
Jon Stewart
Jerry Seinfeld
Barbra Streisand
Robert Redford
Jesse Jackson
Kofi Annan
George Soros

The regime's portrayal of the Establishment represents a kind of inverted Marxist theory of the world. The Establishment is a ruling class, but its power is based on cultural capital than monied capital. Cultural capital, in the form of educational credentials, buys it entrenched positions in Hollywood, the mass media, universities, and, most important, the courts and the huge federal government bureaucracy. It rules over a dispossessed "cultural proletariat" who lack knowledge and cultural credentials. The cultural proletariat is almost everyone who lacks an advanced degree, the majority of America. Since the Establishment has a global reach, it is also threatening cultures around the world, with Hollywood and other leading Establishment forces subverting both Western ideals and the highest moral standards of all the world's civilizations and religions.

The regime has succeeded in persuading a large sector of this culturally dispossessed majority that George W. Bush is one of them, because of his born-again faith, plain speaking, and Texan boots. John Kerry, on the other hand, seems a classic model of the arrogant Establishment, speaking with big words and lacking simple faith and the common touch. Kerry's intellectual powers led him to win the debates but lose the election, since his whole persona fit the model of the Establishment that the regime has created.

The Establishment exploits ordinary people, but not through extracting profit or surplus labor from them. Instead it prevents them from living the lifestyle faithful to traditional American culture. The Establishment dictates the moral fashions that are "politically correct," and these are sandbagging the American way of life based on family, God, and country. The current Establishment is the legacy of the 1960s and 1970s, the white and black civil rights activists, antiwar radicals and hippies who went back to school but never abandoned their countercultural permissiveness and their left-wing politics. The Establishment remains the official sponsor of civil rights, feminism, and affirmative action that are displacing the "anxious class," intensifying their job insecurity, and undermining the level playing field. The liberals running the Establishment are slowly but surely destroying Christianity and the American way of life, imposing their own morality—through the universities, the mass media, and the courts—on ordinary Americans who have no defense against them. This entire story plays especially to the fears, racial prejudices, and moral and religious traditions of Americans in the South and in rural areas throughout the country; in the South, it is hard to separate pseudopopulism from a revival of the Civil War in which the liberal Establishment supposedly is unfairly promoting secular values over evangelical religion and African-Americans at the expense of whites.[10]

It is at this part of the story where the regime steps forward, led by the president himself. The regime offers itself as the voice and political vehicle for ordinary Americans, especially in the South and heartland, who want to save the great religious and cultural traditions of America. As noted in Chapter 2, the corporations joined forces with the religious right in the 1970s to take back the country from a New Deal liberalism that had gone haywire, breeding the political and cultural radicalism of the 1960s and early 1970s. Many of those in the Bible Belt and the heartland, who had looked on civil rights activists, antiwar protestors, long-haired hippies, and liberal New Dealers as undermining everything good in America, now had a political cause to embrace and the money to make good on it. The marriage of televangelist preachers with corporate elites, who came together to create the New Right and elect

Ronald Reagan, was the founding of modern pseudopopulism. It created a crusade of ordinary religious folk and corporate elites against the cultural Establishment and the New Deal regime, finally sinking it.[11]

THE TRUTH AND FANTASY OF THE ESTABLISHMENT STORY

The regime's framing of the Establishment is a series of fantastic but widely believed misconceptions that constitute "the myth of the Establishment":

1. Corporations and conservative political elites are subordinate to more sinister ruling elites and do not run the country.
2. A liberal Establishment, whose power is rooted in its control of culture, rules America.
3. The anxieties and discontents of most Americans are caused not by the corporate regime but by the immoral, antireligious Establishment.
4. Corporations and the president are populist insurgents who have aligned themselves with ordinary people to challenge the reign of the Establishment.

While this story is fantasy, it has gained credibility because it skillfully twists certain realities about cultural authority and social stratification in America based on education. There is, in fact, a cultural elite in America, concentrated disproportionately on the East and West coasts and in urban centers. It is made up of people with advanced degrees and it exercises authority in higher education, sectors of the media, and many professions, as well as the civil service. It leans toward "liberalism" on social values such as abortion, homosexuality, and affirmative action. It promotes separation of church and state. Its educational credentials represent real cultural capital and confer not only economic privilege but, among many, a feeling of superiority. Its language tends to be more like John Kerry's than George W. Bush's.[12]

But the fact that both Kerry and Bush were educated at Yale points to some of the black magic in the Establishment idea. There is no politically unified class of highly educated Americans. Many, like Kerry, are liberals, but many others, like Bush, are conservative and actually are leading figures in the corporate regime. In fact, most of the corporate CEOs and their political allies in Washington that run the third corporate regime have advanced degrees. This seems to suggest the bizarre idea that the regime is actually controlled by the members of the alien cultural Establishment that it claims to be fighting.

The truth is that the mass media and other leading cultural institutions of America under the current corporate regime are largely owned and controlled by corporations rather than by any liberal Establishment.[13] We live in a corporate culture whose materialistic and consumer values dictate America's morality and lifestyle. The federal civil service must follow the dictates of the conservative political elites, including the president, who run the regime. Moreover, Kerry and many other leading "liberal" Democrats, as I show shortly, are themselves part of the corporate regime, throwing more cold water on the very existence of a liberal Establishment that rules the corporations and the country. Nonetheless, the black magic of the regime has turned the idea of the liberal Establishment into powerfully compelling propaganda in large slices of the American heartland, especially among the most mobilized religious conservatives in the Bible Belt. It plays a key role in concealing the existence and ruling power of the corporate regime. And it sustains the absurd proposition that the corporate elite have become the populist allies of American workers, when they are abandoning these very workers for the global labor force that comes far cheaper.[14]

PERMANENT WAR

Wag the Dog was a popular film and novel about how a president invented a war and staged it on television to win reelection. Larry Beinhart, the author of the novel, bases the book on an interpretation of the 1991 Gulf War as a strategy by George Bush, Sr. to win reelection. Bush's ratings were low and he had the reputation of a wimp. According to the novel, while the famous political operative, Lee Atwater, is dying of cancer, he passes a memo to Secretary of State James Baker for Bush. The memo proposes a war made for television that Americans believe will be a real war caused by a vicious aggressor who threatens everything America stands for. Bush will win the war and reelection.[15]

This is war as ultimate black magic fictionalized in a very funny film and novel. But the regime has capitalized on the idea as central to its real-world propaganda system, and this is the third chapter of its master narrative. The regime is fighting a permanent war that is, in large measure, its own invention. The purpose of the war is not just to reelect a corporate president but to sustain the regime as it begins to crack and inflict unacceptable harm on much of the American people.

War has been a tool of political survival for ruling regimes throughout history. It is a part of American history almost from the beginning, when war became part of America's Manifest Destiny to civilize the Indians and the rest of the world. But the war that is at the heart of the corporate regime's current propaganda system is new in several ways. It is a permanent war that cannot ever be won. It is a civilizational war that is essential to save America and all of civilization from barbarians at the gate. The foreign enemy that it is fighting, like the alien Establishment at home, is, in surprising measure, its own creation.

Because the regime's image as guardian of civilization depends on its war against a civilizational enemy, if a suitable enemy does not present itself, the regime will find a way to invent it. Fortunately, there are always threats that can be turned into civilizational enemies, and these have become so central to the regime's survival that the enemy's relation with the regime itself can be equated, in our age of Oprah, with a co-dependent marriage. The regime hates its enemy, just as a co-dependent husband hates his addicted spouse. But because he depends on her for survival, he does whatever is necessary to keep her alive and preserve the hostile relationship. The regime survives only as long as its despised enemies do.

The regime survives, that is, by playing a foreign policy game that I call "marry your enemy."[16]

The regime's first enemy was Communism. President Reagan got elected and created the regime partly by his pledge to destroy the Soviet Union and save the "free world." When the Soviet Union imploded in 1991, the

Communist enemy disappeared, creating a potential crisis of legitimacy for a global regime that faced increasing dissent from American workers who saw their industries outsourcing their jobs to Asia and Latin America. Without a civilizational enemy, the greed and corporate mission of the regime might become more visible, class warfare could erupt, and the cracks in the regime could widen and break it apart.

9/11 provided a near miraculous solution for the regime. Al Qaeda and Osama bin Laden, of course, are very real, as were their attacks on the Twin Towers and the Pentagon. But they afforded the regime a new civilizational enemy and a splendid opportunity to enshrine a version of *Wag the Dog* into the core of its propaganda system. The endless television reruns of the planes hitting the Twin Towers were just the beginning of the reconstruction of 9/11 into a kind of Hollywood production envisioned in the novel, but extended into a permanent war whose aim is to ensure permanent survival of the regime.

For a regime whose propaganda system is based on civilizational warfare, the terrorist enemy is better than any made in Hollywood—or in the Soviet Union. While the Soviets could be portrayed as enemies of the "free world," they advanced an idealistic political and economic agenda that pitted two economic ideologies against each other: capitalism vs. communism. For a corporate regime seeking to hide its economic power and aims, the Communist enemy was not a perfect one, since it threatened to expose world politics as an economic rather than a civilizational conflict.

Al Qaeda and Islamic terrorism are enemies who fit more neatly into the regime's master narrative. While "terrorism" has an elusive meaning, with some people's terrorists being other people's "freedom fighters," terrorism is barbarism by almost any definition. One does not need a Hollywood script writer to persuade most Americans that terrorist acts run contrary to civilization itself, and that the regime's war on terror is the most noble form of civilization defense. Moreover, since the Soviet Union was based in one country, its collapse could make the enemy disappear, whereas since terrorism will always be with us, it offers the prospect of permanent war.

The war on terrorism is now central to the regime's survival. It redefines the corporate regime as a moral rather than an economic force, committed mainly to the defense of American values and the world's civilizations. It plays a central role in the transformation of American politics from class war to civilizational war. This played out very explicitly in the 2004 elections when the majority of American people indicated that they opposed Bush's economic agenda but voted for him because he was protecting their morality and Christian values from both foreign and domestic enemies. As one blogger put it, "He's going to wag the dog until hell freezes over." But this is a political principle for both parties in the regime. Kerry ran mainly on the idea that, as a warrior from the Vietnam era, he could prosecute the war on terror—and in Iraq—even more effectively than Bush, thus collaborating in the regime's story that politics is about civilizational rather than class war.

TERRORISTS AND LIBERALS

Part of Kerry's inability to make his case successfully, however, was because he was implicated as a member of the domestic alien Establishment that itself was threatening American and, by implication, globally shared civilizational values. This hints at the unspoken black magic that links the liberal Establishment at home to the enemy abroad. The regime, of course, did not explicitly identify Massachusetts liberals as a fifth column of terrorists inside this nation, although the Bush Administration occasionally lapsed and implied liberals were traitors, a charge made more explicit by conservative writers like Ann Coulter, who titled her best-selling book on the liberal Establishment *Treason*.[17]

Permanent war adds the central issue of patriotism into the regime's story of civilizational defense. Love of country is at the heart of traditional American morality. The regime's case for itself as guardian of civilization, founded on its equation of wrapping itself in the flag, is a particularly compelling part of its black magic, since, in fact, it is America's first truly global rather than American regime. As discussed earlier, the mission of the American government under the third corporate regime has been trans-

THE NEW TWO-
WAR DOCTRINE

The regime does not have to rely on such explicit, extremist rhetoric because its master narrative identifies both a domestic and foreign threat to American values—and can leave the rest to the imagination of the heartland. Since the alien liberal Establishment at home and the terrorists abroad both represent a threat to the fundamental religious and moral values of ordinary Americans, it does not matter whether they are formally allied. The regime's aim is simply to make clear that it stands firm against both threats—and will do whatever necessary to protect the heartland's morality against both domestic and foreign enemies.[18]

formed to serve the global interests of global companies. Within the regime, the U.S. government is caught in a schizophrenic role, seeking to prove its loyalty to American voters while carrying out a global corporate agenda harmful to their interests.[19]

Patriotism becomes the linchpin of the regime's civilizational case that it is protecting America despite the obvious adverse impacts of corporate globalization on American workers and communities. Yes, the regime is defending the right of corporations to flee abroad and make profits off the cheapest workers on the planet, while turning whole American industries and communities into wastelands. But, since the broader threat to America is civilizational, the regime's economic agenda becomes secondary, and its claims of patriotic leadership in a moral and civilizational war dominate the headlines and feed the fears of ordinary Americans.

THE ELECTION TRAP AND THE RED/BLUE DIVIDE

Americans carry around a new mental geography of a color-coded America, divided into red and blue areas. Red and blue are symbols of Republicans and Democrats, whose partisan divisions have become so bitter that it can make discussion over Thanksgiving dinner very difficult. My students who are "blue" but go home to "red" Republican parents over holidays tell me they have to avoid political discussion, because the differences are so deep that any discussion about politics seems like it might break up the family.

As I discussed in the Introduction, the Election Trap focuses Americans on the next election and the horse race between the two parties. I have already explained how this helps hide the commanding power of the regime and disguise its very existence. As people come to believe that America is run either by Democrats or Republicans, they ignore the reality that the leadership of both parties are dependent on corporate funding and represent different voices of the same ruling regime.

The entire system of American elections is, in this sense, a part of the regime's black magic. The ever-more fierce competition between the parties does little to threaten the regime's control of America. While there are important tactical differences between the parties, they are both bound by the core economic and foreign policy of the third corporate regime. The fervor of the horse race suggests a vibrant democracy but the people lose—and the regime wins—whether the Democrats or the Republicans win the White House and the Congress.

THE RED/BLUE DIVIDE AS BLACK MAGIC

The regime has a deep interest in perpetuating the partisan divide, and not just because it hides its own power. The division between the parties—and the red/blue divide that now symbolizes its intensity—has become an integral part, the fourth chapter, of the master narrative of cultural and civilizational war. In a startling sense, the regime has invented the red/blue divide, in a form of black magic closely related to both the myths of the liberal Establishment and the war on terrorism, to reinforce its image of politics as civilizational warfare and itself as the guardian of American morality.

While red and blue have become symbols of Republican and Democrat, they are largely cultural images. When you think Red, you think of middle Americans in the heartland who come right out of a Grant Wood painting. Thomas Frank has made them Kansans in his best-selling book

What's the Matter with Kansas?[20] But they could be from almost anywhere in the Bible Belt, rural America, or exurbia. They are patriotic plain folk, who care most about family, God, and country. They drive SUVs and pickup trucks, like to hunt, go to NASCAR races, and drink beer. They are Republicans, it seems, largely because they believe the GOP will best protect the American way of life by protecting the country against terrorism and against the moral decay undermining marriage, family, community, and religion.

The blues are seen as bi-coastal liberals who tend to be intellectual, professional, urban, cosmopolitan, secular, and internationalists. They are Democrats because they support affirmative action, gun control, abortion, women's rights, gay rights, the environment, and civil liberties. They drive Volvos, Saabs, or Hondas, they drink wine, they go to foreign films, and they travel to foreign countries. They are viewed as closer in cultural and social sensibilities to Canadians or Europeans than to heartland Americans. That is why you can go to the Internet and find color-coded maps dividing America into the "United States of Canada" (which includes Canada, the Northeast, the upper Midwest, and the West Coast) and "Jesusland" (which includes the rest of the United States).[21]

The images of the United States of Canada and Jesusland essentially suggest a civilizational conflict between red and blue America. The red/blue divide is bitter and emotional—capable of breaking up holiday family dinners—precisely because it seems a matter of core values, spirituality, and personal identity. If you are on the red rather than the blue side of the divide, you are part of a different tribe. It affirms the regime's master narrative that politics has become civilizational, with our fundamental morality and basic values on the line.[22]

Since red and blue are symbols of Republican and Democrat, the new color-coded symbolism sticks a civilizational label on each party. They may be voices of the same corporate regime, but one represents traditional American morality and the other seems nearly identical to the mythical liberal elite Establishment that I have already discussed. The red/blue divide becomes shorthand for describing a new electoral politics in which civilizational conflict has migrated from the Middle East and come home to the Midwest.

The image of the Democratic Party as a civilizational enemy and a voice of cultural elites is widespread in the South and West of the United States, helping to explain not only the swath of red states but the red voters even in places like Minnesota or Michigan or Maryland, historically Democratic bastions. This delegitimation of the Democratic Party carries potential problems for the regime, since it depends on the image of being a democracy for its own survival. But it is also a plus for the regime. It reinforces the image of civilizational war that is growing from within as well as outside the country. It gives a tangible political face, that is, the Democratic Party, to the image of an alien Establishment that threatens Christianity and America's values. It reinforces the view of the Republican Party, the closest to the regime, as a populist force defending the salt-of-the-earth American.[23]

The painting of the Democratic Party as a civilizational enemy—and the entire construction of the red/blue divide —is another remarkable feat of black magic, since the Democratic leaders have become co-opted into the regime, as I document in Chapter 7. Indeed, the polls give the lie to the entire view of the red/blue divide as a civilizational conflict. Yes, there are extremists on the "red" side, such as some evangelical fundamentalists who want to turn America into a Christian kingdom. And there are radicals on the "blue" side, cultural anarchists who want to destroy the state, end the family, and create a world without country or God. But these are groups at the margins. Most Americans, while they are far more likely to describe themselves as philosophically conservative than liberal, and religious rather than secular, have become relatively tolerant on the entire range of moral issues that are the red meat of "civilizational warfare." The majority of Americans support racial equality, women's rights, and even civil unions for gays. They seek compromises on hot-button issues such as abortion.[24]

This is not to say, though, that there is no cultural divide. The regime's civilizational war rhetoric resonates precisely because there are charged, historically rooted cultural differences separating Bible Belt and other social conservatives from more liberal Americans. These differences concern not only abortion, gay marriage, and affirmative action, but also broader attitudes toward authority, religion, and the good life. Millions of ordinary conservative Americans see themselves trying to be good people by following the Ten Commandments and other Biblical codes, while also trusting in and following America's leaders.[25] They pride themselves in the simplicity and goodness of their strict conformity to ancient codes of religion and morality, as well as in their unambivalent patriotism and love of America. Simplicity and acceptance of religious and political authority are part of their core identity. They look back to the morality of the antebellum South, America's Manifest Destiny, and America's Christian heritage as confirmation of their own definition of America and of the simple folk who make it good.[26]

This "plain folk" conservatism is threatened by the value placed on complexity and critical thinking by many intellectuals and liberals. The American liberal tradition—which has taken root most strongly in urban America on both coasts—is rooted in the critical, reasoning mind. It refuses to accept authority and religious doctrine without constantly re-examining it, a view that can be traced back to the Enlightenment mindset of many of the Founders of the country. "My country, right or wrong," may be simple, but it is too simple for this historically rooted liberal imagination. The same can be said for any doctrinaire interpretation of the good life. There is no place in the heart of blueness for absolute good and evil, since, for most liberals, there is appreciation of the complexity and contradictions of the great moral dilemmas of life and politics. They view "plain folk" conservatism as a life based on "recipe rules," a resort to the safety of absolute moral authority in the face of growing social uncertainty and disorder. They identify with the Progressive and New Deal political traditions that enshrined liberal thought in the American pantheon.[27]

What the regime has succeeded in doing is distorting and whipping up these long-standing cultural divisions into a partisan political and cultural war that overshadows class and polarizes deeper social resentments. The strategy is particularly successful because so many of the small-town "plain folk" in the Bible Belt and the heartland, and so many culturally conservative workers in the old manufacturing cities across the nation, have become an "anxious class," facing dire economic and social insecurity. The regime has redefined their problems as moral decay engineered by internal civilizational enemies of the liberal persuasion. While economic anxiety and social resentment creates today's particularly fertile soil for pseudopopulism, the regime's master narrative is a version of conservative thought that has long had resonance to millions of Americans. The fact that there are deep historically entrenched cultural differences between American conservatism and liberalism is the kernel of reality that reinforces the black magic of the regime, helping explain its potency as a political weapon and as a strategy of regime legitimation.

Despite the germs of truth underlying the regime's ideology, the black magic involved in the regime's master narrative is astonishing, since it has invented an Establishment that doesn't exist, concealed the power of the regime that actually rules the country, rendered its ruling power as defense of a nation (which it is actually abandoning for global profits), and turned corporate elites into champions of the workers and the people. We should not be entirely surprised. Historically, pseudopopulism has proved astonishingly powerful—and astonishingly dangerous. Just as it helped create fascist regime changes in Europe, it carries the potential to create an American Orwellian future. In the next chapter, I discuss the ways in which the strategy that the regime is now using to survive could morph into a regime change creating "fascism lite" at home.

CHAPTER 6

FASCISM LITE

Right after George W. Bush was reelected in 2004, thousands of Americans applied to emigrate to Canada. Immigration lawyers in Toronto and Montreal got so many requests for help that they went to San Francisco, Boston, and other bastions of the blue states to answer questions from Americans who didn't want to live in their country anymore. Most of these despairing Americans were not just upset that their candidate had lost the election. Some feared a slow-motion coup, in which a far-right Administration would tighten its grip on the nation, continue its attacks on constitutional rights, and step-by-step undermine American democracy.

We have seen hints of a fascist drift in earlier American eras, although it never created a permanent police state or fascist order. As discussed in Chapter 1, Woodrow Wilson in 1917 launched one of the worst crackdowns against antiwar protest in American history, involving unconstitutional detentions and deportations of thousands of people. The internment of Japanese Americans in World War II and the anti-Communist hysteria of the McCarthy era during the early 1950s were other such periods. McCarthy purged thousands of government civil servants, scientists, professors, journalists, and Hollywood writers and producers. The country's move toward a police state was halted only when McCarthy went after top generals in the military and he was discredited.

This chapter looks at the dangers of an unprecedented tip toward a new regime that I will call "fascism lite." Fascism has long been understood as a police state based on the union of big business and government. Such a regime suspends the most basic constitutional liberties of citizens in the name of a religious or nationalist war against civilizational enemies. I argue in this chapter that several forces could converge to create right-wing regime change toward an American brand of fascism.

In the current regime, we already see the embryonic shape of such a new hypernationalist order, foreshadowed in the Patriot Act, the Homeland Security restrictions on civil liberties, and the Pentagon's suspension of the Geneva Accords and Constitutional safeguards against arbitrary detention and abuse of terrorism suspects. This suggests a creeping authoritarianism that already functions within today's regime and could continue to sustain the current order. But, in another scenario, repressive forces could expand and accelerate to create regime change. By fascism lite, I mean a new regime that would effectively suspend much of our current rights, while still preserving the patina of formal elections and constitutionalism. It would preserve a government-corporate partnership, but, in contrast to the current regime, it would clearly subordinate corporations to the state. It would eliminate unions, formally subjugate the press to government censorship, increase the tie between religion and the state, and subject dissenters and tens of millions of ordinary citizens to the unconstitutional treatment and daily abuse now received by terrorist detainees.

Any form of fascism that might take root in America is radically distinct from the classical forms in Germany and Italy in the 1930s—and will remain a different breed. Fascism lite is not Nazism, Hitlerism, or Mussolini-style rule, and is dangerous precisely because it is likely to retain the framework of constitutional rule that Hitler and Mussolini openly abandoned. Nonetheless, parallels between the conditions in classical European fascist societies and ours today include: the marriage of big business and the state; the rise of militaristic and religious nationalism, and severe economic dislocation at home that creates an "anxious class" of workers and small businesses. Hitler exploited such social anxieties and came to power through elections, promising to respect democracy and the law. He created fascism from within a democratic, corporate order undergoing great destabilization, a situation not entirely different from our own. Both the parallels and differences between fascism and fascism lite in the European and American contexts need exploration.

Another caveat is that fascist regime change in the United States is a possibility, not a certainty. The American people have the ability to stop it if they understand the danger and how to respond. In the last section of this book,

I make clear how Americans can not only prevent fascist regime change but also tip the corporate regime in the opposite direction, toward a reenergized democracy.

THE PROPHET OF AMERICAN FASCISM

At the beginning of the current regime, Bertram Gross, a prominent political scientist, wrote *Friendly Fascism*, a best-selling book that was published in 1982, two years after Ronald Reagan's election. The book was a shot across the bow about the dangers posed by the new corporate order and its structural potential to transform itself into an American breed of fascism.[1] Gross saw the rulers of this new "friendly fascist" order as "members of the Establishment or people on its fringes, who in the name of Americanism betray the interests of most Americans by fomenting militarism, applauding rat-race individualism, protecting undeserved privilege, or stirring up nationalistic and ethnic hatreds. I see pretended patriots who desecrate the American flag by waving it while waiving the law."[2]

Friendly fascism was likely to come to America not through brown-shirted fringe elements on the streets but "as an outcome of powerful tendencies within the Establishment itself." "Big Business and Big Government," he writes, "have been learning how to live in bed together, and despite arguments between them, enjoy the cohabitation."[3] Such cohabitation regimes—what I have called corporate regimes—have had a historical tendency, Gross noted, to slide down a dangerous authoritarian slope. "I am worried," he observed, "by those who fail to remember—

or have never learned—that Big Business–Big Government partnerships, backed up by other elements, were the central facts behind the power structures of old fascism in the days of Mussolini, Hitler, and the Japanese empire builders."[4]

But Gross did not imagine a friendly fascism in America that looked anything like the classical fascist regime. In the United States, "anyone looking for black shirts, mass parties, or men on horseback will miss the telltale signs of creeping fascism."[5] Instead, friendly fascism would have a distinctively American form, preserving the formal constitutional framework and presided over by congenial, folksy leaders. Gross suggested a new kind of authoritarian order built on America's own most basic institutions. Instead of abolishing the Constitution and formal democratic procedures, elections would be subtly subverted, and opposition parties and the general public subtly intimidated and manipulated. Propaganda would come not through direct government-owned media but through the electronic circus of corporate cable media. Dissent would be crushed not by murderous street gangs but by professional and high-tech policing and surveillance.

Unlike classical fascism, friendly fascism arising from a corporate regime would play off the most appealing elements of contemporary American culture. "In America," Gross wrote, friendly fascism "would be supermodern and multi-ethnic, as American as Madison Avenue, executive luncheons, credit cards, and apple pie. It would be fascism with a smile. As a warning against its cosmetic face, subtle manipulation and velvet gloves, I call it friendly fascism. What scares me most is its subtle appeal."[6]

William Shirer, in his epic chronicle of German Fascism,

The Rise and Fall of the Third Reich, wrote that "America may be the first country in which fascism comes to power through democratic elections."[7] Gross admitted his own very personal fear of this possibility. "I am not afraid to say that I am afraid," he wrote. "I am afraid of those who proclaim that it can't happen here."[8]

While Gross's work points to the structural potential of our corporate regime to become fascist, fascism lite is the most likely scenario. Gross could not anticipate 9/11, nor the ideology of the current American war on terrorism. He could not imagine the blatantly unfriendly form of fascist regime change that looms now as a national nightmare. The current fascist drift already evident in the existing regime, as symbolized in the torture chambers of Abu Ghraib and Guantanamo, is far less cosmetically appealing or apple pie than the model Gross forecast.

Fascism lite is not at all friendly. True, it has a corporate flavor, and it has many of the attributes Gross predicted, including the ability to insinuate itself slowly into the American landscape without the most extreme trappings of classical fascism. But the driving thrust is likely to come not so much from the corporations, as Gross would suggest, but from the state, the military, and religion. Corporations would continue to play a major role, but the state would move toward more direct control over corporations themselves, as part of a new, radically militarized social order. Its center of gravity will be the Pentagon rather than Citigroup or Merrill Lynch. Its repression of ordinary people, particularly dissenters, minorities, and immigrants, at home and abroad, will be characterized by violence and inquisition.

CAUSES AND CATALYSTS

Consider the following three potential causes of a fascist lite regime tip.

1. FROM CRACKS TO CHASMS

In Chapter 3, I showed that serious cracks in the regime could potentially destabilize it and lead toward regime change of either a progressive or a reactionary form. Fascism lite could arise from a deepening of the regime's current cracks into unmanageable chasms, leading to vast popular dissent and a decision by regime elites to maintain order by suspending normal constitutional procedures and imposing an American form of police state.

One scenario is a deterioration of the regime's economic crises, creating recessions or even a depression. Mass unemployment, spiraling debt, a collapse in the dollar with a steep rise in interest rates, and dramatic new cuts in health care, Social Security, and other parts of the safety net could trigger mass protests or riots. If the dissent looked like it might spin out of control, threatening the regime's very survival, elites might crack down with brutal new measures outside the current constitutional order, sliding toward right-wing regime change. Another possible scenario is a desperate deterioration of the military situation in Iraq and Afghanistan, or other catastrophic new foreign policy misadventures. As in the Vietnam era, these could produce a huge antiwar movement that would divide the country and threaten regime stability. New terrorist attacks on the homeland are another such eventuality, but I consider these separately because they are historically unique and probably the single most likely catalyst of a fascist regime turn.

We have already seen the rise of a popular movement against corporate globalization, and we also have seen the eruption of one of the biggest peace movements in history against the Iraqi war. The regime's response has not been reassuring. While both the antiglobalization and anti-war movements have been largely peaceful and have not threatened large-scale social disorder, regime elites have responded with growing repression. In the 1999 Seattle protests against the WTO, the police launched volleys of pepper spray and used batons against protestors, rounding up hundreds in detention centers. On the first day of protest, authorities darkened Seattle's sunny skies with clouds of tear gas. By the fifth day of protest, tanks were patrolling Seattle streets.

To deal with hundreds of antiglobalization and antiwar protests in recent years, police have cordoned off whole areas of cities, built walls with barbed wire or electronic shock devices to keep people miles away from the meetings, forced protestors to march in small cordoned areas surrounded by fences and armed guards, begun refusing to issue protest permits of any form, rounded up and detained larger numbers of protestors without charges, beat peaceful protestors violently, and launched judicial proceedings and sentencing that prevented those arrested from going out on the streets again. Before the 2002 Miami protest of the Free Trade of the Americas meeting, authorities described a military approach to "crowd control." Television cameras showed mass detention facilities, humvee-type police vehicles, and prison-like protest areas, as officials made barely disguised threats of police violence. I knew many students, labor activists, religious protestors, and others who were terrified and canceled their decision to go out of fear of being beaten, jailed, or even killed.

I have had my own experience of the new repressive climate:

> I went to jail briefly for civil disobedience in support of a "Janitors for Justice" protest event in Boston in 2002. It was a very different and more frightening experience than my other experiences with the prison system during 1960s antiwar protests before the current regime. All those committing civil disobedience were arrested, fingerprinted, booked, and eventually sent to individual cells. I noticed on the walls of the police station a thick sheaf of daily postings from Washington about terrorism. After we were booked and sent to cells, the police told us that our detention was indefinite, pending word from Washington regarding whether we were suspects for terrorism. They sent our fingerprints and records to Washington to determine whether any of us might be under surveillance by the CIA or FBI. Sitting isolated in a cell, unaware of how long I would be detained and feeling that I might be deprived of my normal rights to talk to lawyers and get help, was quite different than contemplating the Patriot Act from my office. For anyone who doubts whether civil liberties and the Bill of Rights matter, I recommend an involuntary stay in a jail cell under the new conditions.

While the rise of a fascist regime would require more far-reaching constitutional and institutional changes, the assault on dissent suggests a climate where additional catalysts could create a tipping point. The most likely candidate for such a tipping point is more terrorism and an escalating war against it.

2. TERRORISM AND THE WAR ON TERRORISM

In January 2005, Richard Clarke, the country's leading counterterrorism advisor to Presidents Reagan, Bush Sr., Clinton, and Bush Jr., published the article "Ten Years Later" in the *Atlantic Monthly* about what America might look like in 2015. Clarke envisages a series of new terrorist attacks on the country beginning in 2005 and 2006. They are not dramatic disasters on the scale of 9/11 but smaller explosions like the terrorist bombs set off in Madrid train stations. They involve attacks on subway stations or commuter rails, on shopping malls, power plants, and official buildings. American officials respond to the attacks with global military campaigns that intensify anti-Americanism and create more terrorist attacks. Authorities in 2008 and 2009 seek to restore order with a massive extra-constitutional campaign of repression. Civil liberties are dramatically curtailed and the president suspends many constitutional constraints on surveillance, detention, and normal judicial procedures. Key parts of the Bill of Rights fall by the wayside. Clarke concludes with a picture of America as an Orwellian police state, suggesting essentially a regime change to a fascist model in five to ten years.[9]

Clarke acknowledges that this is an exercise in hypotheticals, commonly used by intelligence and counterterrorism analysts to crystallize their planning. But while he takes pains to emphasize that this is only an imagined future, he also emphasizes that his analysis is based on existing threat analyses and policy responses to terror—involving surveillance of all citizens, new detention procedures, lifting of existing bans on torture, and other emergency suspensions of constitutional liberties—that are already laid out in thousands of Homeland Security, Pentagon, FBI, CIA, and Justice Department documents and procedures. He laces his *Atlantic* essay with pages of footnotes based on this official documentary record, essentially creating a fictional future that looks scarily possible based on present evidence.

Clarke's scenario is conservative by his own admission because he does not discuss nuclear or biological terrorist attacks. This is a leading matter of discussion among the nation's top intelligence analysts and political officials. American leaders have already stoked fear of such attacks as grounds for the war on Iraq and suspensions of constitutional rights at home. If a nuclear terrorist attack were actually to occur, it would be the single most likely catalyst of a fascist regime change.[10]

Clarke also does not discuss the deeper economic and political aims of the regime that lock in a dangerous U.S. foreign policy. As already discussed in Chapter 1, the entire regime is structured today around the interests of global corporations whose interests require American global hegemony. The unilateral and militarized excesses of the neoconservatives have captured attention, but even before their coming to power in the Bush Administration, the regime under Reagan, Bush Sr., and Clinton had firmly committed itself to empire. This was built into the regime's DNA, since global corporations depend on a globalization system secured by the U.S. military that can sustain friendly governments and stabilize a global order increasingly polarized between rich and poor.

The regime's interests thus commit it to a permanent expansionist policy that is a recipe for anti-American terrorism and intensified repression abroad and at home. Empires have always faced terrorist attacks, from the Roman to the British Empires, particularly as they decline. The American Empire is no exception; as I showed in Chapter 1, Empire is a pillar of the regime, and the military has become an increasingly central player. The difference from prior empires is that technology has made terrorist attacks, even from the periphery of the Empire, far more lethal to the imperial heartland.

The war on terrorism (and its implications for a fascist turn) will continue even if the Democratic leadership, now securely integrated into the corporate regime and its foreign policy establishment, comes to power. Clarke's scenario is based on the regime's global interests, not just on the radicalism of neoconservative Republicans, and likely would play out under a Democratic administration as well. Terrorism and the war against terrorism remain the most likely catalysts for a fascist regime change under either Republicans or Democrats. Both parties are likely to pursue the regime aim of U.S. hegemony, create blowback of repeated terrorism against America, and unleash the potential of a regime change toward fascism.

3. REGIME RADICALISM AND CIVILIZATIONAL WARFARE

The potential for a fascist tip is far more likely under the Republican Right governed at this writing by President George W. Bush. Bush has turned the third corporate regime into an "extreme regime," and his right wing radicalism and pandering to his evangelical religious base is a third factor that could prove a tipping point toward a fascist regime change.

One way to see this is to look at the master narrative of the regime under Bush, which I described in the last chapter as civilizational warfare. Civilizational warfare was also the master myth of Germany and Italy when they turned fascist. It is the most dangerous ideological myth for stabilizing a regime, since it creates the war between absolute good and evil that fascist leaders use to justify the abandonment of constitutionalism and the creation of a police state. The rhetoric of religion and race is especially dangerous, because it brings God and biology in as justifications for state repression.

Civilizational war propaganda is so dangerous because it suggests politics is now a struggle against barbarians at the gate—and against the more insidious barbarians who have already slipped in. Such barbarians are not really political opponents but devils, since they threaten everything human and everything good about America, Christianity, and the West. If we don't win this fight, we don't just lose another election but we lose thousands of years of the best that religion and human civilization has created, the kind of extreme danger that could legitimate even a fascist response.

When you declare war against an enemy that is absolute evil, the goal of destroying it justifies any means. In 1954, at the height of the McCarthy hysteria, a commission formed by the president and headed by ex-President Herbert Hoover, made exactly that claim about the new Communist threat, arguing that "traditional rules of American fair play" could no longer apply. Bush's radical language of absolute good and absolute evil justifies even more extreme measures, since what is at stake is not just capitalism but the survival of civilization itself. This helps to explain the famous secrecy and constitutional radicalism of his Administration, and explains why he has brought the nation farther down the path toward fascism than any of his predecessors. His increasing reliance on religion and religious extremists waging war on judges and secular politics is especially dangerous, a harbinger of fascist possibilities.

Civilizational war propaganda has always been most dangerous in societies where large sectors of the population are economically threatened or socially displaced. Historians see Hitler's appeal as rooted in the German small-business class that was being displaced by the corporations during the terrible German economic crises of the 1920s and 1930s. Their anxieties became intense enough that Hitler's propagandists could manipulate them at will with their own version of Aryan civilizational warfare. The new anxious working class in America is suffering its own fear of social displacement, with some of the same anxieties and resentments of the German lower middle classes in Hitler's day. The black-magic propaganda of the current regime feeds on the American displaced classes with comparable power, and any further deterioration in the security of American workers, especially displaced males who have always been the backbone of fascist movements, will only make a shift to fascism in the United States that much more likely.

FASCISM TODAY

Might we already have seen a regime tip as the third corporate regime encounters ever-deepening crises—in the context of a war on terrorism that seems tailor-made for the rise of fascism? The explosion of literature in academic circles, in the mass media, and on the Internet about fascism suggests that this possibility is on the public's mind. George Orwell is back in vogue, now required reading in classrooms around the country.

This is not the first American era when there has been widespread discussion about whether fascism "could happen here." But today's conversation is carried out by more educated elites, is marked by a less paranoid style, and is less focused on the rise of extreme right-wing fringe groups such as the KKK or the American Nazi party. Instead, the focus is on the systemic attributes of fascism and how they might arise (or might already have done so) out of tendencies within the ruling elites and the corporate regime itself.

Consider the widely circulated work of political scientist Lawrence Britt, who after a comparative, historical analysis of fascism from Germany and Italy to Franco's Spain, Suharto's Indonesia, and Pinochet's Chile, identifies fourteen defining attributes of fascist regimes.

The list should be nailed on the door of every classroom in the country. It is a generic description of a fascist regime broad enough to encompass both classical and fascist lite models. It hints clearly at the structural vulnerabilities of

THE FOURTEEN
CHARACTERISTICS
OF FASCISM

1. Powerful and continuing nationalism
2. Disdain for the recognition of human rights
3. Identification of enemies/scapegoats as a unifying cause
4. Supremacy of the military
5. Rampant sexism
6. Controlled mass media
7. Obsession with national security
8. Religion and government are intertwined
9. Corporate power is protected
10. Labor power is suppressed
11. Disdain for intellectuals and the arts
12. Obsession with crime and punishment
13. Rampant cronyism and corruption
14. Fraudulent elections

Lawrence Britt, *Free Inquiry Magazine,* Spring 2003

the current U.S. corporate regime to a fascist turn. At minimum, it raises the question of where America is headed and whether some form of fascism could lurk in our future. At worst, it suggests that the United States is already undergoing a regime change toward its own species of "democratic" fascism.

Many of Britt's fourteen attributes have been elements of the third corporate regime from the beginning. On most

of the fourteen criteria, the current regime is clearly becoming more extreme. Look at the items on the list refer-
ring to militarism, patriotism, enemies, and national security. Ever since 9/11, these have become defining staples
of the American political landscape and they are becoming
ever more serious threats to American constitutionalism.
Control of mass media, as discussed below, is a part of a
growing official propaganda apparatus threatening an independent press in America. Much of the rest of the list
relates to corporate power: the dominant role of corporations, their growing ties to government and the military,
and the rampant growth of institutionalized corporate cronyism and corruption. These building blocks of the third
corporate regime—particularly the tight, incestuous link
between big corporations and government—have grown
more blatant and far-reaching as it has aged. The suppres-
sion of labor power is particularly important, a defining
feature of the regime since its birth but increasingly its ruling passion as it seeks to virtually eliminate unions from the
American scene. The similarity here to German fascism is
too strong to miss, since Hitler secured the support of German corporations for his own regime change by crushing
the German unions, a benefit too great for otherwise reluctant German corporate elites to overlook. And the elements related to the disdain for intellectuals, obsession
with crime and punishment, and fraudulent elections are
other frightening signs of a regime turning to repression as
it loses its ability to survive through constitutional means.

The melding of religion and government may be among
the most ominous signs that Britt describes. Religious conservatives have become a driving force in the regime, push-

ing toward a redefinition of the classic separation of state and church. They are assaulting the independent judiciary, a classic fascist threat. Their efforts to bring Christian language, symbols, and beliefs back into the classroom and the courtroom, and to make churches recipients of government funding for social services and broadcast enterprises, dangerously blur the line between religious and political discourse and institutions. The growing dependency of the Republican Party on its religious base, and the willingness of President George W. Bush and Congressional leaders, such as House Majority leader Tom DeLay and Senate Majority Leader Bill Frist, to accommodate and even encourage extremist religious demands are truly explosive ingredients here. In early 2005, DeLay threatened "activist" judges with retaliation, after judges had been shot in the courtroom and religious conservatives themselves had threatened to remove judges who were purportedly attacking people of faith. The willingness of regime leaders to play the religion card, hinting or overtly claiming that their political opponents are enemies of God, is straying into the deep weeds of a new American fascism.

WARNING SIGNS

Three current trends rank among the most alarming signs of the potential for a fascist regime tip:

1. PROPAGANDA

To report the war in Iraq, America's war correspondents became "embedded." The Pentagon assigned them to combat units, and they became a new part of America's fighting forces. Their weapons were their laptops, and they reported the story like good soldiers.

The 2003 Iraqi invasion coverage was one of the great propaganda triumphs of modern times. Americans heard a war story scripted by top political leaders. It was as if the generals "embedded" the software of the reporters' brains and laptops. The programmed journalists told the official story of American liberators who would be greeted by Iraqi civilians showering G.I. Joe with roses.

In fascist regimes, the media becomes officially "embedded" in the government propaganda apparatus. Structurally, the media is absorbed into the government and "institutionally" embedded, with stories prepared and distributed by political hacks. Ideologically, this embedded press reports what it is told and reporters unconsciously parrot the official master narrative of the regime.

In the current corporate regime, the press remains officially independent of government ownership and control, but is increasingly informally embedded. The extent of today's ideological and structural embedding has been widely discussed by authoritative media critics such as Robert McChesney. As huge corporations such as GE, Disney, Newscorp, and AOL–Time Warner have bought up television stations and newspapers, and have become ever more monopolistic, structural embedding has become an obvious fact of life. Of course, the mainstream media varies in its level of embeddedness. Fox has become the model of the most fully embedded media, faithfully disseminating not just the regime's propaganda story, but becoming the quasi-official broadcasting voice of the Republican Party. Other mainstream media, such as CNN, are less partisan in terms of party politics, but uncritically accept most of the regime's underlying ideological assumptions about the virtues of U.S. hegemony abroad and corporate power at home, reflecting corporate ownership and beliefs. The Public Broadcasting System (PBS) and National Public Radio (NPR) are the mainstream media that are more open to critical discourse, particularly on social issues related to race and gender, but are themselves operating increasingly as embedded media on core economic and foreign policy issues. This reflects their growing dependence on corporate funding, the general repression of dissent, and their continued financial dependence on an increasingly conservative Congress that views them as part of the liberal Establishment.

The coverage of the Iraqi war demonstrated the level of ideological programming throughout the mainstream media, as reporters embraced the regime's underlying premises that the United States seeks to rid the world of tyrants and terrorists while promoting freedom not just in Iraq but everywhere. Such ideological embedding is particularly important because it does not require coercive control; reporters learn from childhood to absorb the underlying regime myths and the embedded media requires no formal censorship to ensure conformity with the regime's master narrative.[11]

Beyond the informal media embedding that characterized the third corporate regime almost from the beginning, there are new trends that hint at a shift toward the more formal embedding characteristic of friendly fascism. In January 2005, a scandal broke when it was revealed that the Bush Administration paid $240,000 to a columnist, Armstrong Williams, to write columns in support of its No

Child Left Behind program—and to encourage other journalists to do the same. Soon, similar secret arrangements with other columnists were revealed. This led to outrage because it crossed a long-standing, sacred line separating government and media, making it impossible to know whether a journalist is independent or on the Administration's payroll and just parroting its official line. The arrangements violated U.S. law that prohibits this form of propaganda, although analysts noted that the Administration had devised similar arrangements to promote its Medicare reform and other policies. It was an early mark of the more formal embedding found in fascism.[12]

In 2005, reports implicated far more influential media personalities in a different propaganda outrage. Well-known conservatives, such as Bill Kristol, editor of the influential conservative magazine the *Weekly Standard* and a regular commentator on Fox News, have helped draft speeches and policies for members of the Administration. Then, in their role as media commentators or columnists, they would praise these speeches or policies as "independent" journalists. Kristol and fellow prominent conservative journalist Charles Krauthammer were consultants to President Bush in the drafting of his second inaugural speech. In the January 31 edition of the *Weekly Standard,* Kristol lauded the speech as "powerful," "impressive," and "historical," making similar comments on Fox national news during Fox's live coverage of the event. Fox commentator Krauthammer called the speech "revolutionary," comparing it to John F. Kennedy's inaugural address. There is nothing wrong with conservatives like Kristol and Krauthammer getting involved in or being paid for speech writing. But to appear in print or on television as independent journalists without making clear when and how they have been involved in drafting the very important speech that they are commenting on moves the media closer to being the official organ of propaganda character-istic of fascist regimes.[13]

In January 2005, the Administration required leaders and staff professionals in the Social Security Administra-tion (SSA) to join the regime's full-court media campaign to privatize social security. Top Social Security administra-tors prepared documents about the imminent crisis of the system and the dangers of not moving quickly to privatize. But staff professionals in the agency blew the whistle, dis-closing that this was false information and that the Agency was being forced to shift from its professional indepen-dence to become part of the Administration's propaganda system. The agency's professionals claimed that their in-tegrity and that of the Agency was being destroyed, lead-ing top Bush officials to say that the Social Security officials would not be required to advocate any specific privatiza-tion remedy. But SSA officials continued to promote the Administration's policy under reported pressure from top officials, a sign of a shift to embed not just the media but the civil service.[14]

In 2002, reports emerged that the Pentagon was creat-ing a new propaganda tool involving foreign media. The idea was not different from that in the Armstrong Williams scandal. Through a new internal office, the Office of Strate-gic Influence, the Pentagon planned to pay foreign media or columnists to run favorable stories or to write stories for them involving "spin" or demonstrably false information. As one Washington watchdog group wrote in an online piece called "Paying for Disinformation," "George Orwell couldn't have come up with a better name for a program whose yet-to-be-determined mission may include expensive public relations campaigns using the foreign news media, the Internet, and covert operations to win the hearts and minds of foreign citizens." This revelation set off intense global and domestic storms against the Pentagon's role as chief foreign propagandist.[15]

As noted above, the Administration set the stage for the Iraq invasion of 2003 by running one of the most deceptive propanganda campaigns in American history. To justify the two key false justifications for the war, that Saddam Hussein had weapons of mass destruction and that he helped cause 9/11, the regime put pressure on intelligence officials at the CIA and other intelligence agencies to back their own story of the threat. As in the case of the Social Security Administration, this action compromised the credibility of the most important U.S. intelligence organizations, turning them into embedded instruments of state propaganda. Senior professionals in the agencies who resisted this trend either quit or were fired.

As Baghdad fell in 2003, an Iraqi American exuberantly calls out "Thank you, Mr. Bush, thank you, U.S.A." to a television crew in Kansas City. But it turns out that the television news clip was not produced by the local Kansas City channel but by the State Department, although this was not announced to the viewing public. Some months later, another reporter in a story on U.S. airport security described the changes as "one of the most remarkable campaigns in aviation history." This "reporter" was also fake, a public relations professional from the Transportation Security Agency. In January 2004, another story described the success of the Bush Administration in opening up global markets for U.S. farmers. This "news" was actually produced by the Office of Communications of the State Department, with the public having no way of knowing.[16]

These government-produced propaganda pieces are just three of hundreds of pre-cooked news segments produced by the Bush Administration between 2001 and 2005, and disseminated to local news stations around the country for inclusion in their regular news programming. Typically, the fact that it was government-produced rather than regular news created by the local news department was never revealed. Karen Ryan, a former reporter for ABC and PBS, appeared as a "reporter" for seven different government agencies in 2003 and 2004. During investigations, she said, "I just did what everyone in the industry was doing."[17]

Almost all major government agencies now have vast public relations offices creating "news" for America's home viewers. Local channels may be reluctant to become such official propaganda organs but many are hurting for funds or staff and are happy to get these free pre-packaged segments from the government to insert and fill out their own news.[18] As this remarkable pattern of formal embedding expands, it turns the broadcast media into direct extensions of the state, part of the official propaganda structure.

In fascist states, both the media and official government agencies become explicit organs of propaganda. The media and government bureaucracy in America have historically managed to avoid this fate, despite the many pressures on them to conform to official story lines. But the examples above suggest a crossing of the Rubicon. The regime is moving from cajoling and pressuring journalists and civil servants to embedding them directly into the official government propaganda apparatus, while embedding government propaganda agencies and their public relations reports seamlessly into the mass media's news. If this "deviant" pattern becomes more normalized, as many think it already has, it is a path to the complete disappearance of a free media and professional civil service, one of the hallmarks of fascist regimes.

2. TORTURE

The image of an American-held Iraqi prisoner at Abu Ghraib, hooded, with electrical wires attached to his arms and genitals, has been seared on the consciousness of the world. So have the photographs of naked Iraqi prisoners in a pyramid, forced to masturbate by their American guards. And we have all seen the photos of Iraqi prisoners with leashes around their necks dragged around by American soldiers. We have not seen photos of some of the beatings that have led to severe injuries and even death.

Such abuse has not been restricted to Abu Ghraib. It has been confirmed in American detention centers in Afghanistan, where U.S. guards have used "water board" torture (strapped to a board and held under water) to threaten prisoners with drowning. In Afghanistan and at Guantanamo Bay, journalists have reported other grisly forms of torture, including dog attacks that led to severe bite wounds and beating prisoners so brutally on their legs that at least one died of a heart attack. Indeed, all these practices go well beyond the humiliation of prisoners. At least five prison detainees have been reported killed at the hands of their American guards.[19]

While only lower-level soldiers, such as Sergeant

Charles Graner at Abu Ghraib, have been officially convicted of these practices, internal Pentagon reports acknowledge that they were following orders launched from further up the chain of command. This confirms a shift toward a more official embrace of torture and a repudiation of constitutional procedures at the heart of the American system. Since the beginning of the third corporate regime (and before), the United States has supported governments from Saudi Arabia to El Salvador that have used torture and systemically rejected constitutionalism.[20] But there are new signs that this fascist repudiation of constitutionalism—of which the direct embrace of torture is one of the most frightening signs—is becoming part of the American system itself.

After Attorney General Ashcroft stepped down, the new Attorney General designee, Alberto Gonzales, refused under questioning at his 2005 Senate confirmation hearings to renounce the use of torture. Gonzales was famous as the White House counselor who had aggressively advanced the argument in 2002 that 9/11 had ushered in a new era in which the old rules of the game—such as the Geneva Conventions that forbid torture—were out of date. Thirty-six senators voted against his confirmation, observing that he was one of the principal architects of a new America policy of torture. Senator Edward Kennedy was one of many senators who explicitly argued that Gonzales's policies "have been used by the administration, the military and the CIA to justify torture and Geneva Convention violations by military and civilian officials."[21]

The regime's religion of civilizational warfare is a recipe for torture and broader extra-constitutional measures. The prominent British journalist Jonathan Steele reported in

2005 "that the administration sees the U.S. not just as a self-appointed global policeman, but also as the world's prison warder. It is thinking of building jails in foreign countries, mainly ones with grim human rights records, to which it can secretly transfer detainees (unconvicted by any court) for the rest of their lives—a kind of global gulag beyond the scrutiny of the International Committee of the Red Cross, or any other independent observers or lawyers."[22] The documented record of abuse and torture at Abu Ghraib, Guantanamo and Afghan prisons makes clear that the regime sees torture as an acceptable part of the war on terrorism. The Attorney General's view that the old rules do not apply—including the ban on torture—is a grave step toward fascism.

3. ELECTION FRAUD

The Constitution requires fair and free elections, and the most dangerous extra-constitutional sign of friendly fascism is the corruption or suspension of the electoral process. Classical fascism involved the direct suspension of elections, which Hitler did after the 1933 Reichstag fire. But fascism lite is more likely to take the form, as discussed earlier, of maintaining the formal procedures of elections. Systemic rigging undermines the possibility of fair outcomes, while other factors, including the incorporation of all the leading political parties into the regime, erode real, substantive democracy.

In the 2000 presidential election, in which Bush was selected by the Supreme Court rather than elected by a majority of the voters, at least the following electoral irregularities or blatant fraud surfaced:

The famous butterfly ballots in Florida

Voters, mainly African Americans, who reported being
turned away at the polls

Organized crowds who disrupted recount procedures in
Florida precincts

Prevention of voter registration of convicted felons who
had served their terms[23]

About 40 percent of American voters viewed these irregularities as a pattern of fraud that led them to view Bush
as an illegitimate President. It spurred legislation for electoral reform, the Help America Vote Act, passed in 2002 to
prevent any repetition. But in 2004, more serious charges
of electoral fraud surfaced all over the country but especially in the key state of Ohio, which determined the outcome, as Florida had four years ago. The new election
problems in Ohio, which led to an official recount of the
whole state vote, included:

Disappearance of ballots in some precincts

3,000 more votes for Bush counted than voters registered
in at least one precinct

Citizens were denied legal access to voting records
and lists in Ohio precincts as they tried to check
the validity of the counts

Waits of up to eight hours in some, mainly African
American, districts

Electronic voting without paper records, with the voting
machines manufactured by an Ohio-based company,
Diebold, whose CEO, Walden O'Dell, is on record
as committed "to helping Ohio deliver its electoral
votes" to President Bush.[24]

While many view these irregularities as mistakes and not
fraud, the very fact that the top election officials in Florida

in 2000, Katherine Harris, and in Ohio in 2004, Kenneth Blackwell, were chairs of the Bush reelection campaigns in their states creates unacceptable conflicts of interest. These officials made key decisions about registration procedures, ballot types, machine selection, distribution of voting machines by precinct, and how to investigate allegations and do recounts. Harris, of course, reported to Governor Jeb Bush, the brother of the president.

Beyond the problems in Florida and Ohio, systemic national voting problems increasingly undermine the legitimacy of the American "free elections" system. The problems and their potential remedies are now widely recognized:

> Election machines, particularly electronic machines without paper records, create an unaccountable system and should be banned.
>
> Top state election officials should be prevented from serving on the campaigns of any candidate.
>
> Machines, ballots, and counting procedures should be made uniform within and across all states, with bans on providing more machines for affluent precincts, as occurred in Ohio.
>
> Counts and recounts should be transparent, preventing the shenanigans reported in Ohio of precinct officials throwing whole lists into the garbage.
>
> The Help America Vote Act should be fully funded and expanded to address all of the problems discussed here.
>
> Registration procedures that deny the vote to prisoners, felons who have served their term, and millions of others in the entire voting age population are unac-

ceptable. In European countries, all voting age
citizens are automatically registered when they
are issued passports or driver's licenses.
Voting should be on a holiday, as in many other countries,
so all can vote.[25]

The regime is shifting in the opposite direction of most
of these remedies, introducing more voting machines
without paper ballots, creating more restrictive and
difficult registration procedures, and underfunding its own
voter reform initiatives. It appears to be normalizing what
were seen as deviations in 2000. Should this pattern of normalizing electoral deviance continue, not only will about
half the American public continue to be non-voters, but
those who do vote will doubt whether their preferences
have been counted fairly. The loss of faith in free elections,
and the systemic subversion of a fair electoral system, is the
surest path to fascism lite.

None of this proves that we are already living under a fascist system. Instead, it shows that we have already drastically weakened or eliminated many of our most important
constitutional rights and protections, and have already ex-
perienced what might be described as creeping fascism
within the current regime. If we don't reverse course, the
current path could take us toward fascist regime change.
But there is nothing inevitable about this. The United
States has survived prior eras, such as the 1917–20 repression and the McCarthy period, that temporarily subverted
the Constitution but did not lead to fascist regime change.
Substantial freedom still remains in the United States, as

evidenced by my freedom to publish this book and your freedom to read it. And cracks in the regime could equally open up possibilities for a regime change toward a more humane and democratic society. In the next few chapters, I show how ordinary Americans can exercise their own hidden power to make that happen.

CHAPTER 7

THE AMERICAN RECIPE FOR CHANGE

*T*hree possible futures lie in front of us. One is the survival of the current corporate regime, with the elites managing to patch up the cracks and keep the existing order intact. The second is a reactionary regime change toward fascism lite described in the last chapter. The third is a progressive regime change toward a more humane and democratic order. Since history shows no U.S. regime can survive forever, and typically collapses after several decades, the real question is whether we will see in our lifetimes the reactionary or progressive regime change. The answer depends largely on you.

All through U.S. history, changing a corporate regime

has depended entirely on ordinary citizens. If you believe regime change is necessary, and, along with your fellow citizens, decide that you're going to do something about it, it will happen. And it will be one of the most important and rewarding things you do in your whole life.

Of course, it is hardly surprising that it is up to you. Remember, the whole reason for regime change is that ordinary citizens like you have lost control—in overstressed workplaces, under-funded communities, and unrepresentative governments. The people who run this regime—the fat cats in the corporation and their pals in the White House and Congress—will fight regime change until the end, even as terminal crises weaken their hold. Yes, the regime crises I have described are growing more intense and are weakening the regime. But it takes powerful movements of people like you and me to create regime change and make sure it is progressive. Such movements are revving up, and I show in this chapter that you should help them make history.

You're probably thinking that a person like yourself can't fight city hall, let along the biggest corporations in the world. But when you link up with many more like you, the equation begins to change. When citizens act together, the corporate regime can lose power and eventually be defeated. And the corporations know it. After the 1999 Battle of Seattle, when just 50,000 Americans went out on the streets to protest corporate globalization, corporate leaders went into a panic, sending frenzied e-mails to each other trying to figure out why people were so angry and what they could do to settle them down.[1]

Every change of a corporate regime in U.S. history has been tied to a dramatic growth in popular citizen activity and movements, such as the nineteenth-century populists or the New Deal unions. The explosion of new social movements in the end game of regimes reflects the rise of severe crises. Regimes fall because they can no longer patch up crises that intensify the stress and suffering of citizens like you. In the endgame, people no longer trust the elites, get "mad as hell," and decide to take matters into their own hands.

You may be skeptical of the whole idea that ordinary people can successfully challenge and change a regime based on the power of huge corporations. Such skepticism is one of the reasons the current regime survives, since if ordinary citizens doubt their own capacity to make change, it will not happen. The regime has worked hard to reinforce this doubt, by helping hide from the American people their own proven history to change even the most powerful regimes.

As I discussed in the Introduction, there are two key forms of hidden power in America. One is the hidden power of the regime itself. The other is the hidden power of the people to change it.

The Election Trap is one of the key reasons Americans have lost faith in their capacity to make real change. The Election Trap diverts people from even seeing the regime, focusing them instead on the Democrats and the Republicans. It blinds them from seeing what Teddy Roosevelt called the "invisible government." Instead, it ensnares ordinary citizens into believing that the only real way to make change is to vote and change the party in power within the visible government. But when they look at the choices on the ballot, they see two parties that speak for the current economic system, get their funding from the big corporations, and seem like inside-the-beltway elites who don't care about them. The Election Trap leads Americans toward the couch potato syndrome, since the choices it offers do not offer hope for major change.

But there is another reason why so many Americans doubt their ability to change things. The regime has concealed not only its own invisible government but also the political tradition of populism and progressivism by which Americans have historically challenged corporate power. Populism has a political lineage stretching all the way back to Tom Paine and Thomas Jefferson. It contributed to the American Revolution that created the country and challenged the first corporate regime of the robber barons.[2] The Progressives finished the job and toppled both the first and second corporate regimes.[3]

Our awareness of these traditions—which offer some of the vision, language, and strategy necessary to take on the current corporate regime—has been clouded by the success of the regime's pseudopopulism. Pseudopopulism undercuts populism and progressivism by redirecting popular anger away from corporate power toward the power of an imagined alien liberal Establishment and the civilizational threat of evil enemies.[4] This helps conceal the history of the popular American struggle against corporate greed and power, takes away from people an understanding of their most important national tradition for restoring their democratic rights, and subverts not only their faith in their own abilities to challenge corporate power but also the very notion that there is any reason to engage in such a struggle.

Nonetheless, a new form of progressive populism is

emerging in the form of what I call the Active Citizens' network. It consists of a vast group of mobilized citizens who are exposing the hidden power of the regime and could ultimately topple it. You may be thinking that you're not an activist—but the Active Citizens' Network is bigger than protest groups. You're almost certainly part of it now, in your church, neighborhood association, union, or civic group. If you've ever e-mailed a friend an op-ed piece or even talked with fellow workers or neighbors about some of the issues discussed in this book, you're an active citizen and part of the network. In fact, just by reading this book you're engaging in active citizenship that can help create regime change.

When you do any of these things, you contribute to a process, already under way with the rise of new grassroots citizens' movements—including new unions, antiwar networks, antiglobalization activists, or religious communities —that seek to expose hidden power, change public consciousness, and create a new regime. These citizens' or social movements are the catalyzers of regime change and that is why I devote this chapter to them. I want to give you my view of how they have created regime change in the past and how they are starting to do so again.

Keep three things in mind. First, the movements are ultimately based in the civic associations of people like you. Americans have always been individualists but also civic "associators" who know how to get together and help run their own communities—that's how Alexis de Tocqueville described us 170 years ago to his fellow Europeans.[5] As Howard Zinn has shown in his wonderful *A People's History of the United States*, we have also always been a nation of strong grassroots movements—from the abolitionists to the suffragettes—who have made America the great country it is![6]

Second, even successful regime-busting protest movements are always a small percentage of the population. But they speak for a much larger number of people who lack the time or temperament to get out in the streets. The abolitionists helped bring down slavery but they were just a fraction of the populace, as were both the Populists and Progressives a century ago.

Third, citizens' movements cannot create regime change without transforming the political parties—either by taking over one of the mainstream parties or by creating third parties. I discuss the relation between the new movements and the Democratic Party in the next two chapters.

While I pay a lot of attention to the Democratic Party all through this book, always remember this: regime change has to come from you and me. The Democratic Party calls itself the party of the people but it isn't—and we will have to drag it away from its comfortable perch in corporate America and force it to act as well as speak in our name. If they don't, we will create a new party as the Gilded Age Populists did!

REMEMBER THE POPULISTS!

It is time to recall the populist movements of a century ago, since they exposed both the hidden power of corporate regimes and the hidden power of ordinary Americans to rally against them. By the mid 1880s, Rockefeller, Morgan, Carnegie, and other robber barons had consolidated their control over Washington, elected a long string of mainly Republican corporate puppet presidents, and turned themselves into billionaires. But farmers and workers found themselves facing crises of survival. New social movements—from the Knights of Labor to Christian Socialists to Alliances of heartland farmers—began forming as early as the 1870s to overthrow the first corporate regime. The Populists were the most important, made up mainly of Southern and Western farmers sinking into debt. The leading historian of the Populists, Lawrence Goodwyn, calls them "the flowering of the largest democratic mass movement in American history."[7]

The Populist agenda was to return control of the country from the thieving corporations to the people. Kansan Populist Mary Lease said, "We're going to raise less corn and more hell." She was clear about the enemy: "Wall Street owns the country. It is no longer a government of the people, by the people, and for the people, but a government of Wall Street, by Wall Street, and for Wall Street."[8]

The solution: "The corporation has absorbed the community. The community must now absorb the corporation."[9] This meant:

  Abolishing the private banking system
  Breaking up Rockefeller's trusts and Morgan's
     financial empire
  Getting big money out of Washington
  Rebuilding the economy around new producer
     cooperatives

The Populists sought "legislation as shall secure to our people freedom from the onerous and shameful abuses that the industrial classes are now suffering at the hands of capitalists and powerful corporations." They challenged corporate social Darwinism with a political philosophy of cooperativism and Jeffersonian democracy. The Populists created their own farmers' co-ops, instituting cooperative purchasing and marketing and envisioning a whole economy based on cooperative principles.[10]

In 1892, they founded a third party, the People's Party, and ran a credible race on a platform of economic democracy. Focusing on corporate power and greed, they realized they would be "confronted by a vast and splendidly equipped army of extortionists, usurers, and oppressors." But they refused to be cowed, proclaiming "We are at the dawn of the golden age of popular power."[11] Populism emerged as the classic American form of opposition to corporate regimes, and while the Populist movement was defeated by the big money of the robber barons and its own internal failures to speak to immigrant workers, it helped give rise to the regime change of Teddy Roosevelt's Progressives, who preserved capitalism but reformed the corporate order and helped "bust the trusts."

POPULIST VIRTUES, POPULIST FLAWS

The Populists invented a potent but flawed tradition with the following elements essential to making real change today:

They were regime changers. They set their sights not just on individual tycoons or corporations but on the system of their day: the first corporate regime. In so doing, they brilliantly exposed hidden power, the most important first step in corporate regime change. They liberated ordinary Americans from the Election Trap, showing that the key to saving democracy was not just changing the party in power but attacking the systemic pillars of the invisible government.

They offered real alternatives. These included the creation of an economy based on mutual aid and cooperatives. As just noted, they began to create and operate co-ops in their own farming and local businesses; they saw worker ownership as central to their own job security, economic well-being, and economic democracy. They also had a detailed political program to establish public control over the media, education, and the commanding heights of the economy. They demanded government ownership of the largest banks on Wall Street and the largest corporate empires controlled at the time by Morgan and Rockefeller.[12]

They couched their entire program in a moral philosophy. The Populists lived mainly in what we now call the red states and many were religious. Their entire agenda grew out of their core values and their belief in community, cooperation, and hard work. They spread their word through churches and through their connections with their neighbors. Evangelical Christians played an important role in labor and populist insurgencies as early as the 1870s, leading some Christian socialists loosely aligned with the populist revolt to say that "this movement will either mark the second coming of Christ or be a total failure."[13] In other words, the populists looked a good deal like the New Right activists of today, but rather than allying themselves with the corporations, they saw that corporate power had become the enemy of democracy and was undermining economic security for ordinary Americans.[14]

The Populists were not elitists. Most were not highly educated and they were plainspoken. They were deeply identified with America and its democratic political traditions.

The Populists were radicals but they could not be portrayed as civilizational enemies or part of an alien Establishment (even though the robber barons of the day tried to tar them as socialists or anarchists). Their identity as ordinary folk insulated them from the black magic that might try to paint them as an elite outside the American mainstream.

Their deep moral convictions carry special significance in the light of the current focus on moral values. The Populists were economic radicals who attacked corporations on moral grounds, arguing that it was impossible for America to maintain its values and spirituality under a corporate regime. Christian socialists and many religious populists argued that the robber barons' "Gospel of Wealth" was incompatible with the Gospels of Jesus. The greed and materialism symbolized by the billion-dollar fortunes of Morgan and Rockefeller were at odds with America's spiritual heritage and inconsistent with the American cultural traditions of mutual aid, community, and democracy. This critique had credibility because the Populists walked their

POPULISM IS HIDDEN POWER

These early populists would be formidable challengers to our current corporate regime. Not only would they bring to light the hidden power of the regime but they would exemplify the hidden power of the people to create a movement for regime change.

talk and embodied these American traditions in their own lives.

Nonetheless, the Populists failed and are not perfect models for a democratic regime change movement today. Their failure reflected to a large degree the enormous money and political power fueling the corporate regime's all-out attack on them. But it also reflected their own vices and limitations. These must be recognized and avoided in any new movement by ordinary Americans for populist or progressive regime change. Even according to historians such as Lawrence Goodwyn and Michael Kazin, who view the Populists as one of America's great democratic movements, the Populists fell partly on their own sword.

Despite serious populist attempts to organize or ally with labor groups, they failed—partly because of xenophobic or nativist tendencies—to win over the urban immigrant workers who were flooding into America and whose support and involvement were central to any democratic regime change.

Despite the successful effort of some white farmer alliances to organize or align with black farmers, other Southern Populists shared the racism of their region, leading early populism to be mainly a movement of white, Protestant farmers.[15]

Their agrarian roots led many Populists toward an agrarian philosophy out of synch with the new urban, industrial economy that was America's future.[16]

When they aligned with the Democratic Party in 1896, the Democratic nominee for President, William Jennings Bryan, watered down their program to a narrow focus on "the cross of gold" and the currency debate that greatly weakened the power of their broad systemic critique of the robber-baron regime[17] In demonizing the corporation, they did not recognize the contribution it was making to the industrialization and development of the country, nor did they find a way to allay the fear of Americans that attacking the corporation was killing the golden goose.

For all these reasons, the Populists began to fade after Bryan's lost race for president in 1896. They did not pull off the corporate regime change they wanted. But they established a legacy for the Progressive regime change that did occur just a few years later under the leadership of Teddy Roosevelt.

THE PROGRESSIVES

Roosevelt's new progressivism grew up from the soil of the concern with corporate power made popular by the Populists. Roosevelt was from the elite, he did not identify with the Populists, and much of his progressive regime-change movement ended up strengthening the very corporations that he sought to tame as a trust-buster and corporate regime changer.[18] TR can be seen as watering down populism to make it safe for capitalism. Nonetheless, he did change the robber-baron corporate regime and created a regulatory state that, while it helped corporations stabilize the new national economy, also put constraints on corporate excesses and gave new political avenues for ordinary Americans to challenge corporate power.[19]

The progressive tradition that began with Teddy Roosevelt took a new, more democratic form with Franklin Roosevelt, who took on the second corporate regime and changed it successfully. Progressivism thus changed two corporate regimes, partly by overcoming the limitations of the populists. During the New Deal, the Progressives, who were more urban than the populists, succeeded in making an alliance with the working classes that the populists had not reached. Their greater education helped to weaken prejudice against immigrants, Jews, and blacks that stained some Southern populists. Through their alliance with the rising industrial unions, they were able to shape a regime-change vision that did not hearken back to the agrarian philosophy of the populists. It created a basis for a more powerful political movement rooted in the urban industrial labor force, with an agenda for economic and social security that attracted many culturally conservative American workers, including those in the Bible Belt and the red states. Its similarities to European social democracy opened up a potential for a solidarity with progressive movements all over the world in a rising global economy.[20]

Nonetheless, while the Progressives overcame some of the most important populist liabilities, they had their own faults. The Progressives of both the TR and FDR eras were far less radical than the populists in their critique of the corporate regime, incorporating large corporations into the new regulatory systems they were creating. While this allowed them to make strategic alliances with parts of the business class, which helped their political prospects, it created a less fully democratic transformation than the populists had imagined.[21]

Moreover, the Progressives—and particularly their leadership—were drawn from elites who were urban, highly educated, and economically privileged. Unlike the populists, they were not the plainspoken folk from the American heartland who transparently embodied the American traditions of family, mutual aid, community, and God. They were conveyors of a new cosmopolitan and multicultural America, and their progressive morality was more secular and less traditional than the heartland's populist culture. As such, the progressive elites, and even the entire progressive tradition, could be portrayed—as they have been today by the current regime's pseudopopulism—as an alien liberal Establishment, out of touch with the morality and lifestyle of ordinary Americans.[22]

The elitist attributes of the progressive leadership should not obscure the New Deal regime as an alliance of labor, poor people, minorities, and urban professionals who were successful in making major changes that unseated earlier corporate regimes and contributed immensely to the well-being of American workers and communities. But the Progressives did set themselves up as a target for pseudopopulist attacks. After the South split off from the New Deal coalition, the Progressives retrenched to a blue-state perimeter that the New Right portrayed successfully as alien to American values and part of an elite liberal Establishment.

A successful regime-change movement today needs to integrate the best features of populism and progressivism. It needs the economic radicalism, moral conviction, and grassroots, red-state appeal of the Populists. It needs the traditional blue-state base, the forward-looking labor agenda, the multiculturalism, and the global political vision of the Progressives. Fortunately, we are already seeing signs of such a new progressive populism on the political landscape. While it is in its formative stages, it has the potential to create a new era of progressive regime change.

THE NEW PROGRESSIVE POPULISTS

At the Battle of Seattle, the 1999 surprising explosion of the antiglobalization movement in the United States, I walked through the tear-gassed streets with a cell phone. Every block or so, I got a call from another radio or newspaper reporter with more questions. One talk-show host even caught me at dinner and wouldn't let me finish my meal until I answered his questions.

As Bob Dylan wrote in one of his famous songs, "Something's happening here but you don't know what it is." What's happening is the rise of a new progressive populism. Today, new grassroots progressive movements are sprouting, a sign of the coming battle for regime change. While still largely under the radar screen of the mass media, we are entering a new era of on-the-ground and on-the-Net grassroots political activism. Beyond the antiglobalization activists who pop up at every meeting of the world's financial elites, the most visible new activists are the millions of people all over the world who spontaneously took to the streets in 2002 and 2003 to protest Bush's invasion of Iraq, the largest peace movement in history. These included millions of Americans, many in the mainstream, who had never demonstrated before and remain deeply distressed about the U.S. presence in Iraq.[23]

The 1999 Seattle gathering of "turtles and teamsters," the environmentalists and workers who had never been on the block together, symbolized the first big coming together of social movements unifying against the corporate regime. It was quite an experience. I talked with big burly teamsters, who marched alongside eco-activists and college students with nose rings. There were grandparents and kids in strollers. America was coming together in a new way.[24]

There are literally thousands of progressive populist organizations working in cities all over the United States and the world. It is hard to keep track of them because so many are sprouting up. Based on my own experience, I list some of my personal favorites and include more with their websites in Appendix II.

These movements of ordinary citizens are destined to grow rapidly as the regime begins to crack under the weight of its own crises and contradictions. Four aspects of the new regime-change movements could, over time, carry them to success:

> They are riding the wave of the Internet.
> They are acting globally as well as locally.
> They are blooming on campuses.
> They are multicultural and multicoalitional.

CITIZEN MOVEMENTS.ORG

Regime change is possible because the new movements are on the cusp of a massive growth in their capacity to reach and awaken the general public. One reason is the revolution in grassroots politics that the Internet makes possible. During the Iraq war, a group called MoveOn, known to most activists as MoveOn.org, helped transform the political world. Formed by two people, Wes Boyd and Joan Blades, it emerged as an online network coordinating

PROGRESSIVE POPULIST ORGANIZATIONS TO JOIN

National Labor Committee
United for a Fair Economy
Unitarian Universalists for a Just Economic Community
Global Exchange
Alliance for Democracy
Mainstream Media Project
Public Citizen
MoveOn.Org
Program on Corporations, Law and Democracy
Center for Study of Responsive Law
Women's International League for Peace and Freedom
Third World Network
TransAfrica Forum
American Friends Service Committee
Sierra Club
Service Employees International Union
Campaign for America's Future
Jobs with Justice
United for Peace and Justice
United Students Against Sweatshops
Citizen Works
Free Press

activism among hundreds of thousands of antiwar citizens. For several months before the war, MoveOn helped shape global campaigns that deluged Congressional offices with hundreds of thousands of e-mails on a given day, almost making it impossible for Washington to function.

MoveOn is one amazing organization! It has changed the way politics as usual works in America, showing that the Internet allows movements without much money or visibility to come together and make a vast impact on the public conversation. Along with at least a million other Americans on their listserv, I get e-mails from MoveOn every week, educating me about current initiatives and allowing me to register my views on vital issues to Congress or the White House with a simple click of my mouse. MoveOn has staying power, continuing today to wage battles about militarism and corporate power in Iraq and Washington. When the FCC deregulated the mass media in 2003, allowing a few giant companies such as Fox, Disney, and AOL–Time Warner to own multiple radio, TV, and newspapers in any given city, MoveOn sent e-mails to the people on its listserv, encouraging them to call their Congressional representatives and repeal the FCC rules. Hundreds of thousands made the calls and Congress launched a new major effort to rescind the procorporate FCC decisions, leading the Senate to vote to block the FCC ruling.[25]

MoveOn.org is just one of thousands of new activist networks with their own listservs, mobilizing the new populists around everything from campaign finance to globalization to children's rights. If you care about an issue, I guarantee you can find an online network or listserv that can get you educated and connected. There are websites for coalitions of groups, so many thousands of them that directories have popped up on the Web just to help you find them. Social Justice Connections is one great source.

Social movements are increasingly networks mirroring the structure of the Internet itself and taking the form of new kinds of political actors like MoveOn. They are fluid, multi-issue and coalitional, bringing together hundreds, thousands, or millions of people in a series of evolving and

ONLINE NETWORKS OF NETWORKS

The Institute for Global Communications, whose component networks include PeaceNet, EcoNet, AntiRacismNet, and WomensNet, provides links to a wide range of progressive organizations, as well as information on its own services. (www.igc.org)

Macrocosm USA is an ambitious effort to list peace, environmental, health, and justice resources in a searchable database. (www.macronet.org)

WebActive offers not only directory but current information on progressive activities. (www.webactive.com)

National Organizers Alliance connects progressive organizers and strengthens our ability to do organizing well. Fun is also emphasized. (www.noacentral.com)

CTCNet unites grassroots community technology centers around the nation. High-tech at the grassroots. (www.ctcnet.org)

spontaneous protests and policy initiatives. Far different from a political party, they nonetheless represent an increasingly effective way for ordinary people without money to help shape a new political conversation in the country and the world.

One local example that emerged after the Battle for Seattle is the Boston Global Action Network (BGAN), a coalition of many different labor, immigrant, student, and community groups. The organizations making up the network focus on their own special issues but come together to support each others' initiatives. In the Boston area, they have launched many anticorporate initiatives on immigrant rights, the living wage, social service cuts, and corporate outsourcing that affect all the organizations in the network, trying to help people make the link between local labor and social crises and the global economy.[26] Another such network is United for Justice with Peace (UJP). It is a coalition of traditional peace, community, and labor groups who initially came together to protest the war in Iraq but are committed to a broader transformation in the regime's corporate priorities both at home and abroad. It brings together whites, blacks, and browns, and unites local groups representing working-class communities and upper-middle-class groups focused on antiwar actions. Networks like BGAN and UJP are political "start-ups," and they have many problems in sustaining coalitions across class and race.[27] Many of these early networks will fail but the network model may survive and prove an important new way that progressive populism can combat the fragmentation that has plagued the progressive community and undermined a united front against the regime.

This brings us to another completely new strength of today's regime-change movements. They are linking up with citizens in other countries to create regime change in many nations simultaneously and in the global corporate order itself. This is crucial to regime change since the regime itself is global.

Historically, populist national movements operated in virtual total national isolation from each other. Today, movements all over the world are reconstituting themselves as part of a giant anticorporate, prodemocracy plan-

ATTAC

In the fall of 2003, I did a book tour in Germany and Austria sponsored by the European movement called ATTAC. ATTAC is a remarkable group of international activists in forty-seven different countries. They have a common interest in global justice issues but the ATTAC in each country has its own agenda. While it is a global movement, its strength is the vibrancy of its local chapters, which mobilize people in their local communities around populist issues. When I spoke in Munich, Germany, the local ATTAC group had just successfully organized to prevent a big global company from taking over the local public subway system. While they act locally, they come together in places like the Global Social Forum, a worldwide convention of social movements and NGOs, to chart out a new system of people's globalization.

etary coalition never seen before. Sweatshop activists in Boston are communicating daily by e-mail with sweatshop workers and organizers in Indonesia and El Salvador as well as in New York and Los Angeles. The antiwar activists protesting the U.S. invasion of Iraq coordinated demonstrations of millions of people in scores of countries in the same global spirit.

A NEW GENERATION OF REGIME CHANGERS

You may be surprised to hear it but—in a sign of a generational awakening—regime-change movements are sprouting up on campuses all over the country.

While this new student politics is rarely reported on in the media, activist regime-change groups of this kind can be found on virtually every major campus in the country and they are building a national student network increasingly aligned with broader activist networks around the world.[28] United Students Against Sweatshops, speaking on just one student issue, has more than two hundred campus chapters. It was from these networks that the millions of activists against the war in Iraq appeared out of nowhere and that the global justice movements since Seattle have continued to recruit the global whirlwind of protestors at WTO or IMF meetings every year. Most of these students go on to work in careers that allow them to make a life working for social justice. They are the backbone of a new generation that will ultimately create regime change.

MOVEON ON CAMPUS

At Boston College, my own university, a movement called the Global Justice Project (GJP) has been growing for the past five years. It is a bit like MoveOn on campus, a loose network of hundreds of activist students who communicate with each other largely through the Internet. The group formed around the time of the antiglobalization movements in Seattle and takes up issues ranging from sweatshops and fair-trade coffee to peace in the Middle East to the wages of custodians on campus or the uses of the university's billion-dollar endowment. The students have a global perspective, since many of them come to the group after doing service projects in the shanty towns of El Salvador or Mexico.

The students are passionate and full of hope. Each year they become more numerous and more sophisticated in using the Internet and the "network" to increase their clout on and off campus. In the 2004 electoral season, most were passionately against Bush, and while many today are working for the Democrats, they are looking for more systemic change.

ALL TOGETHER NOW

Noam Chomsky, who has had his finger on the pulse of American activism since the Vietnam war, observes that there is more grassroots progressive action today than there was in the 1960s.[29] Most activists I know agree. There are even hundreds of new insurgent local labor groups, such as

WHAT FOX NEWS WON'T TELL YOU

You may wonder why you don't know about the new activist student generation. Well, here's one reason. Fox News called me to do an interview on a story about student politics today. I agreed, and told them my observations about the vast proliferation of campus activist groups, on my own campus, in Boston and around the country. But Fox ran its own pre-cooked story line, which said that this was the apathetic, conservative generation. They ran maybe a five-second clip of my interview, but it didn't carry my message at all. I guess they didn't want you to hear it.

But no matter what Fox News tells you, social movement groups with a democratic, populist spirit are sprouting up all over the country, and not just on the campuses.

Janitors for Justice, who represent the new generation of multicultural activist workers mentioned above, pushing unions to become a social justice movement. Winning major battles for some of the most low-paid workers in the country, groups like Janitors for Justice, backed by highly politicized unions such as the Service Employees International Union (SEIU), representing immigrants, women, and workers of color, are a powerful force helping to change the labor establishment in Washington. At rallies to support Janitors for Justice, the size, spirit, and diversity of the crowds on the streets remind me of the civil rights protests in the 1960s. Had Martin Luther King, Jr. survived, he would be at the front of the barricades again, leading black, brown, and white workers in a new multicultural and multicoalitional struggle for civil and workers' rights against the third corporate regime.

While grassroots citizen social movements are the heart and soul of regime change, ending the current regime also depends on the transformation of the Democratic Party, something which will require a new relation between the movements and the party itself. Regime change can only arise when the charisma, radicalism, and grassroots energy of social movements infuse a political party with the capacity to change the country. In the next chapter, I turn to the Democratic Party, and how it must change into a voice for progressive populism and regime change.

CHAPTER 8

WHAT'S THE MATTER WITH THE DEMOCRATS?

*W*hen you look at the red/blue map of America, the Democrats seem on the edge of extinction. There's a blue strip up the West Coast, across the Northern border with Canada, and down the East Coast to Washington, D.C. Almost the entire heartland is red. Moreover, even in many blue states, the red splotches are getting larger. It makes you think that the whole country could turn red.

Even though Al Gore won the popular vote for president in 2000 and John Kerry nearly won the electoral college vote in 2004, the Democratic Party is in deep crisis. It has lost control over all three branches of government. The 2004 Congressional losses are perhaps more telling than the presidential votes. And state governors and legislatures, at this writing, are moving red also.

It is time for Democrats to face up to the magnitude of their crisis. In many states, the party has become irrelevant, with the real political contest going on between different factions of the Republican Party.[1] This trend is now surfacing in the federal government, where splits among Republican leaders in Congress and the White House are driving the political debate.

We should not be entirely surprised by this development, since the Democrats have been on this precipice before. In the first corporate regime of the robber barons, from 1865 to 1901, Americans elected only one Democratic president, Grover Cleveland. In the second corporate regime of the Roaring Twenties, Democrats elected no president at all. Corporate regimes are bad news for the party, and the party has historically recovered only by creating regime change. The primary example is the New Deal, a half-century dominated by the Democratic Party. The lesson for today is that the Democrats are unlikely to regain power until they change the third corporate regime.

The cooptation of the party into the regime is the prime cause of its undoing. It locks the party into the iron cage of the Election Trap, focusing on winning elections without any real agenda for change, and thus losing elections. By embracing the regime, it took the populist alternative off the table. This is what allows pseudopopulism to flourish, and in this chapter I show how the Democratic Party has undermined itself and the nation over the life of the

WHAT'S THE MATTER?

BUSH AND
BUSH LITE

The reason that corporate regimes marginalize the Democratic Party is counterintuitive. It is not because the party is an outsider, but because it allows itself to get absorbed within the regime itself. The party loses credibility as a force for change because it is correctly perceived by the people as part of the elite and lacking any real will or agenda to side with the people and change the country. That is why Al Gore and John Kerry lost to President Bush. When people have a choice between two Yalies who are both part of the regime—in other words between Bush and Bush lite—they will choose the real thing. Or, as President Harry Truman put it in 1952, "If it's a choice between a genuine Republican and a Republican in Democratic clothing, the people will choose the genuine article every time."[2]

regime. In the next chapter, I show how it has begun to recover and how it can remake itself into a party of the people.

THE PARTY JOINS THE REGIME

Before indicating what the Democratic Party can do right, we should be clear about how and when it went wrong. The problem goes back to the Vietnam years, when Democratic New Dealers began rejecting the young activists against the war (including John Kerry). But the Democratic integration into the corporate regime was sealed by President Clinton, who by his own admission embraced core regime objectives usually associated with Republicans: globalization and free trade, zero deficits, small government, the end of welfare, and American Empire and continued militarism after the end of the Cold War.[3] Despite the challenge from grassroots and progressive Democrats, these are still core aims of the Democratic Party today.

Influential Democratic insiders created a movement within the party—centered in the Democratic Leadership Council (DLC)—to sever the Democrats from their New Deal past. With financial backing from corporations, secured by DLC players who had been corporate lawyers and lobbyists, they created the vision of a "New Democrat" that has redefined the party, at least until the 2004 defeat to Bush that began to weaken the DLC grip. The New Democrats want the party to abandon their New Deal liberalism and embrace the new corporate regime. They seek modest reforms of the regime—including a minimal safety net, government support for research and development, and enterprise zones for the poor. But their zeal is around creating a new party that sheds the baggage of the New Deal and embraces the regime priorities of corporate expansion and profit, fiscal conservatism, globalization, and smaller government.

The DLC's position seems eminently practical. The Democrats, like the Republicans, are increasingly dependent on corporations for their funding. Reagan and the new regime had severely weakened the unions and other traditional sources of Democratic Party funding. Corporate money is the mother's milk of political success. The DLC argues that joining the regime and moving toward the center is the only way to win back the red states. It might erode the party's capacity to mobilize systemic change for the people, but it keeps them in the game.

What the DLC actually has done is ensnare the party in the Election Trap. The party shifted from a social justice agenda to an electoral obsession. Focus on winning the next election and abandon ideas about systemic change. Go for the center and forget the poor, the base, the non-voters. The whole idea was based solely on winning the next election. But this shift is driving Democrats out of the game and not winning back the red states.

While Clinton did win twice, it was in large measure be-cause ordinary people saw him as one of their own, a tri-umph of style over New Democrat content. Clinton had gone to Yale, but he ate Big Macs, was overweight, had marital problems, was a Baptist, and a "good ol' boy" from Arkansas. Clinton won on personality and lifestyle, not on issues, by shedding the image of an elite Washington in-sider that plagued other Democrats. In the meantime, the party abandoned content, renouncing its populist, pro-gressive, and New Deal roots. After Clinton, whose per-sonal magic seemed to validate the DLC strategy, the real consequences emerged. The party would begin losing elec-tions because its only real agenda was winning them. Al Gore and John Kerry both lost because they advanced the same New Democratic agenda of Bill Clinton, but lacked the charisma that would allow them to win on style.[4]

The party, of course, continued during the Clinton years and after to pursue substantive political agendas and pro-grams, but these mainly reflect the interests of the regime. Consider how this worked out in the New Democrat economics, foreign policy, and "moral values" positions that emerged under Clinton and remain the mainstream Democratic leadership creed today.

ECONOMICS

The New Democrats continue to defend certain popular New Deal programs like Social Security. But no longer does the Democratic Party, as it did in the New Deal, challenge the fundamental philosophy of the market or the governance structure of a corporation increasingly unchecked even by its own shareholders. Despite populist rhetoric during elections, and alliance with powerful unions, no longer does the party stand truly tall for the poor, social welfare, and workers' rights, in an age of corporate globalization when worker insecurity and the outsourcing of the American economy are critical cracks in the regime. Rather than a full-scale attack on the corporate globalization process, advanced by millions of people around the world, the party suggests small adjustments in trade and tax policy that it acknowledges would not fundamentally solve the outsourcing or jobs crisis. Nor does it champion aggressive, systemic efforts to regulate the corporations that would prevent scandals like Enron, stop the attack on unions, or weaken corporate political control of Washington.

In their basic philosophy, the Democrats have embraced the corporatist ideology of the regime, accepting the idea that both the "free market" and corporations are part of the natural order.[5] By collaborating in the regime's central project of globalization, they have accepted a "natural law" concept of the American model as applicable to every nation, including those in the Middle East or Latin America or Africa that don't see the U.S. market system or global corporation as either natural or benign. On the home front, they now embrace the constitutional changes created by earlier corporate regimes that redefined corporations as legal persons protected like you and me under the Constitution. While they promote modest campaign finance reform, they accept the idea that corporations have the rights of persons to speech, privacy, and other cherished freedoms under the Bill of Rights. They do not question the obvious contradiction that as the biggest corporations used these rights to gain overwhelming monopoly power, they not only subverted democracy but the market itself.[6]

Amazingly, as the party embraced the regime in the early 1990s, it delivered to the global corporations some of the biggest prizes that Republicans had never won for them.

The Democrats have happily joined in the competition for corporate dollars as they cling close to the regime and get ensnared in the Election Trap. Their efforts at campaign reform and regulation of corporate lobbying have been cosmetic. Democratic leaders have become inside-the-beltway elites far removed from social movements and communities, thus legitimating the image concocted by the Republicans that they represented an Establishment out of touch with common folk.

Their elitism and timid economics sank both Al Gore and John Kerry. Neither Gore nor Kerry ever seemed to viscerally connect with the daily struggle of workers, nor did they ever seem to understand that the only way that the new American "anxious class" would rise to their cause was

THE NEW DEMOCRATS' BIGGEST HITS

Democrats became the regime's most successful fiscal hawks. The consequence was less money for social welfare but more for corporate welfare involving corporate tax breaks, subsidies, and loopholes.

The Democrats became co-partners in the American project of globalization, thereby losing their credibility as defenders of anxious workers in the global corporate regime. Unions weakened and shrank as much under New Democrats as they had under Reagan and Bush, because the Democrats were just as willing as Republicans to underwrite corporate flight to Mexico or China. Clinton signed NAFTA, created the WTO, and championed "free trade" agreements, which undercut the bargaining power of labor.

The Democrats stopped talking about the poor and instead talked about helping the middle class. But because Clinton and the Democrats were not willing to restrain the corporations, who were madly cutting job security and benefits for both blue- and white-collar workers, the gap between the richest 1 percent and everyone else has grown larger under the New Democrats than at any time since the second corporate regime of the Roaring Twenties.[7]

if they offered serious solutions to the outsourcing of the American economy. Since a majority of voters told pollsters that they were unhappy with the direction of the economy and with the power of big business, Kerry could have made a bold populist case for change, as I told him in a letter.[8]

Dear John Kerry,

Congratulations on becoming the Democratic candidate. After the primaries, the Party Establishment and all your spin guys will say: tack to the center. This is the worst advice you can get. You will lose the passion of the Democratic Party base, lose the chance to turn out millions of new voters, and end up like Al Gore in 2000.

Here's the deal. Bush has $200 million, cash on the barrelhead, and the support of Corporate America, including the mass media. All you've got is the little people: the two million who might give you $100 each or four million who might give 50 bucks each. But if you dull their passion, they'll abandon you. Many will sit it out or vote for a third party, and you'll deserve to lose.

You had a great line in your New Hampshire speech. "I have a message for the influence peddlers, for the polluters, the HMOs, the big drug companies that get in the way, the big oil and the special interests who now call the White House their home: we're coming, you're going, and don't let the door hit you on the way out."

You won't beat Bush unless people feel that you truly share their outrage about the war, their disgust that poverty is increasing, that 45 million Americans have no health care, that job security and wages are dropping like a stone when corporations are getting fatter and more corrupt. Millions of Americans are fed up; they hate Bush and the corporate establishment but they don't believe in the Democrats either. If they believe you will shake up politics and the Democratic Party—and will work to change this horrific, dying regime and bring the nation back to its democratic principles—then you've got a chance to turn out millions of new voters and make history.

Kerry didn't take my advice. His embrace of the corporate regime—and it was aptly symbolic that he was married to a big corporation, the Heinz estate—prevented him from even imagining anything but tepid reforms. His policy proposals on health care and education got no major traction, since they were not big enough to make any real difference. It is a tragedy that Kerry, my own very bright and thoughtful senator, rejected the wisdom of his own long experience in Vietnam and his own very substantial knowledge about the past and present crimes of U.S. interventionism.

FOREIGN POLICY

The Democrats embrace the regime's aim of American hegemony. While there was no clear threat to American security, the Democrats in the Clinton years refused to demilitarize or rethink the idea of American Empire. They went in search of new and old enemies, whether Colombian drug lords or tin-pot "rogue" dictators like Saddam Hussein.[9]

After 9/11, when Bush made the war on terrorism the regime's new religion that could justify intervention anywhere in the world, Democratic leaders instantly closed ranks against the new enemy. They enthusiastically supported the president's concept of the "war on terrorism" as well as the war in Afghanistan and then, most fatefully, the war in Iraq. Their embrace of the regime made it impossible for them to develop a clear critique of the invasion and occupation of Iraq, even when it became clear that it was a war based on lies and was degenerating into a Vietnam-like quagmire, increasing anti-Americanism, and upping the risk of more terrorist attacks against the United States.

John Kerry ran his 2004 campaign almost entirely on the grounds that he could fight the war on terror and the war in Iraq more effectively than the Republicans. He passionately attacked Bush's handling of the war, but on tactical grounds. He denounced Bush's unilateralism, but did not oppose the war itself. Kerry supported U.S. hegemony, but argued it could only be sustained multilaterally.

Kerry could not align the Democratic Party with its own grassroots. Despite passionate opposition to the war within the Democratic base and the progressive organizations like MoveOn that worked for his election, Kerry had long ago embraced both globalization and American Empire. This would sink Kerry's campaign, make the "flip-flop" label on Iraq credible, and distance him from the growing popular despair about a new Vietnam in the making. Kerry argued for thousands of new U.S. forces to be sent to Iraq, blinded to the view that more U.S. soldiers would only fuel the anti-American insurgency and could not create stability in Iraq or anywhere else in the Middle East.

The Democratic Party has been paralyzed by the fear of being tagged as unpatriotic. They have reason to be afraid, since the regime's pseudopopulism explicitly tars the "liberal Establishment" as a subverter of American morals, much like the civilizational enemies abroad. The

While Kerry had led an antiwar movement in his youth, he and the Democrats could no longer run on that populist peace legacy. The party was up to its eyeballs in the corporatist ideology of American global power. Kerry ran as a war hero rather than a peace activist, symbolizing the Democrats' marriage to the regime and its sacred commitment to American Empire.

solution is not to shun peace, but to make clear that it *is* patriotic to critique your own government for a war and foreign policy that are immoral, illegal, increase the threat of terrorism against America, and lead to the death and injury of thousands of young American soldiers.[10]

MORAL VALUES

The common wisdom of the 2004 elections is that the Democrats lost on the issue of moral values. This is, of course, entirely consistent with the pseudopopulist campaign of the Republicans. While pundits are racing to tell the Democrats how to get back to the moral center, this is all concealing the real way that the moral values issues works in American politics. True, the Democrats can be accused of a certain "litmus test" liberalism on social issues that, as distorted by the propaganda machinery of Karl

Rove, is seen by millions of ordinary Americans as an arrogant doctrine of "political correctness." And it is true that Democrats are less likely to be evangelical Christians than Americans in the red states. But the American population, including many in the red states, has become increasingly tolerant and progressive on a wide range of social issues. Despite the mobilization of a committed minority of conservative evangelicals, the gap on moral values between the Democratic Party and the American heartland is more a matter of style than substance.[11]

The Democrats have set themselves up not by becoming morally extreme but by becoming too closely wedded to the ruling regime itself and losing their capacity to see the regime itself as the core source of what so many Americans perceive as a crisis in moral values. Every regime rules through its control of economics, politics, *and* culture. Culture and ideology are one of the five pillars of a regime, and the current corporate regime's culture of materialism and consumerism shapes the moral framework of the nation. Since moral values are embodied in the regime's core economic and political institutions, such as the corporation, and because those institutions own and control much of the cultural system, such as the mass media, it only restates the obvious to say that the moral values of the nation are those of its governing regime. Yet this needs to be highlighted, since the Republicans' propaganda—and the regime's own black magic—suggests that the moral values of the country are being dictated by a cultural Establishment entirely separate from and antagonistic to the regime itself.

Virtually the entire range of problems coded in the "moral values" debate flow out of the regime's imposition

THE DEMOCRATS' REAL MORAL PROBLEM

The moral values crisis faced by the Democrats is not what either the Republicans or the Democrats' own pundits suggest. Instead, the crisis stems from the Democratic Party's cooptation into the third corporate regime, its embrace of that regime's core moral philosophy, and its subsequent inability to critique it.

of a corporate market system whose religion is materialism and whose morality is money. These regime values are built into the legal and political codes of the regime's governing institutions. As shown in the popular documentary film *The Corporation,* the corporation is legally structured as a fictional person who, if put on the psychiatric couch, would be diagnosed as a psychopath.[12] The corporation's directors have a fiduciary obligation to maximize profit for the company, without any corresponding obligation to concern themselves with the costs of this pursuit of profit on workers, their communities, or the environment.

This is an apt metaphor for the morality of the entire third corporate regime, which is a triumph of materialist values over all else. The American Dream has always had a materialist emphasis, but it has become increasingly perverted, emphasizing greed and pursuit of wealth at any price. What I have called moral "wilding" has trickled down from the elites at Enron and WorldCom and Merrill Lynch to the middle and lower strata of the population, so that street gangs among the poor imitate Wall Street hucksters and corporate downsizers to make a fast buck no matter what harm is done to others.[13]

Decency in the media, a key issue in the moral values debate, is an obvious example of how the regime is helping create the moral problems distressing ordinary Americans. Sex and violence are rampant in the media, creating a real dilemma for many parents trying to figure out what their kids should watch on television at night, but this is less a problem caused by an alien liberal Establishment run by Democrats than a corporate-owned media prepared to put on prime time whatever will make them the biggest quarterly return. Sex and violence sell—and in a corporate regime, this ensures that the morality of sexuality and violence will always be driven by money.

Or take the issue of family values. Families are under huge stress, but the prime cause lies not in the Democratic Party or liberals but in the breakdown of the family wage and the social safety network engineered by the regime itself. The latchkey kid is a product mainly of the fact that both parents have to work long hours at low wages, with both the wage and schedule dictated by their companies rather than the needs of the family. One of the biggest causes of divorce and family stress is money. Along with the new job insecurity and the slash in educational, health, and retirement benefits dictated by global companies with cheaper options abroad, the regime nearly guarantees not only the breakdown in families dominating so much of the moral values discussion but the alcoholism, depression, and abuse that mars the lives of so many Americans and also has been portrayed as a prime symptom of moral decay.

The central role of religion in the moral values debate also illustrates the regime's own hidden complicity. Officially, the regime's leaders, like President Bush himself, wear their religion on their sleeve and espouse the importance of religion in public and private life. But the corporate regime is ruthlessly secular, a money-making system that puts materialism over spirituality. Many Americans are genuinely religious, but their religious convictions have to be asserted in opposition to the regime's materialist values and the consumerist lifestyle that it enshrines. Effectively, this converts much religiosity into Sunday rituals, where the preaching in the pulpit becomes increasingly at odds with the reality of ruthlessly competitive corporate work and daily life. But the Democrats have not been able to exploit this hypocrisy, partly because they are fearful of broaching the entire subject of religion and getting stigmatized as "secular humanists," one of the favorite targets of Republican pseudopopulists such as Newt Gingrich.[14] The Democrats, as discussed in the next chapter, should remember that in earlier corporate regimes, populists and progressives effectively challenged the corporate system for institutionalizing the greed and selfishness denounced by nearly all religions.

Their complicity in the regime undermines the Democrats on "moral values" in several major ways. It essentially commits them to much of the institutional matrix that enshrines corporate values and creates many of the moral problems of America. It prevents them from offering a coherent alternative to the black magic of the Republicans, since they cannot present the core regime of which they are part as the real source of moral crisis. It also contributes to their image as an elite, since they are, in fact, partners in

HOW DEMOCRATS CAN LEAD ON MORAL VALUES

The big moral agenda in American life involves challenging the core values and moral philosophy of the regime itself. Framing economic issues as moral issues, as proposed by Democratic advisors such as George Lakoff, is a step in the right direction, but can never be effective simply by using clever linguistic strategies. Whatever the Democrats may say, their moral agenda will never be credible, and will never lead to solutions to moral problems until they extricate themselves from the regime and show that they are prepared to challenge both its core values and its ruling institutions that dictate America's moral conduct.[15]

the ruling regime. This makes them more vulnerable to the pseudopopulism served up by the Republicans, who argue that the Democrats are Washington elite insiders, far removed from the values of ordinary Americans which the GOP is committed to defend.

Joining the regime has another fateful consequence on the moral values issue. Since the Democrats cannot target the corporate regime as the heart of the moral issue, or propose systemic change as a solution, their moral agenda becomes fragmented, a series of disjointed cultural agendas driven by their various core constituencies, including women, minorities, gays, and others. Since each of these groups has its own political and moral agenda, the Democratic Party aggregates them into a shopping list that does not provide a coherent critique of the regime's moral failures or the foundation of a coordinated and systemic moral alternative.

This creates real problems of "political correctness" and moral incoherence among the Democrats. Lacking a coherent master narrative, centered on the regime's immorality, they cannot go to the heart of the moral crisis. This, ironically, ratchets up the moral demands of each of the Democrats' separate constituents, who, without a shared systemic alternative, fight harder to ensure that their own demands are the ones heard. Since the Democrats do not offer its different core constituents a common agenda, the constituents are less disposed to compromise with one another and forge a common front, especially on core moral or identity issues. This drags down the Democrats not just on moral values but on their entire political program. Having joined the regime, they cannot unify their own base or the country at large on a clear, systemic, political and moral alternative. This becomes part of the lure of the Election Trap: what all Democrats share is just one thing, the desire to win the next election. But nobody knows, even the Democrats themselves, what they really stand for and how they are going to solve the very real crises of the regime.

CHAPTER 9

A CURE FOR THE BLUES

*T*he only solution for the Democrats is to move from the Election Trap to regime change. This is a huge change, but it is the only way the Democrats can survive and gain a clear vision of how to save the country from the regime itself.

While regime change sounds utopian, it is the most practical advice that the Democrats can get—for five reasons. First, historically, regime-change politics has been the only way that Democrats have pulled themselves out of the ditch of corporate regimes and regained sustainable power. Second, the cracks in the current regime are serious enough that a regime change of one form or another is not at all impractical. Third, it is the inside-the-beltway leadership of the Democrats rather than the base that has joined the regime; large numbers of ordinary Democrats are fed up with their leaders and looking for a new direction. Fourth, a large number of progressive Democrats and new progressive organizations are challenging the leadership for control of the party. And, fifth, polls suggest that the majority of the entire country is deeply concerned about both the domestic and foreign policy direction of a regime that has gone far to the right under President Bush. If the Democratic Party offered a real alternative, and did so by climbing down from its elite perch and becoming a voice of ordinary people, it could change itself, the regime, and the country.

In the first part of this chapter, I show the new regime-change principles the Democratic Party must follow. In the second part, I show that there are hints that the Democrats are beginning to hear the message.

THE DEMOCRATIC PARTY GETS A MAKEOVER

In Chapter 3, I laid out a few basic principles of regime-change politics. The Democrats must heed them to create the extreme makeover they need.

1. EMBRACE DEFEAT

The Democrats are a defeated party. The first step is to recognize the nature and huge scale of their collapse and what has caused it. If you don't acknowledge the problem, you'll never solve it.

Their loss of all three branches of government since 2000 is just a symbol of the Democratic crisis. While the surface problem is losing elections, the deeper problem is the loss of identity. The Democrats no longer have a vision and nobody is clear about what they stand for and how they will change the country. That is why they are not winning elections.

The Election Trap is one way of describing the Democrats' problem. When a party has lost a vision of real change, it can define itself only by beating the other party. In 2004, the Democrats' only real agenda was "Anybody But Bush." While this need to beat Bush was urgent and perfectly appropriate, the Democrats helped ensure they would lose to Bush because people knew that Bush stood for something, while the Democrats stood for nothing but winning.

The Election Trap becomes a self-reinforcing cycle for a defeated party. The more it loses, the more it wants to win at the expense of everything else. It focuses more of its energy on winning, and in the process abandons the search for vision and change. This is a self-defeating strategy, even if you accept the critical need to defeat a dangerously right-wing president. The Democrats were right to work very hard to win in 2004, if only to ward off "fascist lite" trends. But you are going to lose if you redefine your agenda as just winning.

In 1964, as noted in Chapter 3, the Republicans lost in a landslide to the Democrats, but conservative activists on the ground rejected the seductions of the Election Trap. Instead, the grassroots New Right, inspired by Goldwater and his willingness to stand for losing principles, slowly won over the party with the long-term aim of creating systemic change. Instead of putting everything into winning the next election, they channeled their energy into creating visionary ideas and building a movement for regime change.

The Democrats can learn a lesson from the New Right. The aim of a party is to change the country. The regime-change ideas you will need to transform the country will rarely be popular; they may lose you elections in the short term. Nonetheless, you will only begin winning elections when you have a vision of change that shows conviction and a path to making the lives of ordinary people better.

This is hardly an academic issue, since it is a debate now wracking the Democratic Party. Much of the party's leadership argues that the key to the party's survival is winning —and that you can only win by putting out ideas that appeal to the mainstream center. The party's centrist leadership is ensnared in the Election Trap, as are many progressives both in the leadership and the base. But even if, by embracing Election Trap politics, the Democrats succeeded in winning the next election, it would not change the regime or the country. The 2000 and 2004 elections suggest that such a strategy, in any case, is more likely to lead to electoral defeat.

On the other hand, progressive insurgents in the party, linked in the press to 2004 candidates such as Dennis Kucinich or Al Sharpton, or organizations like MoveOn, ACORN, the Campaign for America's Future, the Sierra Club, and the most progressive unions, are arguing for something closer to a regime-change politics. They may passionately want to win the next election, and some suffer from their own version of the Election Trap, where the goal is still winning but by moving to the left rather than the center. The goal of winning the next election is so powerful in

American politics that it seduces people of all ideologies. But many progressive or insurgent groups recognize that if they don't stand for real change and hold to convictions that might lose them the election, they are doomed. The groups that are prepared to risk defeat have the greatest chance of leading the party to victory. They want regime change and that is why they are the only Democrats capable of changing the country.[1]

2. THINK BIG AND PLAY OFFENSE

Most of the mainstream Democratic leadership have been thinking small and playing defense since the collapse of the New Deal. This is because they have joined the corporate regime and cannot question its basic assumptions. The party's agenda is small because it can imagine only small reforms in the system. Democratic leaders play defense because Republicans argue that Democrats are elitist and not true-blue Americans. In a sense, by joining the regime, the Democrats have to play defense on two fronts: against claims of liberal extremism in red states and claims of selling out to the corporations in blue states.

Thinking big is the core of regime-change politics, but it is the hardest thing for mainstream parties to do. The electoral system and the Election Trap keep driving the parties, especially losing ones, back to the timid thinking that seems to have credibility in the mainstream and win elections.

But if you want to really change the country, you have to take the risk of thinking out of the box. Remember that a regime is a set of ruling ideas, essentially a system of thought control, or hegemony.[2] The regime defines the spectrum of economic, foreign policy, and moral principles that are "respectable" or legitimate. If you want to change the country, you have to be prepared, as Goldwater and the New Right were during the New Deal, to be heretics, and go beyond the respectable ideas of the era.

In other words, real change requires changing the conversation, breaking through the thought control of the regime. But if that thought control has succeeded among the party elite, then it becomes even more difficult. It is not only risky electorally, but it can only be accomplished by grassroots or populist insurgents who are prepared to challenge the party's leaders and splinter the party.

The Democratic Party has to think big and go on the offensive in economics, foreign policy, and "moral values."

In economics, this does *not* mean an anti-business crusade or a repudiation of markets; *a good and productive society requires a pro-business approach that recognizes the deep economic and moral deficits of the corporate economy.* The Democrats have to challenge the constitutional protections, monopolistic power, and sociopathic structure of the global corporation that are undermining democracy and wreaking havoc with the security and well-being of ordinary workers at home and abroad. This means creating a new regime of secure, well-paying jobs at home essential not only to worker prosperity and social stability but to U.S. productivity and competitiveness. Such regime-change economics means resurrecting the populist and progressive tradition that stretches back to Jefferson; it is part of the American creed even though it sounds heretical in the current regime.[3]

In foreign policy, big thinking means unambiguously rejecting American Empire and offering a new foreign policy based on collective security and international law and diplomacy. It also means opposing the regime's war on terrorism, that, along with the debacle in Iraq, is actually making the country less safe by whipping up anti-Americanism around the world. Such big thinking is risky, since it makes the Democrats vulnerable to the regime's propaganda that the Democrats are antipatriotic. But I am suggesting not that the Democrats abandon efforts to combat Islamic terrorism but that they show that the regime's "war on terrorism" is actually aiding and abetting what it claims to be fighting. The Democrats need to forcefully reject even the most "humanitarian" visions of Empire advanced by the reigning neoconservatism, demonstrating that a U.S. military reduction in Iraq and around the world, coupled with a new commitment to collective security, is the only path to reducing the appeal of terrorist groups in the Mideast and to enhancing peace and true national security.[4] This new multilateralist and noninterventionist direction resonates to a growing number of both blue and red Americans who worry that their own children will die in the regime's permanent war or that they themselves will be hit by terrorist attacks on the homeland. Moreover, the biggest danger to the Democrats and the country is another terrorist attack on the homeland, the most likely catalyst for right-wing regime change toward fascism. Changing the big picture of U.S. foreign policy to reduce that risk is one of the most important challenges facing the Democratic Party—and it is entirely consistent with genuine patriotism.

On "moral values," this means challenging the fundamental morality of the regime itself. The third corporate regime is grounded in a morality of materialism, consumerism, and greed. The regime has a sociopathic nature, and its low wages, outsourcing, and profit-oriented media are creating crises in values, families, personal life, and spirituality that drive the moral debate. The Democrats need to go on the offense and not only attack the regime at its sociopathic core but show that they are ready to change it for a new order based on values.

3. MAKE YOUR PARTY
A SOCIAL MOVEMENT

The New Right turned the Republican Party into a social movement of grassroots Bible Belters and corporate elites.[5] The Democrats must heed their success and turn their own party over to the grassroots populist and progressive movements described in the last chapter. They are the party's only possible salvation.

The Democrats have become vulnerable to the propaganda that they are an alien Establishment because the Washington leadership of the party is, in fact, an elite tragically distant from the grassroots. This reflects the transformation of the party into a professional bureaucracy disconnected from grassroots social movements. Reconnecting the party with the movements is the only way for the Democratic Party to rediscover its identity as a people's party that can create regime change for ordinary Americans.

The movements can do three vital things for the party. First, they will liberate it from its suicidal elitism, which puts it out of touch with the population. Grassroots movements are, first and foremost, the organizations of ordinary Americans, who represent the aspirations and values of the American public. It is their voice, their sensibility, and their values that reconnect the party with the "common man and woman." As they infuse the party with their own culture and identity, a new populist spirit, a new plainspeaking language, and new progressive leaders will emerge. The elitism of the party bureaucracy cannot withstand the dynamism of the movements, if and when they open the doors to them.

Second, they will liberate the Party from the Election Trap. Social movements are created for long-term change by people with a systemic alternative vision and passion. They care about elections but their commitment is to the long haul. They will not abandon their core passions for rights and justice to win the next election.

This will create conflicts between the party and the movements, but it will be healthy for both. It will free the party from the obsession with winning at any cost. It will help the movements see the pragmatic compromises necessary to advance their cause.

Third, the movements will bring the big thinking and the spirit of playing offense that the Democratic Party has abandoned since the early New Deal. Movements are visionary because they represent the needs of the people that the ruling regime cannot address. Movements cannot think small because their aim is always regime change. The melding of the movements with the Democrats will light a fire of political imagination that even the party bureaucracy will not be able to squelch.

Movements are also constitutionally suited to play offense. They thrive off confrontation, radicalism, and boldness. They have become movements precisely because they don't want to play by the regime's rules. The activists will force the party into bolder, confrontational thinking and action against the regime. The party can help unify the movements and discipline them to wage more united and winning campaigns.

When the party becomes a social movement, it will resurrect itself as the voice of the people that it is destined to be. I am not suggesting that the party and the movements fuse, since it is healthy for movements to maintain their independent identity and the party has its own needs for national discipline that should not constrain the movements. But the vision and boldness of the movements are the best medicine for the party and the beginning of the cure.

WHY THE DEMOCRATS MIGHT TAKE THE CURE

I can hear your skepticism already. The Democrats might need this cure but they'll never take it. The Democratic leaders are too addicted to corporate money and the Election Trap. You might very well be right, since so much of the leadership is dependent on corporate funding and captive to the regime's hegemonic ideology. But three new circumstances suggest that the Democratic Party might be ripe for a new approach and could move beyond the Election Trap toward regime change. In reading these possibilities outlined below, remember that grassroots movements will remain the key catalyst, and that the Democratic Party will not fight for regime change without the fire of activists outside and inside the party forcing it out of its own comfortable box.

1. THE REGIME MAKES A RADICAL RIGHT TURN

George W. Bush may turn out to have been the best gift history could have given the Democrats. By creating feverish anti-Americanism around the world, taking the country into permanent warfare, attacking Social Security, abolishing or slashing hundreds of programs for the poor, throwing money at corporations, busting the budget, aligning himself with religious zealots, and demonizing the Democrats themselves, Bush has radicalized the regime. By moving so far to the right, he has made it difficult for even the most timid Democrats to play politics as usual. He put the regime into crisis and opened up a new opportunity for the Democrats to persuade Americans across the political spectrum of the need for regime change.

After the 2004 elections, small signs emerged that Democratic leaders were finally rousing themselves from their long slumber within the comfort of the regime. Thirty-six Democratic senators voted against the confirmation of Alberto Gonzales as Attorney General and several made passionate cases against the confirmation of Condoleezza Rice as Secretary of State. The opposition votes to Cabinet nominees of a president were among the largest since Herbert Hoover's presidency, and the grounds of the opposition, particularly against Gonzales, were important. Democrats argued that Gonzales was supporting extra-constitutional measures that gave a green light to torture; they argued he had already violated the Constitution by recommending in secret memos that detainees at Guantanamo or Abu Ghraib were not entitled to protection under the Geneva Conventions or to American due process rights; they pointed out that Gonzales's memos had explicitly indicated that the president, in the new post-9/11 world, stood above the law, an astonishing conclusion that nonetheless appeared consistent to affirm the radical extra-constitutional drift of this new "extreme regime."

Nothing concentrates the mind like the prospect of fascism. The Democratic leaders who had long propped up the third corporate regime were beginning to recognize first, that the regime itself was moving far to the right of the regime that they had been willing to support as a loyal opposition; second, that this extraconstitutional right-turn, driven by regime crises and the triumph of the regime's most right-wing religious and economic ideologies, might eventually create a regime tip; and third, such a regime tip would allow new leaders, particularly in the context of a new terrorist attack on the homeland or a new war in the Middle East, to explicitly brand Democratic Party leaders as traitors and eliminate the possibility of any serious organized opposition. As a result, Democratic senators and members of the House became bolder—during opportunities such as Gonzales's and Rice's confirmation hearings —in challenging the regime's systemic secrecy, its assault on civil liberties, its deceptions and imperial assumptions leading to the occupation of Iraq, and the new arrogant doctrines of preemption and unilateralism. Some liberal Democrats like Senator Edward Kennedy called for an early withdrawal from Iraq, and West Virginia Senator Robert Byrd excoriated the regime for becoming an Empire and undermining American freedom in the name of the war on terrorism. Senator Byrd is accepted by both parties as the Senate's reigning authority on the Constitution, and has, despite his conservative record, become the most eloquent and forceful Democrat rousing the Democrats for all-out struggle against the dangers of American fascism.[6]

The right-wing radicalization of the regime under Bush created other new calculations for the Democratic leadership that pushed much more moderate Democrats, such as Senator Harry Reid, the new Democratic Senate leader, toward a bolder opposition. On the domestic front, Bush's push for privatizing Social Security and eliminating a progressive tax system was a direct assault on the most important Democratic achievements of the twentieth century. This was an assault on the soul of the Democratic Party, and signaled the shift of the regime toward not just co-opting the party but destroying it and its legacy. Even the inside-the-beltway Democratic leaders sensed this threat and had to react. In early 2005, Democrats coalesced as a unified Congressional bloc, taking the position that Bush was misleading the country about the crisis of Social Security, much as he had about Iraq, and that there would be no compromise on private accounts. They would filibuster if necessary—and when Bush sought to nominate deeply conservative judges, Democrats also stood firm against the repeal of the filibuster itself, as well as against the religious extremism of the assault on an independent judiciary. This was not yet regime-change politics, but it represented the beginnings of the Democrats finding their spine.

Moreover, the radicalization of the regime began to make regime change a potential option even for Democratic leaders ensnared in the Election Trap. The regime's right-wing turn and its religious attack on the Enlightenment ideals of the Bill of Rights was firing up the anger and energy of the progressive movements in the party's base— and also fueling fear among the much larger number of

Americans who don't usually vote but were now seeing their Social Security at risk, their kids being sent on too many combat missions to the Middle East, and their culture hijacked by religious extremists. This meant that even inside-the-beltway Democratic leaders ensnared in the Election Trap might see that the best hope for 2006 or 2008 might be relying on the grassroots movements to fire up the base by standing up for a new vision of national and social security in the light of the new very personal threats to disenfranchised, poor, working poor, or couch-potato Americans.

The shadow of fascism lite evokes memories of the fate of Social Democratic and other more leftist parties in Europe as Hitler rose to power. The only chance to stop Hitler was for the Social Democrats (who were the European equivalent of the Democratic Party in the United States) to align with more leftist parties (represented in the United States by the progressive social movements) in a broad anti-fascist coalition—a "united front." They ultimately failed to do this, opening the way for Hitler's election in 1933 and his fascist putsch after the Reichstag fire.[7]

Even the barest memory of this catastrophe should help Democrats transform themselves from pussycats within the regime to a populist united front. When you confront a regime threatening the Constitution and undermining national security, social security, and the religious tolerance of the country, it is no longer credible to advance politics as usual. You need to rethink your relation to the ruling powers of the regime, build a new relation with your base and social movements that seek regime change, and seek a broad new coalition that can unite Democrats, independents, and many moderate conservatives against the regime's drift toward right-wing extremism. As seen below, there were other signs after 2004 that the Democratic Party, with a huge push from grassroots labor, peace, environmental, and minority activists, might be waking up to these possibilities.

2. THE RETURN OF THE DEANIACS

On February 12, 2005, the Democratic National Committee elected Howard Dean as the new chair of the Democratic Party. This can be interpreted as something of a regime change within the party. It did not ensure a Democratic Party commitment to regime-change politics in America, but it put the entire party on notice that there would be a new battle for its own soul.

Dean's coronation was a milestone because it represented deep disaffection with the established Washington leadership, particularly the Democratic Leadership Council and many of the elder statesmen of the Clinton Administration, who had married the party to the third corporate regime two decades ago. Many frantically tried to stop Dean's selection as party chair by putting up more conservative inside-the-beltway candidates who posed no threat of taking the Democrats out of the regime. Such schisms within the party elite are typically a sign of regime change within the party and in the country more broadly. The schism within the Republican Party, discussed as a regime crack in Chapter 3, is now accompanied by important new schisms within the Democratic Party. The threat that Dean represented was less Dean himself than the symbolism of selecting an outsider candidate who didn't play by the normal rules and had a base independent of the DLC and the corporate wing of the party. Even if Dean wanted personally to stay within the regime, his ascendancy gave new access to the populist and progressive forces who might now seek regime change.

Dean himself, while a mainstream politician seen as moderate or centrist by his fellow Vermont Democrats while he was governor, has shown a willingness to entertain all three of the key regime-change principles.

Embrace defeat. Dean went down to defeat in the Iowa primary, a crushing blow that ended his 2004 candidacy for president. Rather than recanting his positions on the war, corporate power, and a new direction for the Democratic Party, he never wavered from them. His "stubbornness," as the media portrayed it, might have led to his defeat, but his subsequent behavior showed that he is willing to lose rather than change his principles.

In other words, Dean does not seem to be a politician locked entirely into the Election Trap. The position of party chair, which assigns him largely the role of raising money to make sure the party wins the next time, is a key test. Dean's challenge is to remain faithful to his principles and try to advance them, even if it doesn't lead to immediate electoral wins. By not reflexively moving toward the center and making deals with big business, he runs the risk of leading Democrats to short-term new losses. But if such a tack leads to greater vision and conviction within the party, Dean could help build a party that rediscovers its historic identity. While he clearly wants the Democrats to win elections, his new approach, which rejects winning at any price, could also teach the entire party a lesson about the futility of the Election Trap. Moreover, since his fundraising is linked mainly to his capacity to excite the grassroots and raise money and time commitments from ordinary citizens, Dean may be able to help Democrats actually win elections by rejecting the traditional wisdom about moving to the center, a lesson the Republicans learned long ago.

Think big. Despite his moderate views on many policies, Dean is thinking beyond the narrow confines of normal politics. His book *You've Got the Power* is a populist manifesto calling for a grassroots transformation of the Democrats and the country.[8] He has gone around the country, rousing students on campuses like my own to see their own power to change the nation. After watching him in action, I can testify that he knows how to excite both mainstream and progressive students about the need to get involved and make a real change in the country. Dean implicitly speaks about both the hidden power of the regime—since he has much to say about corporate power—and the hidden power of the people to change it.

The fact that Dean's positions on many policy issues, such as the deficits, gun control, health care, the environment, regulation, and social spending, are relatively mainstream may increase the credibility of his larger vision. It will sustain his credibility with the moderate and conservative wings of the party—and help him reach out beyond the party's traditional base, including the red states where he pledged to spend most of his time. His mainstream views on many issues and his overt appeals to the red staters and evangelicals may anger many of the progressive movements to his left—and restrain the party's movements toward a genuine regime-change agenda. But the tension between Dean and the movements may be just what the doctor ordered in terms of a new, dynamic conversation between the Democrats and the movements, who will see his ascension as an invitation to join the party and transform it.

Connect with the grassroots movements. Historically, the Democratic Party has only changed the country when it was turbo-charged by the energy of populist and progressive movements. When the party joined the current regime, it cut itself off from the grassroots groups that could propel it beyond the Election Trap and offer it a vision. The Democrats thereby set themselves up for the Republicans' pseudopopulist charge that they were elitist, since they had, in fact, cut themselves off from their roots among ordinary people and no longer spoke for them.

Dean emerged on the stage because he was the only "mainstream" Democratic candidate in 2004 who connected with the grassroots. The more leftist candidates Dennis Kucinich and Al Sharpton also connected strongly with ordinary people, but many Democratic voters who loved the passion and radicalism of both men embraced their own version of the Election Trap and decided to support Dean because they thought he could win.[9] While Dean was less visionary, his dominance early in the campaign came from his blunt antiwar stance that led hundreds of thousands of ordinary people to contribute over the Internet to his campaign. Moreover, progressive unions like the Service Employees International Union (SEIU), America's biggest labor group, and antiwar Internet-based groups like MoveOn signed on to the Dean campaign because they felt he was mainstream enough to gain acceptance in the country but progressive enough to catalyze real change.

The capacity to change the relation between the party

officialdom and social movements is Dean's most intriguing potential legacy. Dean opens the party up to a new conversation with regime-change movements that have the vision the party itself has lost. Since the movements—including the progressive unions such as SEIU, the peace movement, antiglobalization or anti-sweatshop activists, liberal students on campuses who were the original core "Deaniacs," feminist and environmental organizers, and civil rights and civil liberties groups—are mainly interested in systemic change rather than cosmetic reforms of a far-right regime, they are the most important force that can help move the Democrats from the Election Trap to regime change. They will help the party find its spine and identity. In the best scenario, the Democrats will help unify the diverse and often badly splintered grassroots movements into a cohesive force for change, while also helping them to reach out beyond the current activists in the movements to a far larger base of the "anxious class" in the red states and the country at large. A Democratic Party that remembers and speaks in the best traditions of the populist and the progressives can win back the loyalties of millions of displaced and resentful American workers, who have not yet seen the Democrats as their champions but are frightened by the right-wing radicalism of the current corporate regime.[10]

3. THE DEMOCRATS, MORAL VALUES, AND OLD-TIME RELIGION

The 2004 election led to an astonishing refocus within the Democratic Party on the role of "moral values" in politics. A Pew exit poll taken on Election Day that indicated Bush won on moral values will be endlessly debated, but there is no doubt that it changed the conversation among Democrats. The Democratic Party became obsessed with questions about what moral values are, how its own economic policies can be framed as consistent with America's morality, and whether its position on social, family, sexual, or religious issues has put it hopelessly out of touch with Americans around the country. On the whole, this new conversation, while it could lead to very serious misunderstandings and unwelcome directions, is a healthy development for the Democrats. If the moral values issue is properly understood, it could lead them to see that politics is about identity and morality as well as class; that their elitism has led them to be perceived in large parts of the country as either morally arrogant or immoral by the anxious workers in both red and blue states who most need regime change; and that they have bought into the morality of the corporate regime and need to do something about it—fast! Put simply, regime-change politics always involves moral outrage and transformation, and the Democrats now have a chance to find the moral foundations of a politics leading toward regime change.

Historically, a shift toward regime-change politics has been associated with moral or religious movements that infused the Democratic Party with passion about the moral bankruptcy of the existing order. As noted earlier, the nineteenth-century populists and their labor counterparts who challenged the first corporate regime of the robber barons brought some powerful moral outrage and good old-time religion into the Democratic Party. William Jennings Bryan, the quasi-populist Democratic candidate in 1896, was a religious conservative and a man of great moral passion, attributes that characterized the populists as a whole and the early labor movements of the period. An Evangelical Christian, Bryan argued that the robber barons were crucifying ordinary Americans on a "cross of gold." The progressives who created the Progressive regime and then the New Deal, while more secular, were also unabashed in their moral outrage about the injustices of the corporate order, and couched their arguments for regime change in moral terms.[11]

After 2004, Democrats began listening to critics and new advisors like Thomas Frank, George Lakoff, and Jim Wallis, who focused like a laser on the moral values issue that seemed to explode off the red/blue map. Lakoff argued that the Democrats needed to see that politics was all about morality—and that they had to reframe their economic and social agenda in moral terms.[12] Frank argued that the Democrats had been hopelessly outmaneuvered by the Republicans, who had already won the moral argument while the Democrats had abandoned any genuine reason for voters to choose them on grounds related to their own economic self-interest.[13] And Wallis, an ordained minister, argued that Democrats had to get religion and speak to issues of poverty and social justice as Biblical mandates.[14]

The emerging view offered by Lakoff, Frank, and Wallis was that the moral values issue was not a fluke but a sign of serious flaws and misconceptions in the Democratic Party. The main message was that the Democrats had to reframe their message in moral or religious terms. The lesson from Lakoff was that politics is by its nature moral and that people vote their values and identity. This is true, but leads Lakoff to emphasize reframing the current Democratic message without changing the substantive agenda into regime change.[15]

Wallis is more visionary, arguing that Democrats have to live up to the politics of social justice enshrined in the Bible. He wants the Democrats to "get" the necessity of getting religion, a controversial and far from persuasive argument. But Democrats need to debate it, particularly in the context of Wallis's view that this implies major shifts not just in rhetoric but in a bold shift toward a social justice agenda that Jesus could embrace.[16] Frank is less explicit about what the Democrats should do, making it eminently clear, though, that the Democrats made themselves vulnerable to the moral backlash by failing to promote the kind of progressive economic agenda that would redirect Americans back to a class-based conversation.[17]

The moral values conversation has the merits of bringing Democrats back to first principles. Speaking of morality, values, or religion brings people back to what they care about most. Politics—and particularly regime-change politics—requires a vision and commitment to deeply held moral principles. As Frank points out, Republicans in Washington may not care about the moral values they preach—and may not often deliver to their evangelical base—but they recognize that moral claims trump most others in politics. Pseudopopulism is a moral attack strategy to which the Democrats have made themselves vulnerable because of their elitism and embrace of the corporate agenda. It has also allowed the Republicans to advance a persistent regime-change model of politics, since their visionary rhetoric is all about freedom and values that inspire moral passion (see Chapter 5).

When Democrats take up the question of their own moral values, it forces them into a conversation about what they really want. The Election Trap is politics without morality. By committing to a principled moral philosophy that goes beyond winning, Democrats are taking the first step toward a regime-change politics. Moving toward moral discourse has the potential to catalyze conviction and vision in the party itself—and may be a key way to escape the Election Trap.

Second, the moral values issue forces the Democrats to address the issue of elitism, bearing both on the party's message and its messenger. For reasons discussed in Chapter 5, the Democratic leaders and many followers are a cultural class based on cultural capital and educational credentials, thereby alienating themselves in style and substance from ordinary voters. The question of elitism cannot be avoided in the moral discussion, if only because so many red staters keep harping on it. By engaging in the moral values discussion, the Democrats can make progress on issues of style and identity. Style and identity both matter—a lot—not just to win elections but to change the country. The Democrats cannot continue to present candidates who appear to talk down to the people rather than with them. Workers felt they could go enjoy having a beer with Bush. They felt they could sit and chew down a Big Mac with Clinton. This not only made Bush and Clinton electable but helped to erase perceptions of elitism. The pseudopopulist black magic currently plaguing the Democrats—and the widespread view of them as an alien Establishment—will become less true if they actually are comfortable having a beer with ordinary voters.

This goes beyond political theater. The Democrats need

to be in real dialogue with ordinary voters and workers, something that has largely disappeared with the death of the old Democratic Party neighborhood urban machines and the New Deal union halls. Town hall meetings can help restart the process, but only if people feel they can identify with the Democratic politicians, share their fundamental values, and be part of a dialogue, not a lecture. A conversation about values and the morality that we share can help make all of these things more likely.

Such a values conversation requires Democrats to make clear their own ideas of patriotism, family values, and religion. Most Americans are personally identified with the nation, and wonder whether Democrats love their country. Since the antiwar movement of the 1960s, Republicans have tarred Democrats as anti-American, and Democrats have been terrified—one might say terrorized—that the charge will stick. This helped lead to the 2004 debacle in which Kerry, campaigning as a war hero, tried to renounce his 1960s peace activism. This is the worst way of proving patriotism, and Kerry's equivocation—or flip-flopping—on the issue probably lost him the election.

Democrats can do better if they are morally honest. They can make clear that they love this nation's constitutional commitment to protect dissent and oppose unjust war, the highest form of patriotism. Such morally grounded patriotism would have allowed Kerry in 2004—and Democrats today—to break from the slavish adherence to empire and hegemonic wars that is a huge part of the regime's current moral failing—and of the Democratic Party leadership as well. As the nation wakes up to the realities of Iraq, Democrats need to speak for the millions of Americans who oppose permanent occupation of the country and want early withdrawal of U.S. troops. This is true patriotism, since sustained occupation violates U.S. and international law, and bringing the GIs home quickly will bring the United States back into the international community, prevent more of our soldiers from dying for the wrong reason, and prevent more anti-Americanism and more terrorism against the United States. Such dissent also offers the best chance of ending the carnage and killing of innocents in Iraq itself. Antiwar politics is always risky, but it is ordinary Americans who are at risk—physically and morally—when the United States pursues militarism and an immoral foreign policy. Leading Democrats like Senator Ted Kennedy and Senator Robert Byrd, as well as Howard Dean, have helped advance this counterhegemonic moral view, but it will take a vast mobilization at the grassroots—among peace activists, veterans groups, religious communities, and labor unions—to pull most Democratic leaders away from their compromised moral vision of empire. In speaking to red staters and all American citizens, Democrats should recognize and honor the morality of sacrifice that drives many Americans to support the war, or even enlist in the military. They should acknowledge the moral underpinning of such commitment to sacrifice by ordinary soldiers or citizens. But Democrats need the courage to make perfectly clear that sacrifice is patriotic and truly a "moral value" only if it is in the service of a larger moral purpose. Empire is immoral, even when it is an American empire couched in the soothing rhetoric of freedom—and an American patriot must say this over and over and over again.

On the home front, Democrats should make clear that their moral outrage against the regime is partly because it has been so brutally destructive of family life. Yes, Democrats have families too! Divorce rates are higher in the red states than the blue states, and especially high in the Bible Belt. Democrats want a new regime that makes it possible for parents to support families and spend time with them —starting with a living wage that the Catholic Church has described as one of its cardinal spiritual principles. Democrats, like most Americans in red or blue states, value the love and care of children, whom the regime is abandoning to ever-higher levels of poverty and neglect. The Democrats share with most Americans a morality and spirituality that inevitably raises questions about a corporate materialist regime that subordinates the dignity of individual workers and families to global corporate priorities and equates success with money and consumerism. Democrats seek regime change to put individual dignity and respect for family and community—the heart of nearly every religious and moral system—above corporate profit, and to work tirelessly for a new order that subordinates greed to social justice.

Moral politics makes political sense today only when it connects to the moral despair of the anxious working class —especially those socially conservative male workers, now converts to the GOP—known as the Reagan Democrats. The Democrats will not reconnect with such workers, who were once the base of the New Deal Democratic Party, until the party offers a moral vision big enough to embrace both the anxious class's fundamental needs for economic security and a moral philosophy larger than its own self-interest. This melding of economic security and moral principle is precisely how the Populists successfully mobilized the anxious farming class of the first corporate regime against the robber barons and how Progressives won workers across race lines as the base of the New Deal. One concrete approach for the Democrats today is to make an argument for affirmative action based on class as well as race, making it clear to struggling white workers that they will fight as hard for them as they will for women and minorities. Like the nineteenth-century populists, as well as the New Dealers, they need to show that Democrats will not permit the new global corporate robber barons to crucify ordinary Americans again—whether red staters or blue staters—on a twenty-first-century globalized cross of gold.

Despite its potential virtues for Democrats, the arguments for a new Democratic politics of morality can easily lead in counterproductive directions. Much of the conversation after 2004 focused mainly on "reframing." If we can only help the voters understand that our positions on the economy, the war, and the family are not policy wonkery but an expression of our moral, even spiritual values, so Democrats say, then we will have won the moral values issues and may win over the country.

Not so fast. The moral values issue does involve reframing, but as I have argued earlier it begins rather than ends there. The problem with the Democrats lies in the substance of their vision and policy, not just the framing. Ever since joining the regime, as highlighted in the last chapter, the Democrats have abandoned the substance of a meaningful agenda for change on economic, social, and foreign policy matters. If the moral issues debate leads them to focus on reframing rather than transforming their fundamental agenda, it will prove disastrous for the party.

The party needs a momentous change in the substantive vision and programs they promote. Reframing will not extricate the party from the regime—it could lock them in even deeper, if their present timid economic and foreign policy is couched within a language of values. But if a focus on morals leads the party to challenge the underlying source of moral crisis in America—the morality of the third corporate regime itself—the result would be entirely different. This would provide a moral springboard for the party not just to reframe but to transform itself into a party of regime change. In the next chapter, I lay out a specific programmatic agenda that would translate a new Democratic moral philosophy—centered ironically on the regime's own rhetoric of democracy—into concrete economic, foreign policy, and social policy initiatives. It would take us beyond the corporate order, ward off fascism, and move us toward a renewed and real democracy.

CHAPTER 10

SAVING DEMOCRACY

We need regime change at home quickly but it won't happen until we know where we want to go. This requires big thinking by social movements, the Democratic Party, and especially readers like *you*. A new regime, as I'm sure you've concluded, cannot just be a token reform of the corporate order. It has to be driven by a truly bold new vision based on America's own core values.

All corporate regimes transfer sovereignty away from the people. Our third corporate regime has been extreme, with transnational corporations unashamedly hijacking our government for their own ends. This has been accompanied by a disastrous loss of citizen empowerment and social security. The new regime must return sovereignty to the people in a democracy tailored for the new century: what I call "New Democracy."

It's hard to take seriously the very idea of democracy —old or new—in a globalized era of transnational companies, corporate-dominated campaign financing, corporate-owned media, two corporate political parties, a new military-industrial complex, and Florida-style elections. New Democracy can only work if it is inspiring enough to turn a population of exhausted workers and cynical couch potatoes into active citizens who believe they can make a better world. It's a tall order but we have a history suggesting that it is possible. The Populists, Progressives, and New Dealers all had to refashion democracy in the face of their own corporate regimes. They succeeded in regime change. If they could do it, we can too.

PULL 'EM DOWN

New Democracy requires that you and I get together to take down the *pillars* of the third corporate regime. The pillars have become huge hurdles to citizen action and democracy itself. Recall the house this regime built and the long shadows cast by its pillars.

The corporation itself, the first pillar of the current regime, must be reconstructed in the coming new order. New Democracy is based on a regime change transforming the current corporate model of business enterprise. What I call "corporate abolitionism" *does not mean demonizing or abolishing business, even big business, but means eliminating its antidemocratic features.* We need to change the DNA of today's corporation, which has become inherently political, parasitical, and predatory. We also have to limit the exit power of corporations that subordinates countries to companies.

WHY WE MUST TAKE DOWN THIS REGIME'S PILLARS

Pillar 1: The Corporation

Turns us from active citizens into entertained, passively managed, and, yes, brainwashed consumers.

Pillar 2: Corpocracy

*Turns Washington, D.C. over to corporate raiders who are running **your** government for **their** profit.*

Pillar 3: Social Insecurity

Forces most of us to spend our days just running in place to survive, anxious about whether we can pay the bills, get affordable housing and health care, and afford retirement.

Pillar 4: Empire

Builds American military power while undermining relations with our allies, breeding more hatred of Americans around the world, and decreasing our national security.

Pillar 5: The Corporate Mystique

Promotes the ideology of freedom while robbing us of the values and capacity to escape our condition as servants of the corporate order.

PRO-BUSINESS AND PRO-DEMOCRACY

> Abolishing the current corporate structure is a long-term goal but we must make it a central aim, educating our fellow citizens about the ways in which corporations are deadly to both market competition and democracy. It is not just the ripped-off workers at Enron who need a more accountable business system: we all do!

As I spelled out in the Introduction, the current regime is based on a horrific corporate/government marriage that dominates America. The new regime must decisively end corporate domination of politics, that is dismantle corpocracy, the second pillar of the current regime. Senator John McCain gained early political support by proclaiming in his 2000 presidential campaign that getting big money out of politics was his top priority. He echoed President Theodore Roosevelt, who proclaimed in 1910: "There can be no effective control of corporations while their political activity remains. To put an end to it will be neither a short nor easy task but it can be done."[1] Campaign finance reform today, McCain said, "is a fight to take our government back from the powerbrokers and special interests, and return it to the people and the noble cause of freedom it was created to serve."[2] Amen!

The third pillar that must go is social insecurity, a consequence of the corporate rollback of the health, education, and worker protections created by the New Deal. Social insecurity is where politics gets personal for ordinary people. The third corporate regime has delivered a severe, sustained kick in the stomach to millions of poor, working, and middle-class Americans who live under the new conditions of temporary and outsourced employment and downsized services. We're all feeling the pain in one way or another.

If the New Deal could help save Americans in a Depression, we today can create a new model of social security. As observed in Chapters 2 and 3, the New Deal ended partly because it was too timid, failing to deliver the real security that all Americans of every race, age, and gender needed. We need to ensure that all of us can live without fear of chronic or catastrophic job loss, of wages that do not bring us out of poverty, of a bankrupt public education and health system, and of air or water that can make us ill.

The fourth pillar of the current regime that must go is Empire. Empire and democracy are irreconcilable, and the regime's foreign policy is leading to anti-Americanism that endangers the security of every American.

While New Democracy has deep American roots, it can only emerge with a transformation of culture and values. The third corporate regime has enshrined the corporate

"In an opinion poll of 7,000 Europeans conducted recently by the European Commission in Brussels, respondents ranked Bush the number two threat to world peace, tied with North Korean leader Kim Jong Il and behind Prime Minister Ariel Sharon of Israel."

New York Times, November 18, 2003

mystique, its fifth pillar that helps support all the rest. Its remarkable accomplishment has been to create among so many of us the illusion that the giant American corporation and citizen democracy go hand and hand.

New Democracy is based on values of citizen empowerment rather than corporate sovereignty. The third corporate regime speaks the rhetoric of citizenship but transforms it into the art of consumerism. The citizen has become a consumer of politics as entertainment, an extension of the passive and privatized culture of the couch potato. Thus the easy rise of Ronald Reagan and now Arnold Schwarzenegger, actors turned politicians, makes sense. Most of us still believe abstractly in citizen participation but we don't believe it can make any difference in a corporate world. The mall is where the action is.

BUILD IT UP

The first pillar of New Democracy is what I call the Active Citizens' Network. It is a vast network of all the civic associations, nonprofits, labor unions, nongovernmental organizations (NGOs), and social movements in America organized to take back control of the country from big money. The network already exists, and is huge, in fact, bigger and more historically rooted in America than in any other country. You are almost certainly part of the network already! But the network lacks the money and political organization of the big transnational firms. Regime change will take place when civil society—meaning you, me, and others in the network—organize ourselves to eclipse the corporations as the dominant force in America. I can see

BUILD THE FIVE PILLARS OF NEW DEMOCRACY

Dominant Institution—Active Citizens' Network
Ordinary citizens get involved in their communities and in Washington, D.C.

Mode of Politics—New Democracy
Ordinary people like you and me actually run the house.

Social Contract—Real Social Security
The tenants get ownership and legal protection.

Foreign Policy—Collective Security
The house helps create a neighborhood association.

Ideology—Citizen Empowerment
The house walks its freedom talk.

your skepticism rising again, but remember, collectively, we are the overwhelming majority.

The political aim of the Active Citizens' Network is to replace corpocracy with New Democracy, an idea really as American as apple pie. I call it new only because there are new hurdles to democracy in an age of global corporations. We as citizens now have to take back control of our businesses, our media, our educational and health systems, and ultimately the Democratic Party and our federal government itself.

Active citizens will seek regime change for very self-interested reasons: our own real social security, the third pillar of New Democracy. I am not just talking here about protecting the Social Security program that FDR put in place during the New Deal. Every regime change requires rewriting the social contract, in this case moving toward a new social order that rewards ordinary citizens like you with health care, education, secure jobs, living wages, and other forms of social well-being. If you ask what will get couch potatoes off their rear ends and into the political sphere, it is the prospect of a better and more secure life for themselves and their families. Won't you fight for your own social security? Won't your neighbors?

Self-interest will also drive the construction of the fourth pillar of the new regime: collective security. We Americans will be safe only when we fight for a world of international cooperation and law, something that presidents from George Washington to Franklin Roosevelt to Dwight Eisenhower all urged as the American way. In a globalized economy, you should know that democracy and safety at home depend on renouncing unilateralism and turning toward cooperation with other nations.

Finally, all this obviously depends on empowerment of ordinary citizens—meaning, again, you. The current regime depends, as just noted, on your passivity and disbelief in the possibility of regime change. Cultural change cannot be legislated but the idea that you and all other citizens have the right and responsibility to be active in governing themselves is what the Constitution is all about.

THE NEW DEMOCRACY PROGRAM

Below I outline a bold New Democracy platform for regime change. It pushes the envelope, like all regime-change agendas. The New Deal ideas of government regulation, powerful labor unions, and Social Security would have looked totally utopian in the late 1920s under the second corporate regime, and they took decades to implement. Some of the ideas here may seem equally unrealistic, and, yes, I know they will have to be implemented in small steps through a long reform process. But they are the recipe for real regime change and they are *not* anti-business: most of them should help business become more efficient as well as more accountable.

"Take the country back from big business and create a new government, of, by, and for the people." This is the preamble tying all the New Democracy proposals together. The American creed is one person, one vote—not one dollar, one vote. Corporations have stolen our government and it is time for you and me to reclaim it.

REWRITE CORPORATE CHARTERS TO ENSURE THAT BUSINESS SERVES THE PUBLIC RATHER THAN VICE VERSA

The idea of corporate charters—the state laws defining corporate rights and obligations—may make your eyes glaze over, but a charter is a corporate constitution and what it says affects *your* freedom, *your* well-being, and *your* happiness. We need to return to the vision of the Founders, who proclaimed that corporations are businesses created by the public to serve the public interest.

James W. Rouse, the founder of The Rouse Company, writes that "Profit is not the legitimate purpose of business. The purpose is to provide a service needed by society."[3] Rouse is a CEO and his idea is identical to that of the Founders. The earliest corporate charters stated that corporations must ensure the public interest and be directly accountable to the citizens' representatives in state legislatures. The new charter today should legally redefine big business as a public entity with three chartered missions:

Serve the public and be accountable to it
Return profit to shareholders
Protect workers, consumers, and other stakeholders,
    including the environment and democracy itself

Although weakened by three corporate regimes, the concept of a public mission for the corporation still resonates in American law. Broadcast companies today, since they operate on public airwaves, are expected to abide by legal public interest standards requiring fair access, community programming, transparency in financial sponsorship, diversity of ownership, and other major considerations.[4] Similar public interest standards should be written and enforced for all big business, and enshrined in their charters.

Rewriting charters is not as radical as it sounds. Thirty-one states have already changed their corporate chartering legislation to permit directors to make decisions that benefit all stakeholders, a first step on the road we need to take to New Democracy. Such chartering reform requires two other major steps.

Require directors to take into account the interests of
    the public at large as well as stakeholders such as
    workers.

SAVING DEMOCRACY

In the new global economy, we need charters to establish enforceable codes of conduct at the global and
national as well as state levels. We should retain state
charters, but also have limited provisions within federal and U.N. authority governing corporations at
higher levels. Otherwise, corporations will simply exit
to other states or countries where they can abuse the
public interest as they please!

STRIP CORPORATIONS OF CONSTITUTIONAL RIGHTS THAT BELONG ONLY TO FLESH-AND-BLOOD CITIZENS

Regime change requires a conversation about fundamen-
tals: in this case, the Constitution of the United States.
Thomas Jefferson would roll over in his grave if he knew
that presidents are appointing judges who are awarding
corporations protections under the Bill of Rights, including the First, Fourth, Fifth, Sixth, Seventh, and Fourteenth Amendments.

You can have a constitution that protects real citizens or
a constitution that protects corporations, but not both. This
is a point that the Founders understood well, and explains
why the word "corporation" never appears in the Constitution and why corporations were never awarded constitutional protections until the robber barons stacked the Supreme Court in the first corporate regime.

Here's what we have to do—and urgently! We need to
reassert—by amending the Constitution, or securing re-
versals of earlier Court decisions—that corporations are
not legal persons protected under the Bill of Rights. Most

important, they do not have First Amendment protections to give political contributions. As a start, the Supreme Court has affirmed as recently as its 2003 upholding of the McCain-Feingold Act for campaign finance reform that corporations do not have rights to unlimited donations. More dramatic Court restrictions need to follow, including innovative state provisions for "clean money" campaigns, as in Arizona and Maine, that give candidates the right to opt for public funding, which should be the foundation of all national campaigns. There is nothing more important to New Democracy than campaign finance reform that leads toward complete public financing of campaigns, as is the case in most European societies.

Business enterprises deserve clear legally enforceable rights, but not those in the Bill of Rights intended to protect live citizens like you and me. An example close to home: District Court Edward Nottingham recently threw out the Do Not Call Registry that allowed individuals to screen out unwanted phone solicitations because it allegedly violated corporate rights to free speech. Only when corporations are denied constitutional protection under the First Amendment can we enjoy uninterrupted dinners and our own rights to privacy. Millions of Americans realize this and are working for complete public financing of campaigns; scores of active citizens' groups seek to abolish corporate personhood in their own states.[5]

GET CORPORATIONS OUT OF POLITICS FOR GOOD

Corporations larger than most countries snuff out democracy, and we need to restrain them with strong regulations and every creative initiative that you can think of. I would start with the following political changes:

> In addition to public financing of campaigns, work on
> every other campaign reform initiative that drains
> the swamp of corporate money in Washington.
> Curb corporate lobbying and restrict the right of
> industries to draft laws governing themselves.
> Outlaw use of shareholder funds for political causes.
> Prevent former high-level politicians from becoming
> business lobbyists for at least ten years.
> Prevent former or present high-level corporate officers
> from serving on commissions regulating their own
> industries.
> Criminalize threats by corporate officials to influence
> employees' votes.
> Rescind the "investor rights" clauses of trade agreements,
> which allow foreign corporations to sue governments
> for passing labor or environmental laws.
> Penalize corporations that explicitly extort political con-
> cessions by threatening to leave a state or country.
> Limit corporate subsidies that can be poured back into
> influencing votes in Washington.

We also need to rewire the corporation to make it more attuned to public concerns. We can start breaking up some of the world's biggest companies like Wal-Mart, which is bigger than 161 countries. We need an antitrust policy that busts trusts whose very size makes them dangerous for democracy.

We also must make big business more participative and democratic, both to make it more efficient and to align its interests with the public good. More than ten thousand companies have employee stock-ownership plans, and workers in many of the biggest companies already have enough company stock in their pension funds to be a pivotal bloc. Workers in Germany, even if they own no stock, are guaranteed 50 percent of the seats on their company's board because they are viewed as the key stakeholders. In the United States, we need a corporate board that is one-third workers, one-third shareholders, and one-third public representatives. This make-up would help align the corporation's politics with the common good, and since it would give workers a stake in the company, it would also increase loyalty, efficiency, and productivity.

PASS LAWS TO PREVENT CORPORATIONS FROM OWNING AND RUNNING SCHOOLS, HEALTH CARE FACILITIES, MILITARY SERVICES, AND THE MASS MEDIA

Democracy and active citizenship require that public services remain public. This is a very simple idea, consistent with the original U.S. constitutional framework, but it has been severely eroded over the course of three corporate regimes.

Privatizing everything from education to medical care to prisons leaves a shriveled public sector and transfers the most important powers of the people from government to corporations. The business of the people must reside where the Constitution requires, in civil society and the hallowed halls of democratic government. Corporations must be constitutionally prevented from owning and running the sources of information on which democracy depends, especially the mass media and the educational system.

Regime change is emerging as a battle between "privateers," who seek to put a "for sale" sign on anything profitable, and "public guardians," the active citizens who are trying to preserve the vital public sector essential to democracy. The battle to preserve a vital public media has already become intense, as a few giant corporations—such as Fox, AOL–Time Warner, and Clear Channel—use their influence on the FCC to privatize and deregulate the media further, allowing conglomerates to monopolize media markets in your town and across the planet. As I noted in Chapter 7, when MoveOn launched a petition campaign to reverse the FCC edict, hundreds of thousands of grassroots citizens sent e-mails and made phone calls to Washington, forcing the Senate to block the FCC ruling. This was the start of a battle for control of the media that will spread to ownership of the schools, the health care system, and the government itself.

PUT AN END TO CORPORATE GLOBALIZATION IN A GLOBAL ECONOMY REGULATED BY GLOBAL CITIZENS

One reader told me, "Yeah, fine, but U.S. corporations can simply move their headquarters to another country if they fear that a regime change here will undermine their ability to maximize profits or dominate Washington." She is right.

We, the citizens, can prevent this only through global regulation of international investment and to keep giant companies from terrorizing poor (and rich) countries with constant threats to leave. Here's how to help stop this:

Tax on short-term, speculative global investment.
Give favorable tax treatment to long-term global investors.
Write global corporate charters with codes of conduct enforceable by the United Nations and regional authorities, as well as by national governments.
Adopt global labor and environmental protections at the heart of trade treaties.
Offer debt relief to empower poor nations.
Create democratically structured new global trade and financing authorities.

If global companies know that they will have to respect labor and the environment wherever they go; that they will have to answer to the public in every country; that they are required by a global charter to be accountable to the workers in every free-trade zone; that they will have to pay taxes in every host country to ensure that they contribute to social development; and that they will face global consumer and judicial sanctions if they abuse the public trust, we will know we have begun to achieve a global regime change that sustains regime change at home.

The WTO, IMF, and World Bank are the corporate regime's global handmaidens, and regime change requires that we trade them in for more democratic and transparent entities protecting workers and the environment in both rich and poor nations. The money changers in the temple are now global, and we can have no regime change at home without planetary regime change that puts people before profit and global citizens' networks at the helm of the global economy. This means that global NGOs, global social movements, and democratic states will replace global corporations as the stewards of the global economy.

CHANGE THE MORAL VALUES CONVERSATION AND PASS LAWS TO GUARANTEE AMERICANS FOOD, HOUSING, MEDICAL CARE, EDUCATION, JOBS, AND A LIVING WAGE

Moral values are at the center of every regime. In this regime, the core values crisis stems from corporate morality that is leading money to be valued over the most basic human needs—and over human life itself. Regime change requires that the debate about morality be broadened from issues of abortion and other hot-button items on the Evangelical Christian agenda to the central moral issues of social justice and human rights. Corporate morality is stripping ordinary Americans of medical care, good education, and a living wage, and creating violence and wars that violate our own moral codes and Constitution.

You have a moral, human, and legal right to real social security, according to the U.N. 1948 Declaration of Human Rights, which the United States helped draft and signed. Only the manipulations of the current regime have made these social rights seem like socialism, when in fact they are embraced by market societies all over the world and simply ensure that Americans will get the decent education, health care, affordable housing, and secure retirement that Franklin D. Roosevelt saw as the American birthright.

We must guarantee—as a fulfillment of our most basic values—that every child can live free of poverty and get a good education and health care, that every worker is entitled to a living wage, and that you and every other citizen are assured health care and retirement security. Americans increasingly favor universal health care, a barometer of the desire of Americans for real social security.

When computer programmers as well as auto workers are seeing their jobs disappear overseas, Americans need a regime change guaranteeing them the means to a livelihood. *Full employment was the core of the moral philosophy and social security policy of the New Deal, and in the global economy we need it more than ever if we are to live up to our most important values.* Living up to our moral principles means putting unemployed, underemployed, outsourced, and temped Americans to work building schools, clinics, or roads and serving old people, children, and other needy or abandoned citizens. FDR, Lyndon Johnson, and even Richard Nixon argued for a minimum income and work for all.

The United Nations has affirmed that everyone has a basic human right to a job that pays a living wage. The U.N. Declaration of Human Rights declares that "Everyone who works has the right to just and favourable remuneration ensuring for himself [*sic*] and his [*sic*] family an existence worthy of human dignity."[6] In 1891, Pope Leo XIII, in his famed encyclical on "the rights of labor," proclaimed the right of the worker to a job with dignity and a living wage, a moral and legal principle that has been reaffirmed by the Catholic Church ever since.[7] *It is time that America caught up with the United Nations and the pope.*

RENOUNCE EMPIRE, END UNILATERAL WARS, AND EMBRACE COLLECTIVE SECURITY

The Iraqi debacle and the disastrous impact of the current regime's effort to dominate the world should set the nation on a new foreign policy course. As conservative politician and writer Pat Buchanan has proclaimed, we were founded as "a Republic, not an Empire."[8] Our Constitution and democratic spirit, and perhaps the survival of the world, require that we stay that way.

We should abandon our imperial foreign policy and embrace the United Nations that we helped build. We must now work with our allies to build a robust system of international law and multilateral peacekeeping, signing on to the International Criminal Court, nonproliferation and arms agreements, and funding for a permanent U.N. peacekeeping constabulary. Such multilateralism is necessary to keep the world from blowing itself up, to end our long sponsorship of state terrorist regimes, to end anti-Americanism, and to preserve our own democracy.

When we renounce empire, we can massively reduce U.S. spending on nuclear and conventional weapons. We can also withdraw most U.S. forces from Europe and other parts of the world, close U.S. bases abroad, and commit our forces mainly to international and regional peacekeeping efforts under U.N. authority. By downsizing the military, we can pay down our looming debt and reinvest in social security at home. The conversion from a war economy to a peaceful one should have begun right after World War II, or certainly after the Cold War, but it is not too late. It will help remedy the economic and moral damage that U.S. warrior politics has caused to the rest of the world and to ourselves.

The U.S. "war on terrorism" will be no more effective than its war on drugs. Terrorists have been redefined as anyone opposing U.S. interests, and our own war on terrorism ignores the state terrorist regimes that we support, including Saddam Hussein's when he was our ally. When defined properly as those who use violence against civilians for political causes, terrorists can best be dealt with by dealing with legitimate political grievances. Terrorists who refuse political negotiation or political solutions can be tracked and apprehended mainly through the cooperation of human intelligence operatives in the countries where they operate. The only way to keep us and our communities safe is multilateral diplomatic partnership, led by the United Nations and regional security networks, to track the funding, share the intelligence, and seek resolution to the political crises that give rise to terrorism.

END OUR RUSH TO 1984 AND PRESERVE OUR CIVIL LIBERTIES

The war on terrorism is aimed as much at undermining civil liberties and active citizens as it is at stopping terrorists. It is the umbrella for the new surveillance state, which not only suspends constitutional rights for any terrorist "suspect," but seeks to collect information on you by snooping on emails, snail mail, course curricula, credit cards, and book-borrowing from libraries, and by installing video cameras in public and private space. Civil liberties are at the heart of active citizenship, and they are the essential foundation of both citizen empowerment and New Democracy.

The Patriot Act should be repealed and its sequel, "Son of Patriot," should be denounced, making clear that these acts are the prelude to an Orwellian future at home as well as overseas. In times of crisis, we need to extend rather than slash and burn our constitutional freedoms by embracing the new constitutional protections of the International Criminal Court and many U.N. covenants on the rights of workers, children, women, and immigrants. You might be next on the regime's list.

ANSWERS TO YOUR HARD-NOSED QUESTIONS

Parts of this list are appealing, but what are the trade-offs? Can these changes ever be achieved in America? They cannot, in fact, be achieved in the current regime, and it will take regime change based on a major political realignment to make it happen over many years. Below, I look at tough questions you may have about the practicality, trade-offs, and costs of this vision.

Q. HOW CAN YOU ARGUE FOR CORPORATE ABOLITIONISM WHEN CORPORATIONS HAVE PRODUCED THE GREATEST PROSPERITY IN HISTORY?

A: Corporations have undoubtedly contributed to progress by amassing the vast amount of capital required for innovation and production in capital-intensive industries. They have also created a cheap consumer culture that is the envy of the planet. Corporations are the symbols of American power and wealth.

But this corporate triumph, as I have shown, derives largely from corporations' success using *your* taxpayer money and *your* government to *their* own ends. Your government created the limited liability that allows corporations to concentrate vast capital with minimal risk, and it pays for the huge, public research and development effort that generates basic discoveries. Your government educates the corporate labor force, creates the physical infrastructure, discourages unionism, shapes the macroeconomic policies that stabilize the inherently cyclical instability of the market, and pays for the environmental, social, and human costs that corporations acting as cold cash registers leave in their wake. *We have to create a business system that does not drain the federal treasury, steal from the poor, and ravage the social order to promote the economy.*

Corporations are huge command systems, a bit like the failed communist states or the hierarchies of the medieval church, that concentrate power and wealth among unaccountable leaders. They win monopolies through price gouging, political favors, collusive alliances, and other anti-competitive strategies that erode efficiency. They discourage worker productivity not only by making workers disposable, but also by legally disenfranchising them; only shareholders have legal claims on corporate profit or control.

By breaking up the biggest monopolies and rewriting the charter to empower workers and other stakeholders, we create a more open, inclusive, entrepreneurial, and accountable organization whose DNA is now socially wired.

That wiring cuts workers into governance and thereby increases loyalty and productivity, and it reduces the social and political costs of a corrupt inner circle that cannot run the organization profitably without looting its own workers and the rest of society.

We need to retain the parts of the business order that yield economic efficiency and innovation, while changing the anticompetitive, hierarchical, and deeply politicized corporate elements that are destructive for the economy as well as for democracy and society. Most jobs are generated in the small and midsize business sector where genuine entrepreneurship still exists. New Democracy would encourage these forms of business and create more of them by encouraging worker-owned firms and other local or democratic businesses.

Q: AREN'T YOU REALLY A NEW DEALER IN DISGUISE? ISN'T THIS AN OLD SET OF IDEAS FOR THE TWENTIETH CENTURY RATHER THAN A NEW VISION FOR THE TWENTY-FIRST CENTURY?

A: My father was a New Deal economist and it's true that I have much admiration for what FDR and the New Dealers achieved. The New Deal's values of community and social justice, and its defense of a strong labor movement and true social security for the anxious class are still vital for the twenty-first century. The New Deal was the most popular and best deal for ordinary Americans.

But I am not proposing a return to the New Deal. For one thing, it was focused too much on government. Although the twenty-first century will require activist but streamlined government, New Democracy is not a big government agenda, and its core principle is citizen activism. Since the New Deal, we have seen the dangers of a large government that almost always ends up working for big business rather than ordinary Americans. We need an Active Citizens' Network to ensure that government is lean, efficient, and accountable to the people rather than the corporations.

The New Deal depended too much on experts and professionals. This laid the groundwork for the elitism that plagues the Democratic Party today and supports the pseudopopulism of the current regime. New Democracy favors the populist emphasis on grassroots participation, and that is why its foundational pillar is the Active Citizens' Network, not government. The Citizens' Network will work for more participatory institutions—from parent-driven schools and patient-friendly hospitals to democratically structured businesses in which ordinary workers play a vital decision-making role. The political parties and government itself will have to be debureaucratized and governed according to the same participatory principles.

Q: YOU STILL SEEM TO BE MOVING LEFT RATHER THAN BACK TO THE CENTER, WHICH IS THE ONLY WAY THE DEMOCRATS CAN WIN AND CHANGE THE COUNTRY. ISN'T THIS A PRESCRIPTION FOR FAILURE THAT WILL SEND INDEPENDENTS AND MODERATES RACING TO THE REPUBLICAN PARTY?

A: The Republicans have taken the opposite of a centrist tack for the last forty years. Lose or win, they kept moving to the right. As a Democrat, whenever you start thinking "move to the center, move to the center," think about the Republicans. In 2000, they could have chosen John McCain, a centrist, over George W. Bush. They chose the far more conservative candidate and played to their right-wing Evangelical base. It worked for them and it just keeps working, expanding their base and even attracting Independents who appreciate conviction.

When you suggest moving to the center, I say the Democrats are already there. Remember that Bill Clinton acknowledged that he was governing like an Eisenhower Republican, and both Al Gore and John Kerry essentially ran as close to the stripe in the center of the road as Clinton governed. The Democrats have been moving to the center for the last thirty years, and look where it has gotten them.

The "move to the center" message reflects the hegemony of the Election Trap. Yes, in a two-party system, there is plausibility to moving toward the center if your goal is simply winning the next election. But if your goal is changing the country according to your principles, then the move to the center is folly, pure capitulation to the Election Trap. You'll abandon your principles and probably lose the next election because your only real goal is winning. You'll shrink your base, fail to win over nonvoters, and lose Independents or conservatives who might be afraid of the far right or fascism.

New Democracy defies traditional labels. The Populists were both conservative and radical. Democracy has become the rallying cry of the neoconservatives as well as the left. Ironically, as George W. Bush has made democracy the rhetorical centerpiece of his own Administration, he is opening up space for a discussion of what democracy is all about. If we want to advance democracy all over the world, we need to dismantle our own Empire and make good on our own democratic promise at home. New Democracy is a program to get there.

Q: I STILL FEEL THAT YOUR AGENDA HAS A "PIE IN THE SKY" FEELING. WHAT MAKES YOU BELIEVE THAT THIS SEA-CHANGE IN AMERICA IS POSSIBLE?

A: Can this really happen in America? *Can a nation of couch potatoes become active citizens?* We may need the change, you think, and you may want to move beyond the Election Trap, but Americans are too brainwashed, apathetic, or powerless to get up from the couch.

I sometimes feel discouraged myself, despairing about a country whose citizens seem so vulnerable to the seductions of the mall and the manipulations of fear and patriotism from on high. Even though millions of people protested the war in Iraq, most Americans are not in an activist frame of mind. Many are working too hard or watching too many sitcoms to think about politics, let alone to try to make big social change. Moreover, every regime tries to drum into our heads that things cannot be different, and this one has the electronic media and the big money to indoctrinate the population more than any previous one. Evangelical or other forms of right-wing populism could take the country down the road to American fascism.

But while New Democracy is far from inevitable, it *is* possible. In fact, the prospects for hope are far stronger than you might think. Here's why:

HISTORY. None of us can read the future, but reliable clues come from our past. As I emphasized earlier, all of our earlier corporate regimes have succumbed to reform movements that created regime change and a better America. If you don't believe regime change is possible now, you are taking the position that history will not repeat itself. This would itself be a first in history! All the historical evidence suggests that regimes are transient; in fact, most do not last more than thirty years. This one already is twenty-five years old and it is showing its age. History tells me that change, if not imminent, is blowing in the wind.

SELF-INTEREST: Americans now work, on average, a month longer than Europeans and get a lower wage and far fewer social benefits. Put simply, most Americans need regime change for selfish reasons. It will improve their job security, their social security, and their quality of life. As the government keeps shoveling pots of money to the wealthy, and the gap between the very rich and everyone else keeps growing, self-interest will lead the majority of Americans to see that this really is a regime of, by, and for corporations.

THE PEOPLE'S HISTORY: Grassroots movements for democracy and human rights are in the American bloodstream. All you have to do is read Howard Zinn's *A People's History of the United States* to see that this has always been a country of social movements. In fact, you could argue that no country has ever had as many different and powerful social movements as the United States has: abolitionists, suffragists and feminists, civil rights activists, antiwar legions, environmentalists, the labor movement, and the Populists themselves. These movements have always kept the flame of democracy alive in America, and they are very much alive today, more active now and more technologically empowered than probably at any earlier time in history. If you don't believe me, listen to such movement stalwarts as Studs Terkel, Pete Seeger, Noam Chomsky, and Zinn himself, who say the same thing.

TRADITION: The changes I propose sound radical, but they really have a conservative foundation: The Declaration of Independence and the Constitution. We need regime change not to undermine the American creed of democracy but to preserve it, particularly given the drift of the regime toward fascism lite. In other words, the regime is out of step with American tradition and regime change is necessary to restore basic American truths. What's radical and extremist is not New Democracy but the sham democracy of the current regime. Regime change is the conservative thing to do today.

THE BIG TENT: Precisely because the regime is violating Americans' own heritage of democracy, New Democracy can appeal to Americans across the political spectrum. Regime change always seems radical, thus creating a "pie in the sky" feeling before it happens, but today, in the light of Bush's extremism, it is also a conservative impulse. Regime change is something that will increasingly attract Independent and Republican Americans as well as Democrats and progressives.

A: This is a very reasonable question, given the strength of the "me, me, me" culture in America today. But there has always been a strong community-oriented bent in the United States, right alongside the individualism. We are individualistic, but we are also activists and a nation of joiners.

Ironically, one of the most powerful examples of this is in the red states today, among conservative activists. The Evangelical churches have helped drive one of the most powerful grassroots movements, rooted in local neighborhoods and a strong sense of moral community. While they are currently supporting the current regime, we have seen that in earlier historical eras, these same red states relied on their churches and local community spirit to pursue Populist and Progressive regime change. They are beginning to do so again, as I show below. Urban America has also historically seen strong neighborhood and labor movements that gave rise to the New Deal. Yes, this was in the past, but individualistic values were also very powerful just before the New Deal in the 1920s. The individualism gave way very quickly to a vision of social solidarity. This could happen again today.

Try a thought experiment. First, imagine the kind of society you would most like to live in. Would it not be a society with strong communities and a powerful drive for social justice? Try another experiment: imagine a "good society" while you are in a group of friends or colleagues.

Doesn't that also produce images of a much more humane, community-oriented, and more democratic society than the current regime? Then, spend some time in the group imagining how you can begin creating that kind of society now, starting in your own life and community. Such experiments might give you new hope for the possibility of real social change—and your own *very* important role in making it happen.

Groups in communities all over the country are doing exactly this, showing that people can shed their individualism to work together against hidden power in their own communities. Think of the thousands of community groups, some listed in Appendix II, that are organizing their neighborhoods or communities to keep out a Wal-Mart, pass a city council ordinance that declares corporations are not legal persons in their communities, or actually banning corporations from their town. The night that I was giving a book reading in 2004 in Berkeley, California, members of the Berkeley City Council passed a resolution declaring their unanimous support for an amendment to the United States Constitution that would declare corporations are not legal persons and are not entitled to corporate constitutional rights.

Some of the most exciting communities are in red areas, like the townships in rural Pennsylvania that in 1998 mounted what has become one of the most innovative populist campaigns of the new century.[9] These small, mostly Republican communities mobilized themselves when threatened by corporate assaults on their environment and economy. Factory hog farms promised to decimate small family farms and cause extensive pollution to the water and air. Land-applied sewage sludge, brought in from distant cities and bearing any combination of 800,000 toxic contaminants, had already left two teenagers dead from massive infection due to resistant bacteria from hospital waste.

Working with attorney Thomas Linzey, who collaborates with Richard Grossman, the co-founder of the Program on Corporations, Law, and Democracy (POCLAD; see Appendix II), these communities have passed township ordinances declaring that the citizens of the townships have the authority to decide whether offending corporations have the right to operate in their localities. The companies are preparing to fight back, declaring that their constitutional rights are being violated and gathering in backrooms with the legislators they have bought to pass laws against local control.

But the communities are standing firm in the view that it is only flesh-and-blood citizens, not the fictional legal persons called corporations, that have sovereignty. Using community organizing and legal strategies pioneered by Linzey and Grossman,[10] these citizen farmers are courageous, in the best spirit of the American Revolution. Two of the townships, Licking and Porter, challenging over a century of Supreme Court decisions and state and federal law, have even passed ordinances stripping corporations of their constitutional rights in their jurisdictions. Perhaps these Republican farmers are offering the best new lessons about what democracy is all about—and maybe we can challenge hidden power best by listening to them and finding our own creative strategies for reasserting the power of *we the people.*

APPENDIX I

WHAT YOU CAN DO NOW

1. Join one of the social movement groups discussed in this book.
2. Join one of the progressive groups inside the Democratic Party discussed in this book.
3. Start an organization in your town to fight for the change that matters most to you.
4. Educate yourself about hidden power by reading and joining discussion groups and reading a foreign newspaper.
5. Get on your favorite listservs that coordinate action on issues you most care about.
6. Educate others about hidden power by sending them the books and articles and websites that excited you.
7. Get your city council to pass a local ordinance declaring that corporations are not persons in your community.
8. Get your city council to zone out or ban corporations that are harming your community.
9. Read one of the magazines listed in Appendix III.
10. Join one of the organizations listed in Appendix II.

APPENDIX II

ORGANIZATIONS TO JOIN

You can't create regime change alone. But there's hope because there are so many organizations seeking to bring down the old pillars and build new ones. Here are the websites of a few of my favorites, organized by their focus on specific pillars:

I. Organizations on Corporations and the Economy

NATIONAL LABOR COMMITTEE www.nlcnet.org

CENTER FOR DEMOCRACY AND THE CONSTITUTION
www.constitution411.org

COMMUNITY ENVIRONMENTAL LEGAL DEFENSE FUND
www.celdf.org

CENTER FOR STUDY OF RESPONSIVE LAW www.csrl.org

PROGRAM ON CORPORATIONS, LAW, AND DEMOCRACY
www.poclad.org

GLOBAL TRADE WATCH www.tradewatch.org

GLOBAL EXCHANGE www.globalexchange.org

FIFTY YEARS IS ENOUGH www.50years.org

CITIZEN WORKS www.citizenworks.org

THE SIERRA CLUB www.sierraclub.org

II. Organizations on Politics and New Democracy

TOMPAINE.COM www.tompaine.com
PUBLIC CITIZEN www.citizen.org
COMMON CAUSE www.commoncause.org
MOVEON.ORG www.moveon.org
ALLIANCE FOR DEMOCRACY www.thealliancefordemocracy.org
CAMPAIGN FOR AMERICA'S FUTURE www.ourfuture.org
RECLAIM DEMOCRACY www.reclaimdemocracy.org

III. Organizations on Social Security and Social Justice

JOBS WITH JUSTICE www.jwj.org
AFL-CIO www.aflcio.org
UNITARIAN UNIVERSALISTS FOR A JUST ECONOMIC COMMUNITY www.uujec.org
PEOPLE FOR THE AMERICAN WAY www.pfaw.org
UNITED FOR A FAIR ECONOMY www.stw.org
ECONOMIC POLICY INSTITUTE www.epinet.org
CITIZENS FOR TAX JUSTICE www.ctj.org
UNITED STUDENTS AGAINST SWEATSHOPS www.studentsagainstsweatshops.org
TEAM X/SWEATX www.sweatx.net
TRANSAFRICA FORUM www.transafricaforum.org
SERVICE EMPLOYEES INTERNATIONAL UNION (SEIU) www.seiu.org

IV. Organizations on a New Foreign Policy

OXFAM www.oxfamamerica.org
GREENPEACE www.greenpeaceusa.org
INSTITUTE FOR POLICY STUDIES www.ips-dc.org
BOSTON MOBILIZATION www.bostonmobilization.org

AMERICAN FRIENDS SERVICE COMMITTEE www.afsc.org
UNITED FOR PEACE AND JUSTICE www.unitedforpeace.org
**WOMEN'S INTERNATIONAL LEAGUE FOR PEACE
AND JUSTICE** www.wilpf.org

V. Organizations on New Values, Democratic Media, and Citizen Empowerment

CENTER FOR A NEW AMERICAN DREAM www.newdream.org
FAIRNESS AND ACCURACY IN REPORTING www.fair.org
MAINSTREAM MEDIA PROJECT www.mainstream-media.net
GRASSROOTS SOLUTIONS www.grassrootssolutions.com
FREE PRESS www.freepress.net

APPENDIX III

MAGAZINES

Multinational Monitor
The Progressive
Mother Jones
The Utne Reader
In These Times
Tikkun
The American Prospect
The Nation
Z Magazine/Z Net
Corporate Crime Report
Business Ethics
The Progressive Populist
Dissent
Dollars and Sense

NOTES

Introduction

1. See Charles Derber, *Regime Change Begins at Home: Freeing America from Corporate Rule* (San Francisco: Berrett-Koehler, 2004). As noted, the current book is a sequel to my earlier book on regime change and uses the concept of regime that is developed in that work.

2. This quotation from the Progressive Party Platform is cited in Theodore Roosevelt, *An Autobiography* (1912; repr., New York: Da Capo Press, 1998), Appendix B.

3. James Madison, "Monopolies, Perpetuities, Corporations, Ecclesiastical Endowments," unpublished essay in collection of James Madison Papers, reel 26, series 2, volume 8, folio pages 2215–20. Cited online at http://www.sunnetworks.net/ ~ggarman/estaorel.html.

4. The Election Trap is a sign of a perversion of the electoral process and a corruption of the concept of democracy. While I may appear to be critiquing elections, I believe they are a key underpinning of democracy. But the Election Trap is an ideology that falsely equates free elections as the primary mechanism by which democracy operates. Elec-

tions are a central part of "procedural democracy" but they do not ensure "substantive" democracy. That is, they are a necessary democratic procedure but do not ensure that leaders are accountable to ordinary citizens or that citizens ultimately control the direction of the country. The rest of this book will help explain this paradox. See also Charles Derber, *People Before Profit: The New Globalization in an Age of Terror, Big Money, and Economic Crisis* (New York: Picador, 2003), and Derber, *Corporation Nation* (New York: St. Martin's Press, 2000).

5. For a collection of Marx's political and economic writings on this theme, see Karl Marx and Frederick Engels, *The Marx-Engels Reader* (New York: Norton, 1978). See also Karl Marx, *The Communist Manifesto,* reissued ed. (New York: Signet Classics, 1998).

6. On Jefferson's thinking and how it is connected to Madison's ideas, see Adrienne Koch, *Jefferson and Madison: The Great Collaboration* (New York: Oxford University Press, 1950).

7. Bill Gates's Personal Wealth Clock. Posted on http://philip

.greenspun.com/WealthClock. Forbes Fortune 400 put Gates's wealth in 2004 at $48 billion.

8. Joseph Kay, "Forbes List of 400 Richest Americans: Snapshot of a Financial Oligarchy," *Forbes* magazine, September 27, 2004. Posted on http://www.wsws.org/articles/2004/sep2004/forbes27.shtml.

9. For documentation of the concentration of global power and wealth in the top 200 global firms, see Sarah Anderson and John Cavanaugh, *Field Guide to the Global Economy* (New York: New Press, 2000). See also Anderson and Cavanaugh, "Top 200: The Rise of Global Corporate Power," Corporate Watch, Washington, D.C., February 13, 2005, posted on http://www.globalpolicy.org/socecon/tncs/top200.htm.

10. Power, both hidden and visible, has always been wielded, as the great nineteenth-century French social thinker Emile Durkheim wrote, partly by those who assert the reigning moral values and manage the culture and ideology of a nation. If Durkheim were alive today, he would have been among the first to predict that religion and "moral values" would help determine the outcome of elections, and that they would do so in ways that are not always visible or understandable to the people. For a good selection of Durkheim works, see Anthony Giddens, ed., *Emile Durkheim: Selected Writings* (Cambridge, Eng.: Cambridge University Press, 1972). See also Emile Durkheim, *Suicide*, reissued ed. (New York: Free Press, 1997).

11. Thomas Frank, *What's the Matter with Kansas? How Conservatives Won the Heart of America* (New York: Metropolitan Books, 2004).

12. For a good collection of Gramsci's writings on the concept of hegemony and related concepts, see David Forgacs, ed., *The Antonio Gramsci Reader: Selected Writings—1916–1935* (New York: New York University Press, 2000).

13. Antonio Gramsci, *Selections from the Prison Notebooks* (International Publishers, 1971).

14. C. Wright Mills, *The Power Elite* (New York: Oxford University Press, 1956).

15. Following Mills two decades later, William Domhoff pioneered new studies of the evolving power elite. In several best-selling works, Domhoff dived into the hidden worlds of the "Bohemian Grove" and other cloistered institutions and hideaways where increasingly corporatized elites came together and built a coherent political identity and mission. Domhoff named names and pulled back the curtain on hidden places of power. As his work progressed, he moved closer

to the concept that hidden power in American democracy lies not just in elites but in a systematic structure of largely hidden and unaccountable power that I call the corporate regime. See William Domhoff, *Who Rules America?*, updated ed. (New York: McGraw-Hill, 2001).

Chapter 1

1. This box is reprinted from Charles Derber, *Regime Change Begins at Home* (San Francisco: Berrett-Koehler, 2004). As mentioned in the Acknowledgments, this book is a sequel to my earlier book, and I have drawn key concepts and passages from the earlier book to orient new readers. The boxes and several sections in Chapter 2, 3, and 10 of this book are reprinted from *Regime Change*, which offers the first presentation of the regime idea.

2. The concept of relative autonomy has been widely discussed in the social science literature in an effort to understand who controls the state and how much freedom it has to pursue its own, autonomous agenda. For a good review of theories of the state and state autonomy, see Peter Evans, Dietreich Rueschemeyer, and Theda Skocpol, eds., *Bringing the State Back In* (Cambridge, Eng.: Cambridge University Press, 1985).

3. The state's relative autonomy from the monied classes can work to provide a sense of genuine democracy that legitimates the corporate order even further. This concept of relative autonomy giving rise to hegemony is consistent with Antonio Gramsci's theory of how capitalist societies legitimate themselves. See Gramsci, *The Prison Notebooks* (cited in Introduction).

4. The best discussion of the robber barons, including the railroad tycoons, and the social order they built is by Matthew Josephson, *The Robber Barons* (New York: Harvest Books, 1962).

5. President Rutherford B. Hayes, cited in Harvey Wasserman, *Harvey Wasserman's History of the United States* (New York: Harper and Row, 1972).

6. Wasserman, ibid. See also Derber, *Corporation Nation* (cited in Introduction), 19.

7. Josephson, *The Robber Barons,* 359.

8. President Grover Cleveland, cited in Howard Zinn, *A People's History of the United States* (New York: Harper and Row, 1980), 367.

9. Ibid. See also Derber, *Corporation Nation,* Chapter 1.

10. See Derber, *Corporation Nation,* Chapters 6–7.

11. Josephson, *The Robber Barons.*

12. Richard Hofstadter, *The*

Progressive Movement (Englewood Cliffs, N.J.: Prentice Hall, 1963).

13. Historians Charles and Mary Beard and William Appleman Williams offered this interpretation of Manifest Destiny. See Charles A. Beard and Mary R. Beard, *The Rise of American Civilization* (New York: Macmillan, 1920), vol. 2. See also William Appleman Williams, *The Tragedy of American Diplomacy* (New York: Norton 1988). For a synthesis of their works and corporate interpretation of Manifest Destiny promoting market expansion in America itself and outside the country, see Andrew Bacevich, *American Empire* (Cambridge, Mass.: Harvard University Press, 2002), Chapter 1.

14. John D. Rockefeller, cited in Derber, *Corporation Nation*, 27.

15. Bill Clinton, cited in James Fallows, "A Talk With Bill Clinton," *Atlantic Monthly*, October 1996, 20–26, quotation on 22.

16. One of the most prominent analysts developing this case is Kevin Phillips. See Phillips, *The Politics of Rich and Poor* (New York: Harper Collins, 1991). See also Phillips, *Wealth and Democracy: A Political History of the American Rich* (New York: Broadway, 2003). See also Derber, *Corporation Nation*, Chapter 1.

17. Cited in Wasserman, *History of the United States*, 74, 77.

18. The literature on the Populists and related Gilded Age movements is extensive (see Chapter 6). The best book on the radical anti-corporate and democratic spirit of the Populists is Lawrence Goodwyn, *The Populist Moment* (New York: Oxford University Press, 1978). For a far more critical and still controversial perspective that describes anti-Semitism, racism, anti-intellectualism, and xenophobia as populist failures, see Richard Hofstadter, *The Age of Reform* (New York: Vintage, 1960).

19. Martin J. Sklar, *The Corporate Reconstruction of American Capitalism: 1890–1916* (Cambridge, Eng.: Cambridge University Press, 1995), 203ff.

20. Gabriel Kolko, *The Triumph of Conservatism* (New York: Free Press, 1963).

21. Henry Davison, cited in Gabriel Kolko, *Main Currents in Modern American History* (New York: Pantheon, 1984), 13.

22. See Derber, *Corporation Nation*, Chapter 8.

23. The work of Sinclair and Steffens best symbolizes the muckraking zeitgeist of the Progressive era. See Upton Sinclair, *The Jungle*, new ed. (1905; repr., New York: Sharp Press, 2003); and Lincoln Steffens, *The Shame of the*

Cities (1904; repr., New York: Dover Books, 2004).

24. See Robert Justin Goldstein, *Political Repression in Modern America* (Champaign-Urbana: University of Illinois Press, 2001), for one account of this era. See also Howard Zinn, *People's History of the United States,* Chapter 14, for a detailed account of the 1917 Espionage Act and its use as a brutal tool to silence antiwar dissent.

25. I am grateful to Yale Magrass for his insights in linking Progressive antiwar repression and imperialism with the isolationist Republican success after the war in creating a new corporate regime at home.

26. See the discussion of Hooverism and corporate self-government in William E. Leuchtenburg, *Franklin D. Roosevelt and the New Deal* (New York: Harper Torchbooks, 1963), Chapter 1.

27. Ibid.

28. See Ted Nace, *Gangs of America* (San Francisco: Berrett-Koehler, 2003), 125. I am grateful to Nace for his personal communications regarding progressive regime repression and the need for a nuanced presentation of the Progressive regime and its complex relation to corporate power.

29. Stewart Ewen, *Captains of Consciousness: Advertising and the Social Roots of the Consumer*

Culture (New York: Basic Books, 2001).

30. This notion of consumerism as a means of mitigating worker alienation with consumerism's rewards is highlighted in Ewen, ibid.

31. I have learned about Plan America from Elly Leary, a United Auto Workers official and labor historian, in personal conversations and from unpublished drafts of her work on the history of the labor movement.

32. John Kenneth Galbraith, *American Capitalism: The Concept of Countervailing Power* (Boston: Houghton Mifflin, 1951).

33. Leuchtenburg, *Franklin D. Roosevelt and the New Deal,* 154ff.

34. See Milton Derber, *The American Idea of Industrial Democracy, 1865–1965* (Champaign-Urbana: University of Illinois Press, 1970), 302ff.

35. Ibid.

36. For a discussion of the role of different corporate sectors in the New Deal, and an extended treatment of retail and finance, see Yale Magrass, *Thus Spake the Moguls* (Cambridge, Mass.: Schenckman Publishers, 1982).

37. See the discussion in Derber, *People Before Profit* (cited in Introduction).

38. I am grateful to Yale Magrass for suggesting the importance in the New Deal of the evo-

lution from "social Keynesianism," pump-priming by domestic spending, to "military Keynesianism," reliance on Pentagon spending in World War II and afterward.

39. See Robert Lekachman, *The Age of Keynes* (New York: Random House, 1966), for a discussion of the details of the shifting financial priorities of the New Deal during and after World War II. He shows an overwhelming shift from social to military spending in the two phases of the New Deal era, with spending on the military boosting overall government spending to as much as five times in the five years after the war compared to the first five years of the regime.

40. See Seymour Melman, *The Permanent War Economy* (New York: Simon and Schuster, 1983).

Chapter 2

1. Citigroup, Inc., Annual Financials, Hooveronline. www.hoovers.com/citigroup/ —ID__58365—/free-co-fin-annual.xhtml.

2. Stan Cox, "Wal-Mart Gets Greedy," AlterNet, October 28, 2003. Posted at http://www .alternet.org/story.html? StoryID=17060.

3. Anderson and Cavanaugh, *Field Guide to the Global Economy* (cited in Introduction), 68.

4. This global theme has been developed by Noam Chomsky. Most recently, on global control, see Noam Chomsky, *Hegemony or Survival* (New York: Broadway, 2004). For the corporate roots, see also Chomsky, *Deterring Democracy* (New York: Hill and Wang, 1992).

5. Conference Board, cited in Leslie Sklair, *The Transnational Capitalist Class* (Oxford: Blackwell, 2001), 19.

6. This distinction is made by Sklair, *The Transnational Capitalist Class*.

7. Cited in ibid., 50.

8. For a discussion of exit power in globalization, see Derber, *People Before Profit* (cited in Introduction).

9. Ibid.

10. Wall Street Journal Market Data Group, August 31, 2004.

11. *Forbes* magazine calculates one of the most comprehensive rankings of major corporations, by assets, market value, profits, number of employees, etc. As of this writing, the latest data are available from 2003. These rankings are posted at the site: http://www.forbes.com/lists/results .jhtml?passListId=38&passYear= 2003&passListType=Company& searchParameter1=&search Parameter.

12. See Chapter 1 and Wasserman, *History of the United States* (cited in Chapter 1).

13. Bennett Harrison, *Lean and Mean: The Changing Face of Corporate Power in the Age of Flexibility* (New York: Basic Books, 1994).

14. Sklair, *The Transnational Capitalist Class.*

15. Ibid., 21.

16. For the official biographies of the Bush Administration cabinet, which include the corporate histories of cabinet officials, go online to http://usinfo.state.gov/usa/infousa/politics/biograph.htm.

17. Eric Schlosser, "The Cow Jumped over the USDA," *New York Times,* January 2, 2004.

18. For extensive documentation of these corporatized political trends, see Lee Drutman and Charlie Cracy, *The People's Business* (San Francisco: Berrett-Koehler, 2004).

19. The profitability of the pharmaceutial industry is well documented. See the report by the Minnesota Attorney General's Office, "Follow the Money," September 30, 2003, posted at http://www.ag.state.mn.us. For an overview of trends in health care costs and pharmaceutical profits compiled by the Democratic National Party, which refers the reader to more detailed research by government investigators and academic researchers, go to the website at http://democrats.org/specialreports/healthcare_costs.

20. Data on the Medicare Overhaul bill and pharmaceutical spending can be found at the website of the Center for Responsive Politics, from figures compiled by Congressman Sherrod Brown (D, Ohio) at his office, and from the following posting of the watchdog group FAIR (Fairness and Accuracy in Reporting): http://www.fair.org/activism/medicare-networks.html.

21. Robert McIntyre, "Congress Passes $210 Billion in New Corporate Tax Breaks" (newsletter), Washington, D.C., Citizens for Tax Justice, October 13, 2004. This report, along with others from McIntyre and Citizens for Tax Justice, offers extensive details on corporate tax benefits delivered by the Bush Administration.

22. See Donald L. Bartlett and James B. Steele, *America: Who Really Pays the Taxes?* (New York: Simon and Schuster, 1994), 140.

23. Chuck Collins and Felice Yeskel, *Economic Apartheid in America* (New York: New Press, 2000), 100–102.

24. Ibid. For the data on the changing new corporate tax burden, see McIntyre, "Congress Passes $210 Billion in New Corporate Tax Breaks."

25. Ted Nace, *Gangs of America* (cited in Chapter 1), 167.

26. Ibid., 169ff.

27. William Bridges, "The End of the Job," *Fortune,* September

19, 1994, 62–74, quotation on 62. See also William Bridges, *Jobshift* (Boston: Addison Wesley, 1994).

28. Jeremy Brecher and Tim Costello, *Global Village or Global Pillage* (Boston: South End Press, 1998).

29. This "race to the bottom" is well documented in Brecher and Costello, ibid.

30. See Charles Derber, *The Wilding of America*, 1st ed. (New York: St. Martin's, 1996).

31. Cited in Derber, *The Wilding of America*, 3rd ed. (New York: W. H. Freeman, 2003), 93–94.

32. See John B. Williamson, "A Critique of the Case for Privatizing Social Security," *The Gerontologist* 37 (5): 561–571.

33. Andrew Bacevich, *American Empire* (cited in Chapter 1). Chalmers Johnson, *Sorrows of Empire* (New York: Metropolitan Books, 2004).

34. See Bacevich, *American Empire,* especially Chapter 1 and his discussion of the work of Charles Beard and William Appleman Williams.

35. John Perkins, *Confessions of an Economic Hit Man* (San Francisco: Berrett-Koehler, 2004).

36. The division between the Southwestern-based military and oil sectors vs. the Eastern financial and service sectors has been discussed by a growing number of authors since the very beginning of the regime. It is getting increasing

attention under Bush II, who has accelerated the division.

37. William A. Galston, "Perils of Pre-Emptive War," *The American Prospect* 13(17), September 23, 2002.

38. Richard Falk, "The New Bush Doctrine," *The Nation,* July 15, 2002.

39. For the new "free market" Iraqi economic system imposed by Paul Bremer before his departure as U.S. overseer, see Derber, *Regime Change Begins at Home,* Chapter 6.

40. Derber, *Corporation Nation,* Chapters 10 and 13.

Chapter 3

1. Thomas Kuhn, *The Structure of Scientific Revolutions* (Chicago: University of Chicago Press, 1996).

2. Ibid.

3. See Rick Pearlstein, *Before the Storm: Barry Goldwater and the Unmaking of the American Consensus* (New York: Hill and Wang, 2003), for a very similar analysis of Goldwater's impact on catalyzing the conservative movement.

4. For a summary and assessment of these legislative acts, see Milton Derber, *The American Idea of Industrial Democracy* (cited in Chapter 1), especially Chapter 11.

5. Ted Nace, personal communication to the author, 2003.

6. Ibid.

7. I rely heavily on Ted Nace, *Gangs of America* (cited in Chapter 1), for this account of the corporate movement for regime change that he calls the "revolt of the bosses."

8. Cited in ibid., 140.

9. Ibid., 143ff.

10. Cited in ibid., 142.

11. Ibid., 142.

12. For an entertaining account of the rise of the New Right, by an insider who eventually rejected the movement, see Michael Lind, *Up from Conservatism* (New York: Free Press, 1997). See also Robert Liebman, ed., *The New Christian Right* (New York: Aldine de Gruyter, 1983).

13. Proceedings of the Thirty-Fifth Annual Meeting of the National Association of Manufacturers, New York, October 6–9, 1930, 14–15.

14. Washington *News,* July 30, 1932. For a graphic, full account of the Veteran Bonus protest and movement, see Leuchtenburg, *Franklin D. Roosevelt and the New Deal* (cited in Chapter 1).

15. Leuchtenberg, *Franklin D. Roosevelt and the New Deal,* 24.

16. Ibid.

17. Theodore Salutos and John D. Hicks, *Agricultural Discontent in the Middle West: 1900–1939* (Madison: University of Wisconsin Press, 1951).

18. Leuchtenburg, *Franklin D. Roosevelt and the New Deal,* 25.

19. Letter of Spreckels to Franklin Hicborn, June 14, 1932, cited in ibid.

20. Ibid., 61.

21. Ibid. See also Milton Derber, *The American Idea of Industrial Democracy,* especially Chapter 11.

22. For documentation and further elaboration of these actions, see ibid., 111ff.

23. Ibid., 299.

24. Ibid., 301.

25. For descriptions of the Wagner and Fair Labor acts, see the classic work by Milton Derber and Edwin Young, eds., *Labor and the New Deal* (New York: Da Capo Press, 1972).

26. See Alan Wolfe, *Rise and Fall of the Soviet Threat* (Boston: South End Press, 1980), for a discussion of how domestic credibility issues shaped U.S. politics during the Cold War.

27. Gramsci, *Prison Notebooks* (cited in Introduction).

28. See Goodwyn, *The Populist Moment* (cited in Chapter 1).

29. Leuchtenburg, *Franklin D. Roosevelt and the New Deal.*

Chapter 4

1. The contradictions that lead to cracks in the regime are related

to underlying contradictions in capitalism described by Marx. But Marx was wrong about how such contradictions would transform capitalism. Instead of destroying it, the contradictions lead to fundamental reconfigurations of power within capitalism itself. That is why regime changes are not revolutions but instead are profound changes in the direction of the nation and the institutional organization of American capitalism. For Marx's analysis, see Karl Marx, *Capital,* vol. 1 (New York: Penguin Classics, 1992). For an analysis of "stages of accumulation" in capitalism, a different way of conceptualizing institutional reconfigurations similar but not identical to what I call regime changes within capitalism, see D. M. Gordon, "Stages of Accumulation and Long Economic Cycles," in *Processes of the World-System,* ed. T. K. Hopkins and I. Wallerstein, 9–45 (Beverly Hills, Calif.: Sage, 1980); see also David M. Kotz, Terrence McDonough, and Michael Reich, eds., *Social Structures of Accumulation* (Cambridge, Eng.: Cambridge University Press, 1994).

2. This simply reflects the contradictions within capitalism itself. Since all U.S. regimes are restructurings of capitalist systems, they all are ensnared in the tension between profit maximization and human need. This produces differ-

ent kinds of tensions in different forms of corporate regimes, and reflects the way profit and human need are balanced in different capitalist systems. Marx proved wrong in his prediction that capitalism would collapse because of this contradiction; instead, it keeps reconstructing itself in different institutional arrangements.

3. Three literatures make similar arguments about the inability of capitalist systems to resolve internal contradictions without fundamental reorganizations. One is classical Marxism itself, which has the conceptual problems I already described. The second is world system theory, which focuses on hegemonic restructurings of transnational capitalist systems or world economies. See Giovanni Arrighi, *The Long Twentieth Century* (London: Verso, 1992). The third is the work of contemporary economic sociologists who have focused on "stages of accumulation" within the capitalist order. See Gordon, "Stages of Accumulation and Long Economic Cycles." See also Kotz, *Social Structures of Accumulation.*

4. A leading historian of the Gilded Age and Progressive Era, Gabriel Kolko has fleshed out this argument about the regulatory crisis in persuasive depth. See Kolko, *The Triumph of Conservatism* (cited in Chapter 1).

5. This is the central argument of Kolko, ibid. It is also the perspective of Martin J. Sklar, a brilliant historian of the era, in *The Corporate Reconstruction of American Capitalism* (cited in Chapter 1).

6. Cited in Wasserman, *History of the United States* (cited in Chapter 1), 31.

7. Richard Hofstadter, *The Progressive Movement* (cited in Chapter 1), 25.

8. See Kolko, *The Triumph of Conservatism.* For an in-depth analysis of the transition between the two regimes and the rise of the new regulatory state, see also Sklar, *The Corporate Reconstruction of American Capitalism.*

9. For a systematic comparison of the Gilded Age and the current regime, see Derber, *Corporation Nation,* Chapter 1.

10. See Derber, *People Before Profit* (cited in Introduction), for an examination of the contradiction between national sovereignty and global economic requirements, and how it creates a schizophrenic dilemma for U.S. leaders.

11. See Lori Wallach and Michelle Sforza, *The WTO* (New York: Seven Stories Press, 1999).

12. Paul Kennedy, *The Rise and Fall of the Great Powers* (New York: Vintage, 1989).

13. Kennedy is focusing mainly on the economic burden of empire, and of competing with other economic powers, while I see this as only one dimension of the regime's "overstretch" crisis. See Kennedy, *The Rise and Fall of the Great Powers.* World system theorists such as Giovanni Arrighi and Immanuel Wallerstein do not use the "overstretch" concept, nor my regime framework, but develop similar ideas about core contradictions within a global system that create hegemonic contradictions and hegemonic decline. See Giovanni Arrighi and Beverly Silver, *Chaos and Governance in a Modern World System* (Minneapolis: University of Minnesota Press, 1999). See also Immanuel Wallerstein, *The Decline of American Power* (New York: Norton, 2003).

14. The extent of the debt crisis has been chronicled by both conservative and liberal sources, who are equally concerned about the prospects of national bankruptcy. For a conservative's perspective on the national debt, see Peter J. Peterson, *Running on Empty* (New York: Farrar, Straus and Giroux, 2004). On the liberal side, see Paul Krugman, *The Great Unraveling* (New York: Norton, 2003).

15. Paul Krugman, "Don't Look Down," *New York Times,* October 14, 2003.

16. Jeff Faux, "Rethinking the

Global Economy," April, 2003, posted online at the Global Policy Network's website, http://www.gpn.org/faux-rethinking.html.

17. For a graphic portrayal of growing U.S. poverty and inequality since the regime's beginning in 1980, see Collins and Yeskel, *Economic Apartheid in America* (cited in Chapter 2).

18. See Derber, *Regime Change Begins at Home* (cited in Introduction), Chapter 6, for an extended discussion of the Iraqi war as a regime crisis.

19. ABC News, "Poll: President's Year-End Job Approval," December 20, 2004, posted on http://abcnews.go.com/Politics/story?id=346282&page=1.

Chapter 5

1. Gramsci, *The Prison Notebooks* (cited in Introduction).

2. For an analysis of the rise of the New Right, and the corporate roots of pseudopopulism, see Nace, *Gangs of America* (cited in Chapter 1).

3. Pseudopopulism, as I use it, is closely related to what other researchers describe as right-wing populism. I have called it pseudopopulism here because I am discussing a movement heavily comprised of elites who are disguising themselves as champions of the people. Nonetheless, they have aligned themselves with religious and other grassroots groups that are genuine right-wing populists. Pseudopopulism and right-wing populism are thus related but not identical. For an outstanding history of right-wing populism in the United States that also explores elements of pseudopopulism, see Michael Kazin, *The Populist Persuasion* (New York: Basic Books, 1995).

4. The classic account of the rise of German fascism, and the pseudopopulist movement that Hitler led, is in William Shirer, *The Rise and Fall of the Third Reich* (New York: Simon and Schuster, 1959).

5. For the best discussion of the resonance of pseudopopulist ideology in Germany, see George Mosse, *The Crisis of German Ideology* (New York: Schocken, 1981).

6. Samuel Huntington, *Clash of Civilizations* (New York: Touchstone, 1996).

7. Since Huntington is focusing only on the second civilizational war, it might appear confusing to use the terminology. Nonetheless, the regime has skillfully synthesized the Huntington narrative into its overall story while explicitly denying it. The regime's denial is a half-truth, since its concept of civilizational war is different from Huntington's while also integrating

a form of Huntington's idea as a subplot of its own master narrative.

8. This argument was made in a slightly different form by Thomas Frank in his brilliant work on right-wing populism. While Frank does not use the analysis of the regime offered here, he marvels at the capacity of the Bush Administration to take class warfare off the political radar screen of ordinary Americans. See Frank, *What's the Matter with Kansas?* (cited in Introduction).

9. The number of books positing the existence of this liberal Establishment is mind-boggling. Mostly by conservative authors, they range from works on the liberal media to works on Hollywood, the Democratic Party, and the mass media. For a classic example focusing on the media, see Bernard Goldberg, *Bias* (New York: Regnery, 2001). See also Goldberg, *Arrogance: Rescuing America from the Media Elite* (New York: Warner, 2003). For an overall indictment of the liberal Establishment, and the linking of it with evil abroad, see Newt Gingrich, *Winning the Future* (New York: Regnery, 2005). See also Sean Hannity, *Deliver Us from Evil: Defeating Terrorism, Despotism and Liberalism* (New York: Regan Books, 2004). And also see Ann Coulter, *How to Talk to a Liberal (If You Must)* (New York: Crown, 2004), as well as Coulter, *Treason:*

Liberal Treachery from the Cold War to the War on Terrorism (New York: Crown, 2003).

10. This point is made without any sugarcoating by pundits like Hannity and Coulter. See Hannity, *Deliver Us from Evil,* and Coulter, *Treason.*

11. See Derber, *Regime Change Begins at Home* (cited in Introduction), Chapter 3. See also Nace, *Gangs of America* (cited in Chapter 1).

12. I have argued in an earlier book that credentialed knowledge is, in fact, a basis for class formation and that a knowledge class, while not consistently liberal, exists within the class structure of the United States. See Charles Derber, William Schwartz, and Yale Magrass, *Power in the Highest Degree: Professionals and the Rise of a New Mandarin Order* (New York: Oxford University Press, 1991).

13. See Robert McChesney, *Rich Media, Poor Democracy* (New York: New Press, 2000).

14. See also Frank, *What's the Matter with Kansas?*

15. Larry Beinhart, *Wag the Dog* (New York: Nation Press, 2004).

16. See the discussion in Derber, *Regime Change Begins at Home,* Chapter 4.

17. Coulter, *Treason.*

18. The explicit linking of liberals with terrorists is made not only

by Coulter but also by other influential conservative pundits such as Hannity in *Deliver Us from Evil.*

19. For more discussion of the schizophrenia that the global corporate system imposes on the U.S. government, see Derber, *People Before Profit* (cited in Introduction), Chapter 3.

20. Frank, *What's the Matter with Kansas?*

21. Such cultural portrayals, both of urban liberals and exurbanite conservatives, have become a growth industry in the publishing industry. As a prime example, see David Brooks, *Bobos in Paradise* (New York: Simon and Schuster, 2001).

22. It is interesting that Huntington, in *Clash of Civilizations,* did not explore civilizational politics inside the United States. But in a newer book, Huntington does focus on a shift toward domestic civilizational politics, although with an entirely different focus than described here. Huntington examines the clash between classic WASP culture and immigrant culture, particularly from Mexico. Some analysts argue that this native/immigrant divide—and the rapid growth of the Hispanic population—may become the real cultural divide that could ultimately threaten Republican control, if not the survival of the regime itself. See Samuel Huntington, *Who Are We? The Challenges to America's National Identity* (New York: Simon and Schuster, 2004).

23. This image of the Democratic Party and liberals as traitors has been assiduously cultivated by the conservative pundits rallying the Republican base. See Coulter, *Treason,* and Hannity, *Deliver Us from Evil.*

24. For survey evidence documenting this broad cultural consensus, see Alan Wolfe, *One Nation, After All: What Americans Really Think About God, Country, Family, Welfare, Immigration, Homosexuality, Work, the Right, the Left and Each Other* (New York: Penguin, 1999).

25. See Thomas Frank for his particularly vivid portrayal of this conservative zeitgeist in *What's the Matter with Kansas?* For a historical account of such culture, and its conflict with the progressive and liberal American tradition, see Richard Hofstadter, *Anti-Intellectualism in American Life* (New York: Vintage, 1966). For a discussion of how this conservative mindset has been mobilized into a right-wing populist force during much of the twentieth century, see Kazin, *The Populist Persuasion.*

26. I am grateful to Yale Magrass for helping alert me to the importance of this conservative tradition and its critical role in creating "resonance" to the regime's master narrative.

27. The concept of "recipe rules" is developed by Peter Berger. See Berger, *Invitation to Sociology* (New York: Anchor, 1963). See also Berger and Thomas Luckmann, *The Social Construction of Reality* (New York: Anchor, 1967).

Chapter 6

1. Bertram Gross, *Friendly Fascism* (Boston: South End Press, 1982). Ted Nace suggested the term "fascism lite" to distinguish my concept from Gross's.

2. Ibid., 1–2.

3. Ibid., 2.

4. Ibid., 3.

5. Ibid.

6. Ibid.

7. William Shirer, cited in Gross, ibid., 6.

8. Gross, *Friendly Fascism*, 4.

9. Richard Clarke, "Ten Years Later," *Atlantic Monthly*, January/February 2005.

10. Nuclear or biological attacks are, of course, a real possibility and are at the center of the threat presented by the Bush Administration to justify its war against Iraq and its overall war on terrorism. For a discussion of the prospects for and policy planning in regard to nuclear terrorism, see Graham Allison, *Nuclear Terrorism* (New York: Times Books, 2004).

11. See the corpus of McChes-ney's work, especially Robert McChesney, *Rich Media, Poor Democracy* (New York: New Press, 2000). See also the work of Noam Chomsky, including Chomsky, *Media Control: The Spectacular Achievements of Propaganda* (New York: Seven Stories Press, 2002).

12. For discussion of the Armstrong Williams case, see Greg Toppo, "Education Dept. Paid Commentator to Promote Law," *USA Today*, January 7, 2005, posted online at http://www.usatoday.com/news/washington/2005-01-06-williams-whitehouse_x.htm.

13. For discussion of the Kristol and Krauthammer incidents, see "William Kristol" on Media Matters.org, January 24, 2005, at http://www.mediatransparency.org/people/bill_kristol.htm.

14. For an account of the Social Security propaganda debacle, see Robert Pear, "Social Security Enlisted to Push Its Own Revision," *New York Times*, January 15, 2005, posted at http://www.freerepublic.com/focus/f-news/1321506/posts.

15. "Paying for Disinformation," posted by *The Wastebasket, A Weekly Bulletin on Government Waste*, February 22, 2002, at http://www.taxpayer.net/TCS/wastebasket/nationalsecurity/02-22-02osi.htm.

16. I have drawn here and below

on a detailed investigative report in the *New York Times:* David Barstow and Robin Stein, "Under Bush, a New Age of Prepackaged News," *New York Times,* March 13, 2005.

17. Ibid.

18. Ibid.

19. For a comprehensive account of the recent scandals and the changing U.S. policy toward torture, see Mark Danner, *Torture and Truth: America, Abu Ghraib and the War on Terror* (New York: New York Review of Books, 2004). See also Karen J. Greenberg, ed., *The Torture Papers* (Cambridge, Eng.: Cambridge University Press, 2005).

20. See Derber, *Regime Change Begins at Home* (cited in Introduction), Chapter 4.

21. Senator Kennedy quoted in "AG Nominee Gonzales Grilled," CBSNews.com, January 30, 2005, posted at http://cbsnews.com/stories/2005/01/07/politics/main665519.shtml.

22. Jonathan Steele, "New War on Terror," ZNET, January 15, 2005. http://Zmag.org/showarticle.cfm?sectionID=40&ItemID=7029.

23. For a comprehensive analysis of electoral irregularities in Florida in 2000, see essays in Greg Palast, *The Best Democracy Money Can Buy* (New York: Plume Books, 2003).

24. Congressman John Conyers initiated proceedings for a Congressional hearing on voting fraud in Ohio in 2004. Official commissions of the American Academy of Social Sciences and a vast number of citizen groups have also reported on numerous and deep voting fraud or irregularities in Ohio and other states in 2004. For some of the most comprehensive reporting, see the website of BlackBoxVoting.org, which has initiated some of the nation's most important lawsuits and investigations into electoral fraud. For an overview of its reports, see http://blackboxvoting.org.

25. For another website source of comprehensive research into voting irregularities, fraud, and proposed remedies, go to "Election Fraud in 2004," posted at http://betterworldlinks.org/book109h.htm.

Chapter 7

1. See Derber, *People Before Profit* (cited in Introduction), Chapter 9.

2. For excellent discussions of populism, see Goodwyn, *The Populist Moment* (cited in Chapter 1). See also Kazin, *The Populist Persuasion* (cited in Chapter 5).

3. For a discussion of the Progressive tradition at both the beginning of the twentieth century

and during the New Deal, see James A. Monroe, *The Democratic Wish* (New York: Basic Books, 1990), Chapters 3 and 4. For a critical assessment of the populists under Teddy Roosevelt, see Kolko, *The Triumph of Conservatism* (cited in Chapter 1). For a more sympathetic treatment, see Michael McGeer, *A Fierce Discontent* (New York: Free Press, 2003).

4. As observed in Chapter 4, two books that look at right-wing populism in the twentieth century and illuminate its relation to the nineteenth-century populists are Kazin, *The Populist Persuasion*, and Frank, *What's the Matter with Kansas?* (cited in Introduction).

5. Alexis de Tocqueville, *Democracy in America* (New York: Signet, 2001).

6. Zinn, *A People's History of the United States* (cited in Chapter 1).

7. Goodwyn, *The Populist Moment*, vi.

8. Mary Lease, cited in ibid., 71.

9. Cited in Goodwyn, *The Populist Moment*, 72.

10. Ibid., 71ff.

11. Cited in Ibid., 71.

12. For a colorful account of the populists and their bold political vision, see Wasserman, *History of the United States* (cited in Chapter 1), Part II.

13. Cited in Paul H. Boase, ed., *The Rhetoric of Christian Socialism* (New York: Random House, 1969), 95. The discourse of the

Greenbackers, the Knights of Labor, the Christian Socialists, and the populists—all anticorporate movements flourishing in the late nineteenth century—was deeply embedded in a religious language and philosophy. See the discussion in Kazin, *The Populist Persuasion*, 31ff.

14. For a discussion of the moral values of the populists, both in their attack on corporate morality and the special role of women in embodying populist morality, see Kazin, *The Populist Persuasion*, 34–42.

15. See Kazin, ibid., 40–41, for a discussion of the tortured position of the Populists on issues of race in America.

16. This theme of outdated agrarianism is emphasized by Richard Hofstadter in his critical discussion of the Populists. See Hofstadter, *The Age of Reform* (cited in Chapter 1).

17. See Kazin, *The Populist Moment*, 42ff, for a discussion of Bryan's 1896 Presidential race, its narrowing of the populist political agenda (thus many radical Populists refused to support Bryan), and the decline of the Populists after 1896.

18. For an outstanding treatment of how Teddy Roosevelt's Progressivism strengthened corporate capitalism by creating regulatory reform, see Kolko, *The Triumph of Conservatism*. From

Kolko's point of view, TR may have created regime change but it did not succeed in displacing the power of corporations; it only created an institutional transformation by wedding corporations to the regulatory state. My own view is that TR launched a stronger anticorporate assault than Kolko acknowledges. But the new progressive regulatory state was, indeed, a regime change that, while bringing key anticorporate reforms, saved capitalism from itself. For perhaps the best treatment of TR's and Progressivism's approach to corporate capitalism, see Sklar, *The Corporate Reconstruction of American Capitalism* (cited in Chapter 1).

19. For the contradictory impact of progressives on corporate power, see Sklar, ibid., who admirably treats progressive reforms as both limiting and saving corporate capitalism.

20. For a sympathetic account of the New Deal from this perspective, see Derber and Young, eds., *Labor and the New Deal* (cited in Chapter 3).

21. This is strongly emphasized by Goodwyn, who sees populism as by far the most authentic democratic tradition in America. See Goodwyn, *The Populist Moment*.

22. The role of experts and elites in the progressive tradition, especially in the New Deal but also in the age of TR, has been noted

by numerous observers. James Monroe calls the New Deal progressive transformation "Progressive Administration Without the People." See Monroe, *The Democratic Wish*, Chapter 4.

23. One of the keenest observers of these movements has been Naomi Klein. See Klein, *Fences and Windows* (New York: Picador, 2003), for a lively journalistic account of the movements.

24. See my detailed account of the Seattle protests in Derber, *People Before Profit*, Chapter 9.

25. MoveOn has proved that it is more than a flash in the pan. At this writing in 2005, MoveOn has survived the defeat of Kerry in 2004 and continues to play a dual role as social movement in its own right and a new progressive/populist constituent in the Democratic Party, trying to push it toward regime-change politics. Beyond its continuing grassroots initiatives on the Internet, directed at Congress, regulatory agencies, and the like, it is an active player within the Democratic Party and has put out its own book for citizens on how to change the world. See MoveOn, *MoveOn's Fifty Ways to Love Your Country* (Maui, Hawaii: Inner Ocean Press, 2004).

26. I am grateful to Michael Prokosch, one of the organizers of BGAN, for helping me understand its organization and agenda.

27. I am grateful to Deb Piatelli,

who is currently studying UJP, for her help in understanding the structure of the organization and how it seeks to organize coalitions across race and class lines.

28. While this progressive drift of students is not widely reported in the media, it is one of the most vocal complaints of conservative writers and pundits. They argue that the university has become the most solid bastion of the liberal Establishment. Indeed, a significant majority of both faculty and students on campuses across the country voted for Kerry, and Howard Dean found many of his supporters for a more progressive, regime-changing Democratic party precisely among this student base.

29. Noam Chomsky, in a personal communication.

Chapter 8

1. This is particularly true in many "red states." For a discussion of how this plays out in Kansas, between the corporate "mod" Republicans and the evangelical "con" Republicans, see Frank, *What's the Matter with Kansas?* (cited in Introduction), Chapter 5. The Democratic Party in Kansas has become, according to Frank, essentially irrelevant.

2. Harry Truman, quoted on May 17, 1952.

3. For a more extensive analysis of how the Democratic Party under Clinton embraced the regime, see Derber, *Corporation Nation* (cited in Introduction).

4. Clinton's success does indicate the importance of style and personality in politics. Politics is always partly about identity, with people choosing "one of their own." Because of pseudopopulism, the messenger is as important as the message. As long as the Democrats put forward candidates who appear to fit the mold of the pseudopopulist stereotype—that is, an elitist who speaks, dresses, and lives a lifestyle conspicuously different from ordinary Americans—they will find it hard to succeed even with a regime-change message. Style matters!

5. This embrace by the Democratic Party of corporations and the market as part of the natural order occurred in both prior corporate regimes as well. Grover Cleveland, the only Democratic president in the first corporate regime, supported the corporations in their struggle to crush unions and never questioned the constitutional rights being awarded corporations. In one of his first statements, he said "Big business has nothing to fear from my Administration," a point he proved true when he refused to intervene in famous strikes where

robber barons were killing striking workers. Only during the New Deal, where the Democrats rejected the corporate regimes, did they take political and constitutional changes that limited corporate sovereignty and questioned the fundamental ideology of the "free market" system.

6. While the Democrats accept all this, a vigorous challenge to all these corporate constitutional rights is being mounted by social movements to the left of the party, and by figures like Ralph Nader. This has helped to shape a divide between the party and the movements that will only be resolved when the Democratic Party begins to challenge the corporate regime. See Chapter 10, "Saving Democracy," for a specific programmatic agenda outlining how the party could join the movements in challenging market orthodoxy.

7. For a more extensive discussion, see Charles Derber, *Corporation Nation*.

8. This unhappiness among an American majority with Bush's economic policies continued after his reelection in 2004. See the ABC News, "Poll: President's Year-End Job Approval," December 20, 2004, posted at http://abcnews.go.com/Politics/story?id=346282&page=1.

9. For an analysis of the continuity of the regime's foreign policy under Clinton, see Andrew Bacevich, *American Empire* (cited in Chapter 1). See also Chalmers Johnson, *Blowback* (New York: Metropolitan Books, 1999).

10. While there is not space here, this critical analysis of U.S. foreign policy has been developed by many critics. See Chalmers Johnson, *Sorrows of Empire* (cited in Chapter 2). See also William Blum, *Rogue State* (Monroe, Maine: Common Courage Press, 2000). See the entire corpus of Noam Chomsky, most recently Chomsky, *Hegemony or Survival* (cited in Chapter 2).

11. See Alan Wolfe. *One Nation, After All* (cited in Chapter 5), for comprehensive surveys documenting the relatively progressive consensus across red and blue states on issues of "moral values." This, of course, does not deny bitter differences at the extremes of both camps.

12. The film *The Corporation* is based on a useful book by Joel Bakan, *The Corporation: The Pathological Pursuit of Profit and Power* (New York: Free Press, 2004).

13. Charles Derber, *The Wilding of America* (cited in Chapter 2).

14. Gingrich is unsparing in his critique of the Democratic Party as the bastion of Establishment "secular humanism." See Gingrich,

Winning the Future (cited in Chapter 5).

15. Lakoff's work is valuable in its critique of Democratic framing of issues, but it is less helpful in moving beyond the semantics and understanding the structural embeddedness of the Democratic Party in the regime. No semantic reframing can solve this problem. For Lakoff's analysis, see his most popular work: George Lakoff, *Don't Think of an Elephant: Know Your Values and Frame the Debate —The Essential Guide for Progressives* (New York: Chelsea Green Publishing House, 2004).

Chapter 9

1. It is important to note that the Election Trap seduces many Democrats on the left—especially left-leaning leaders in the party— as well as the center. This binds much of the party together in an unspoken pact, whatever their ideology. This can help the party in elections but it sabotages the underlying need for fundamental change in the party's aims and direction out of the regime toward regime change.

2. In this sense, many U.S. regimes tend toward an American version of a propaganda state, with strong affinities to fascism. This concept of a regime as a system of thought control is linked to the Italian theorist Antonio Gramsci's concept of ideological hegemony. See Gramsci, *The Prison Notebooks* (cited in Introduction). For a brilliant discussion of the U.S. ideological system as propaganda, see Noam Chomsky and Edward Herman, *Manufacturing Consent* (New York: Pantheon, 2002).

3. For a useful discussion of such economic ideas, see Charles A. Beard and Mary R. Beard, *Basic History of the United States* (New York: New Home Library, 1944).

4. For the neoconservative vision, read Max Boot, Robert Kagan, Paul Wolfowitz, or even the speeches of George W. Bush, all increasingly speaking openly of "democratic empire" or "humanitarian imperialism." The new blending of hawkish imperialism with Wilsonian idealism is what makes the neoconservative view seductive even to many liberal Democrats, such as Harvard's Michael Ignatieff. One of the most explicit defenses of "democratic empire" is British neoconservative fellow traveler Niall Ferguson, who writes that "empire is more necessary in the twenty-first century than ever before" as a means to "contain epidemics, depose tyrants, end local wars and eradicate terrorist organizations." See Ferguson, *Colossus: The Price of Empire* (New York: Penguin,

2004). For a compelling response that will deter Democrats from this logic, see the works of Chalmers Johnson, especially *Sorrows of Empire* (cited in Chapter 2).

5. See Nace, *Gangs of America* (cited in Chapter 1), for a compelling account particularly of the corporate model of the New Right social movement.

6. Byrd has become the most prophetic and important voice in the Democratic Party, especially regarding the preservation of American constitutionalism in the face of the regime's pursuit of Empire. See Robert Byrd, *Losing America* (New York: Norton, 2004).

7. For a classical and very readable account of this tragedy, see Shirer, *The Rise and Fall of the Third Reich* (cited in Chapter 5).

8. See Howard Dean and Judith Warner, *You Have the Power: How to Take Back the Country and Restore Democracy in America* (New York: Simon and Schuster, 2004). See also Howard Dean, *Winning Back America* (New York: Simon and Schuster, 2003).

9. The Election Trap has seduced many ordinary voters as well as leaders, making it even more difficult to escape from it. The need to escape from the crushing minimalism of Election Trap politics thus involves a broad conversation across the whole population. In 2004, it was ultimately the primary voters who chose Kerry around the slogan, Anybody But Bush. Voters need to understand that this mindset undermines the prospects not only of the Democrats winning but also of them making any real difference even if they do.

10. For an elaboration of the problems in the movements themselves, see Charles Derber, *People Before Profit* (cited in Introduction), Chapter 9.

11 See Kazin, *The Populist Persuasion* (cited in Chapter 5). See also Goodwyn, *The Populist Moment* (cited in Chapter 1).

12. George Lakoff, *Don't Think of an Elephant* (cited in Chapter 8).

13. Frank, *What's the Matter with Kansas?* (cited in Introduction).

14. Jim Wallis, *God's Politics: Why the Right Gets It Wrong and The Left Doesn't Get It* (San Francisco: Harper, 2005).

15. Lakoff, *Don't Think of an Elephant.*

16. Wallis, *God's Politics.*

17. Frank, *What's the Matter with Kansas?*

Chapter 10

1. Theodore Roosevelt, speech, 1910, cited on http://

www.edheritage.org/1910/
pridocs/1910roosevelt.htm.

2. John McCain, September 27, 1999, speaking in Nashua, New Hampshire.

3. James W. Rouse, quoted in Joel Makower, *Beyond the Bottom Line* (New York: Simon and Schuster, 1994), 31.

4. The Media Access Project has information about broadcasters' obligations at http://www.mediaaccess.org/programs/broadcastingoblig.

5. For a review of these efforts, see Thom Hartmann, *Unequal Protection* (New York: Rodale Press, 2002).

6. U.N. General Assembly Declaration of Human Rights, Article 23.3.

7. A summary of encyclical letters by the Pittsburgh diocese, posted at http://www.diopitt.org/resource1.htm.

8. Patrick J. Buchanan, *A Republic, Not an Empire* (New York: Regnery, 2002).

9. I am grateful to Adam Sacks for offering me the detailed description of the work of the Pennsylvania townships and the work of Linzey and Grossman. See

Linzey's website, the Community Environmental Legal Defense Fund, posted at http://www.celdf.org where you can find a description of the legal community work. See also the article by Jeffrey Kaplan, "The Consent of the Governed," *Orion,* November–December 2003, posted at http://www.oriononline.org/pages/om/03-6om/Kaplan.html. Adam Sacks's work in this area includes collaboration with Linzey and Grossman to offer "Democracy Schools." These weekend seminars offer historical background and local approaches to community action in the spirit of the Pennsylvania actions. Contact the Center for Democracy and the Constitution at http://www.constitution411.org.

10. For the pioneering legal and organizing work of Thomas Linzey, and if you want to contact him to help your own community, go to the website of the Community Environmental Legal Defense Fund, posted at http://www.celdf.org. To read Grossman's critically important work, or contact him, go to the website of POCLAD, http://www.poclad.org.

INDEX

ABC, 173
abolitionists, 186
abortion, 73, 82, 136, 145, 147, 268
Abu Ghraib, 155, 174, 175, 176, 234
ACORN, 227
Active Citizens' Network, 185, 257, 258, 275
activism; organizations to join, 197,199; today, 203–205; tools of, 78
activist government: during New Deal regime, 36; and social democracy, 37
activist judges, 132, 167
advertising, modern, 33.
See also Madison Avenue
affirmative action, 79, 134, 136, 145, 250
affordable housing, 268
Afghanistan, 156, 176; torture in, 174; war in, 216
AFL, 90
airport security, 172
Alcoa, 50, 82
alien Establishment, 125, 129–137, 231, 246; characteristics of, 130–131; linked to the enemy abroad, 141; and the media, 220; symbols of, 131–132; truth and fantasy of, 135–137. *See also* liberal Establishment
Al Qaeda, 128; and civilizational warfare, 139, 140
American dream, 40, 58, 219
American Empire, 108, 208, 229; and anti-Americanism, 115. *See also* American overstretch; Empire
American Federation of Labor (AFL), 90
American overstretch, 107, 108–110, 111. *See also*

American Empire; Empire
American Protective League, 30
American Revolution, 20
Americans for Fair Taxation, 81
Analysis and Research Association, 82
anti-Americanism, 51, 216, 230, 234, 248, 256; spread of, 115; and terrorism, 161
anticorporate campaigns, 48–49
antiglobalization movement, 157, 185, 195, 242
antireligious activists, 132
anti-sweatshop activists, 242
antiunionism: and the New Deal regime, 37; during the second corporate regime, 33
antiwar activism, 79, 156, 185, 202, 248
anxious class, 59, 112, 120, 149, 212, 213, 242, 274; and the alien Establishment, 134; creation of, 79; and farmers, 249; and fascism, 152, 163–164; and morality, 243; and need for economic security, 249; and the neoconservatives, 80
AOL-Time Warner, 168, 266
Ashcroft, John, 175
Atlantic Monthly, 159, 160
ATTAC, 201
Atwater, Lee, 137
auto workers, 85

Baker, James, 137
banking crisis and the New Deal regime, 87
Bank of America, 44, 50

Battle for Seattle, 157, 182, 195, 200, 202
Beinhart, Larry, 137
Bible Belt: and the alien Establishment, 134; and Barry Goldwater, 71; and preachers, 81–83; and religious conservatives' coalition with global corporations, 118; revolt, 77–80; and the U.S. cultural divide, 147
big business and big government, 153, 154; and the New Deal regime, 36
big thinking, 72–77, 232
Bill of Rights, 158, 159, 212, 236, 262, 263
Blackwell, Kenneth, 178
Blades, Joan, 196
Bloomingdale's, 1
Borch, Frederick, 82
bosses' social movement, 80–84
Boston College, 2; activist students at, 203
Boston Global Action Network (BGAN), 200
Brandeis, Louis, 90
Bridges, William, 57
Britt, Lawrence, 164, 165
Bryan, William Jennings, 27, 191, 192, 243–244
Bureau of Corporations, 27
Bush, George H.W., 42, 70, 95, 159; and Wall St., 63; and Empire, 160; and the Gulf War, 137; and multilateralism, 64; and the 1992 election, 98; social policies of, 59
Bush, George W., 2, 5, 70, 95, 96, 159, 208, 213; and alienation of fellow Republicans, 117; and alien Establishment, 133; cabinet of, 49–50; and corpocracy, 49–50;

and corporate taxes, 54; and cultural elite, 136; and Empire, 160; and extremist religious demands, 167; and fascist regime change, 162; and the Iraq invasion, 195; and moral values, 242–243; and move to the right, 276; and multilateralism, 64; and oil and military companies, 63–64; and pharmaceutical industry, 53; pseudo-populism of, 122; reelection of, 150; right-wing radicalism of, 119–120, 234, 236; second inaugural address of, 65, 170; social policies of, 60–61; and Social Security, 60–61; style of, 246; and Terry Schiavo, 118; and third corporate regime, 41, 42; as threat to world peace, 256; and 2004 election, 8, 97–98

Bush, Jeb, 178

Bush administration: and the Armstrong Williams scandal, 169–170; differences between it and John Kerry, 117; and liberals as traitors, 141; and normal politics, 73; propaganda and media campaigns of, 169–173; radicalism of, 119–120; and speech writing by media personalities, 170–171

Bush Republicans and thinking big, 72

Business Roundtable, 50, 82

Byrd, Robert, 235, 248

campaign finance, 198, 253; reform of, 117, 212, 255, 263, 264

Campaign for America's Future, 197, 227

campus activism, 196, 202, 203, 204. See also activism

capitalism: contradictions within, 99; and hidden power, 9–10; vs. communism, 140

capitalist democracy, 9–10, 12

Carnegie, Andrew, 105, 186

Catholic Church, 249, 269

The Center, 275–277

Chafee, Lincoln, 117

Chao, Elaine, 50

Chase National Bank, 25

Cheney, Richard, 49, 80

children's rights, 198

China, 114, 213

Chomsky, Noam, 203

Christian New Right, 79–80

Christian Socialists, 26, 187, 189, 190

church, as the dominant institution of a regime, 17; and church/state separation, 73, 136, 167

CIA, 158, 160, 172, 175

CIO, 85, 90

Citigroup, 6, 25, 44, 47, 155

citizen empowerment, 252, 257, 258, 259, 272

citizen movements, 196–202

citizenship, 67

civic associations, 185

civilizational conflict, 138, 184; with Islam, 126–128; between red and blue America, 145–146; the red/blue divide as, 146–147

civilizational warfare, 123, 126–129, 139–140, 147; Aryan, 163; and fascism lite, 162–164; propaganda, 162, 163; and the third corporate regime, 162; and torture, 175

civilization under threat, 122, 125–129

civil liberties, 145, 158, 159, 271–272; activists, 242; assault on, 120; and permanent war, 116

civil rights, 79, 134; activists, 242; legislation, 37, 71, 76

civil unions for gays, 147

Civil War, 18, 21, 24, 44

Clarke, Richard, 159–161

Clash of Civilizations (Huntington), 126

class warfare, 128–129

Clinton, Bill, 42, 70, 95, 159; and American Empire, 160, 215; and the corporate regime, 209; as an Eisenhower Republican, 276; and the Gilded Age, 25; and multilateralism, 64; as a New Democrat, 213; social policies of, 59–60; and style over content, 210, 246

CNN, 131, 168

Cold War, 76, 208, 270

collective security, 230, 258, 259, 270–271

communism, 85, 138, 140, 163

Conference Board, 45

Congress of Industrial Organizations (CIO), 85, 90

conservatism, 27, 148

conservative populism, 83

conservatives: and the 1901 GOP schism, 99; and coalition of religious and corporate, 118–119

constitutionalism, 175

constitutional rights, 23, 120

Constitution, U.S., 5, 236, 262

consumerism, 32, 66, 218, 230, 249, 257; and the second corporate regime, 33–34

cooperativism, 187

corpocracy, 22–23, 254; deregulated, 32, 33; global, 43, 44–45, 49–56; in the first corporate regime, 21; and New Democracy, 255; of the second corporate regime, 32, 33

corporate abolitionism, 253, 272–274

corporate campaign financing, 253

and economic crises, 156–159; and military crises, 156–157, 159–161; and regime radicalism, 162–164; and the Social Democrats, 236; and terrorism, 159–161
fascist drift in America, 150–151, 155
FBI, 158, 160
FCC, 198, 266
federal bureaucracy, 130, 133
federal government: abolishment of, 73; during New Deal regime, 34, 36
feminism, 79, 134, 242
Fifth Amendment and corporate rights, 262
First Amendment, 55; and rights of corporations, 55–56, 262, 263
first corporate regime, 18, 21–26, 184, 249; abolition of, 26; central contradiction of, 102–104; challengers of, 243; corruption in, 104–105; and the courts, 23, 55, 262; cracks in, 103, 104–105; and the Democratic Party, 207; and history of its failure, 101–106; and the social movements that ended it, 187; and split among the elites, 103, 105–106; tipping point of, 103. See also Gilded Age
flat tax, 73
Florida elections, 177, 178, 253
Forbes magazine, 10
foreign labor, 44
foreign policy: of the first corporate regime, 21, 24–25; imperial, 270; of the New Deal regime, 34; of the New Democrats, 215–217, 258; of the progressive regime, 27, 30–31; as a regime pillar, 17; of the second corporate regime, 32; and thinking big, 229–230;

of the third corporate regime, 43, 61–65
foreign threat, 125–126
Fortune 500, 48, 54, 78
The Founders: and corporate rights, 262; Enlightenment mindset of, 148; and intentions in drafting the constitution, 5; and vision of corporations, 260
Fourteenth Amendment, 23, 105, 262
Fourth Amendment rights of corporations, 55–56, 262
Fox News, 168, 204, 266
Frank, Thomas, 11, 144, 244, 245
freedom: and hegemony, 12; as mantra of the third corporate regime, 65–67
free markets, 65–66, 106, 211
free speech, 55
free trade, 47, 59, 208, 213; and Free Trade of the Americas meeting, 157
Frist, Bill, 118–119; and extremist religious demands, 167
fundamentalism: and the corporate social movement, 83

Galbraith, John Kenneth, 35
gap between rich and poor, 10, 99, 213; during the first corporate regime, 103, 105
gays, 73, 145, 147, 223. See also homosexuality
General Electric, 43, 47, 54, 82, 168
General Motors, 6, 43, 44, 47, 48, 54
Geneva Conventions, 151, 175, 234
Germany, 201; fascism in, 162, 163, 164, 166; pseudopopulism in, 122
Gilded Age, 5, 18, 21, 24, 29, 32, 75; end of, 87;

and the Populists, 186; regime of, 21–26, 35; second, 25. See also first corporate regime
Gingrich, Newt, 59, 221
Glass-Steagall Act, 74
global citizens, 266–268
global competition, 83
global corporations, 118; sovereignty of, 50
global democracy, 47, 61, 67
global economy, 193, 266–268; and capital, 63; financial crises of, 111; and mismatch with national sovereignty, 106–108
global governing institutions, 106–108
globalization, 67, 94, 198, 208, 213; and the Bible Belt revolt, 79; justification for, 47; during the New Deal regime, 38, 39; people's, 201–202; and regulatory crisis, 106–108; and the third corporate regime, 42
Global Justice Project (GJP), 203
global social movements, 201–202, 268; and Global Social Forum, 201
global warming, 81, 93, 114
Goldwater, Barry, 70–71, 72; campaign of, 78; and the Election Trap, 226–227; on moderation, 77; and thinking big, 229
Gonzales, Alberto, 175, 234–235
Goodwyn, Lawrence, 187, 191
Gore, Al, 70, 95, 206, 208, 210, 214, 276; elitism of, 212
Gould, Jay, 21
government: as the dominant institution of a regime, 17; propaganda apparatus of, 168–171; public relations offices of, 173

71; Republican base in, 80
South Africa, 44
Southern populism, 90
Southwest petrochemical complex, 117–118
Soviet era, 1–2
Soviet Union, 1, 138; as "Evil Empire," 73
Spain, 164
Spanish-American War, 30
spirituality, 221
splits in the elite in the third corporate regime, 116–119
Spreckels, Rudolph, 87
stagflation, 39, 84, 97; and the corporate social movement, 83; as an economic crack in regimes, 99
Standard Oil, 22, 25
State Department, 130, 172
state-labor alliance, 36–37
Steele, Jonathan, 175
Steffens, Lincoln, 29
stem cell research, 118
stock market collapse of 1929, 34
strikes: during the first corporate regime, 104; and labor movement of the 1930s, 89–90; and the New Deal regime, 87; during the second corporate regime, 33; wildcat, 85
striking workers' demonstrations, 87
suffragettes, 186
Supreme Court, 80, 262, 263; decisions, 55; during the first corporate regime, 23, 104–105; during the New Deal regime, 55; during the third corporate regime, 55–56
sweatshop activists, 202, 203
Syria, 3
systemic credibility crises, 93

Taft, William Howard; and GOP split, 99, 105
Taft-Hartley Labor Act, 37
tax cuts: under George W. Bush, 60, 110; under Ronald Reagan, 59
taxes, 53, 54, 73
tax system, progressive, 236
Teapot Dome, 33, 99
technology: and the move offshore, 63
tenant organizers, 85
terrorism, 14, 128, 271; and civilizational warfare, 140; and fascism lite, 156, 159–161
terrorists and liberals, 141–143
thinking big: and the Democratic Party, 228–231; and Howard Dean, 240–241; and regime change, 72–77
third corporate regime, 18; beginning of, 41–43; birth certificate, 42; central contradiction of, 106–110; and civilizational warfare, 126–129; and civilization under threat, 125–129; and Communism, 138–139, 162; and corporate mystique, 65–67; and the courts, 55–56; cracks in, 98, 106–120; creeping authoritarianism of, 151; creeping fascism of, 179; definition of citizenship, 67; dismantling the pillars of, 253–257; economic cracks in, 107, 110–112; and the Election Trap, 143–149; and Empire, 61–65; environmental cracks in, 114; as an extreme regime, 162; and fascism, 165–167; foreign policy of, 160–161; and global corpocracy, 49–56; hegemonic strategies of, 51, 56, 66; hidden power in, 119; identity politics, 127; and labor, 57–59; melding of

religion and government, 166–167; military cracks in, 107, 114–116; moral values propaganda, 217–219; and oil and military companies, 63–64; and patriotism, 141–143; and permanent war, 137–143; pillars of, 43; political cracks in, 107, 113–114; and pseudopopulism, 122–123, 124; and the red/blue divide, 143–149; right-wing radicalization of, 119–120; and similarities with German fascism, 166; social contract of, 57–61; social cracks in, 107, 112–113; and social insecurity, 57–61; splits in the elite during, 107, 116–119; strategies to continue, 119; survival of, 140–141; tipping point, 107; and torture, 175; and transnational corporations, 43–49; and the two-war doctrine, 142; and unions, 166. See also Reagan Revolution
Tocqueville, Alexis de, 185
Top Ten transnational corporations, 47
torture, 155, 160, 234–235; by the U.S., 174; as a warning sign of a fascist tip, 174–176
town hall meetings, 247
Toyota, 44–45, 48
Toys R Us, 48, 67
trade deficit, 111–112
transnational capitalist class (TCC), 48
transnational corporations, 43, 252, 253; network system of, 48; and the third corporate regime, 42, 43–49; and the U.S. government, 49–50
Transportation Security Agency propaganda, 172
Truman, Harry, 38, 64, 208

ABOUT THE AUTHOR

Charles Derber is Professor of Sociology at Boston College and former director of its graduate program on Social Economy and Social Justice. Derber received his undergraduate degree at Yale University and his PhD at the University of Chicago. He is a prolific scholar in the field of political economy, international relations, and society. He has written nine earlier books and received major research grants from the U.S. Department of Education and the National Institutes of Mental Health.

Derber's books have been translated into Chinese, German, Arabic, and Polish, and have been reviewed by *The New York Times, The Washington Post, The Boston Globe, The Boston Herald, The Washington Monthly,* and other publications. His op-eds and essays appear in *Newsday, The Boston Globe, Tikkun,* and other newspapers and magazines, and he is interviewed frequently by *Newsweek, Business Week, Time, Bloomberg,* and *The Los Angeles Times* for stories about business and politics.

Derber is an outspoken advocate for social change and works closely with many grassroots movements focused on peace and justice.

Derber is married and lives in Dedham, Massachusetts.

ABOUT BERRETT-KOEHLER PUBLISHERS

Berrett-Koehler is an independent publisher dedicated to an ambitious mission: Creating a World that Works for All.

We believe that to truly create a better world, action is needed at all levels —individual, organizational, and societal. At the individual level, our publications help people align their lives and work with their deepest values. At the organizational level, our publications promote progressive leadership and management practices, socially responsible approaches to business, and humane and effective organizations. At the societal level, our publications advance social and economic justice, shared prosperity, sustainable development, and new solutions to national and global issues.

We publish groundbreaking books focused on each of these levels. To further advance our commitment to positive change at the societal level, we have recently expanded our line of books in this area and are calling this expanded line "BK Currents."

A major theme of our publications is "Opening Up New Space." They challenge conventional thinking, introduce new points of view, and offer new alternatives for change. Their common quest is changing the underlying beliefs, mindsets, institutions, and structures that keep generating the same cycles of problems, no matter who our leaders are or what improvement programs we adopt.

We strive to practice what we preach—to operate our publishing company in line with the ideas in our books. At the core of our approach is *stewardship*, which we define as a deep sense of responsibility to administer the company for the benefit of all of our "stakeholder" groups: authors, customers, employees, investors, service providers, and the communities and environment around us. We seek to establish a partnering relationship with each stakeholder that is open, equitable, and collaborative.

We are gratified that thousands of readers, authors, and other friends of the company consider themselves to be part of the "BK Community." We hope that you, too, will join our community and connect with us through the ways described on our website at www.bkconnection.com.

This book is part of our BK Currents series. BK Currents titles advance social and economic justice by exploring the critical intersections between business and society. Offering a unique combination of thoughtful analysis and progressive alternatives, BK Currents titles promote positive change at the national and global levels. To find out more, visit www.bkcurrents.com.

BE CONNECTED

VISIT OUR WEBSITE

Go to www.bkconnection.com to read exclusive previews and excerpts of new books, find detailed information on all Berrett-Koehler titles and authors, browse subject-area libraries of books, and get special discounts.

SUBSCRIBE TO OUR FREE E-NEWSLETTER

Be the first to hear about new publications, special discount offers, exclusive articles, news about bestsellers, and more! Get on the list for our free e-newsletter by going to www.bkconnection.com.

PARTICIPATE IN THE DISCUSSION

To see what others are saying about our books and post your own thoughts, check out our blogs at www.bkblogs.com.

GET QUANTITY DISCOUNTS

Berrett-Koehler books are available at quantity discounts for orders of ten or more copies. Please call us toll-free at (800) 929-2929 or email us at bkp .orders@aidcvt.com.

HOST A READING GROUP

For tips on how to form and carry on a book reading group in your workplace or community, see our website at www.bkconnection.com.

JOIN THE BK COMMUNITY

Thousands of readers of our books have become part of the "BK Community" by participating in events featuring our authors, reviewing draft manuscripts of forthcoming books, spreading the word about their favorite books, and supporting our publishing program in other ways. If you would like to join the BK Community, please contact us at bkcommunity@bkpub.com.